I0715341

Paul Gauguin

Masterpieces of Art

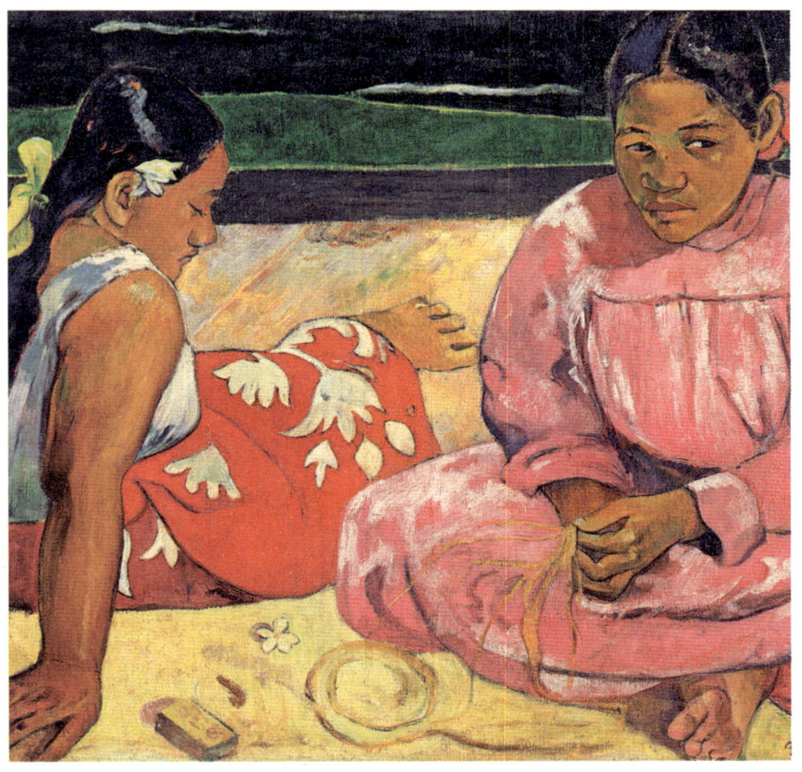

Publisher and Creative Director: Nick Wells
Commissioning Editor: Polly Prior
Senior Project Editor: Catherine Taylor
Art Director: Mike Spender
Layout Design: Federica Ciaravella
Copy Editor: Ramona Lamport
Proofreader: Amanda Crook

Special thanks to Leah Chrisbacher and Bethany Gooding.

FLAME TREE PUBLISHING

6 Melbray Mews
Fulham, London SW6 3NS
United Kingdom

www.flametreepublishing.com

First published 2017

24 26 28 27 25
3 5 7 9 10 8 6 4 2

Front cover: *When Are You Getting Married? (Nafea Faa Ipoipo?)*, 1892, courtesy Rudolf Staechelin's Family Foundation, Basel, Switzerland / Bridgeman Images.
Back cover: *The Siesta, c.* 1892–94, courtesy Metropolitan Museum of Art, New York / Bridgeman Images.

Every effort has been made to contact image copyright holders. We apologize in advance for any omissions and would be pleased to insert the appropriate acknowledgement in subsequent editions of this publication.

A CIP record for this book is available from the British Library upon request.

Image Credits: Courtesy of the following: **Bridgeman Images:** 1 & 105, 10 & 38, 22 & 74, 51, 54, 60 & 87, 84, 110, 123 Musee d'Orsay, Paris, France; 3 & 115, 21 & 76 & 128, 27 & 50 State Hermitage Museum, St. Petersburg, Russia; 4 & 109 Rudolf Staechelin's Family Foundation, Basel, Switzerland; 6 & 66, 68 Van Gogh Museum, Amsterdam, The Netherlands; 7 & 33, 24 & 118 Museum of Fine Arts, Boston, Massachusetts, USA; 8 & 88 De Agostini Picture Library / G. Dagli Orti; 11 & 62 De Agostini Picture Library; 12 Gift of Helen W. Ellsworth in memory of Duncan S. Ellsworth '22, nephew of Archibald A. Hutchinson, benefactor of the Hutchinson Wing , 1996.218; 12 Kunstmuseum, Basel, Switzerland; 14 & 65 Bridgestone Museum of Art, Tokyo, Japan; 15 Fete Gloanec, 1888 (oil on canvas), Gauguin, Paul (1848-1903) / Musee des Beaux-Arts, Orleans, France; 16 & 95, 18 & 36 National Galleries of Scotland, Edinburgh; 19 Norton Museum of Art, West Palm Beach, Florida, USA; 20 & 102, 113 Albright Knox Art Gallery, Buffalo, New York, USA; 25br & 88, 26 & 89 Museum Folkwang, Essen, Germany; 28 & 44 Philadelphia Museum of Art, Pennsylvania, PA, USA / Gift of Mr & Mrs Rodolphe Meyer de Schauensee, 1980; 30 Indianapolis Museum of Art, USA / Bequest of Kurt F. Pantzer; 31 Museum of Fine Arts (Szepmuveszeti) Budapest, Hungary; 32 Musee des Beaux-Arts, Rennes, France; 35 Indianapolis Museum of Art, USA; 37 , 52, 60 & 87, 63, 78, 94 Museum of Modern Art, New York, USA; 40 Museum of Fine Arts, Boston, Massachusetts, USA / Gift of Harry and Mildred Remis and Robert and Ruth Remis; 42 The Art Institute of Chicago, IL, USA / Gift of Kate L. Brewster; 45 Thyssen-Bornemisza Collection, Madrid, Spain; 47, 58, 67, 82, 112, 116, 122 Pushkin Museum, Moscow, Russia; 48 Private Collection / Photo © Christie's Images; 55 Musee de l'Orangerie, Paris, France; 57 Museum of Fine Arts, Boston, Massachusetts, USA / Bequest of John T. Spaulding; 70 The Barnes Foundation, Philadelphia, Pennsylvania, USA; 71 The Art Institute of Chicago, IL, USA / Joseph Winterbotham Collection; 72 Nelson-Atkins Museum of Art, Kansas City, USA; 73 Ny Carlsberg Glyptotek, Copenhagen, Denmark; 75 The Art Institute of Chicago, IL, USA / Gift of Mr. and Mrs. Charles Deering McCormick; 77 Brooklyn Museum of Art, New York, USA / Museum Collection Fund; 79 Fogg Art Museum, Harvard Art Museums, USA / Bequest from the Collection of Maurice Wertheim, Class 1906; 81 De Agostini Picture Library / E. Lessing; 90 & 104 Minneapolis Institute of Arts, MN, USA / The William Hood Dunwoody Fund; 92 Neue Pinakothek, Munich, Germany; 93 © Tyne & Wear Archives & Museums; 94 Private Collection; 97 The Art Institute of Chicago, IL, USA / Mr. and Mrs. Lewis Larned Coburn Memorial Collection; 98 Ordrupgaard, Copenhagen, Denmark; 99 Musees Royaux des Beaux-Arts de Belgique, Brussels, Belgium; 100, 120 Samuel Courtauld Trust, The Courtauld Gallery, London, UK; 101 Cleveland Museum of Art, OH, USA / Gift of Mr. and Mrs. William Powell Jones; 114 The Art Institute of Chicago, IL, USA. **The National Gallery of Art, Washington:** 9 & 41, 108 Gift of the W. Averell Harriman Foundation in memory of Marie N. Harriman; 17 & 69, 46 Chester Dale Collection; 25tl & 125 Gift from the Collection of John and Louise Booth in memory of their daughter Winkie; 34, 96, 121 Collection of Mr. and Mrs. Paul Mellon; 117 Gift of Sam A. Lewisohn. **REX:** 13 & 64 Kharbine-Tapabor/Shutterstock. **The Metropolitan Museum of Art, New York:** 23 & 103 Bequest of Sam A. Lewisohn, 1951; 53, 86, 106 The Walter H. and Leonore Annenberg Collection, Gift of Walter H. and Leonore Annenberg, 1997, Bequest of Walter H. Annenberg, 2002; 85 Gift of William Church Osborn, 1949; 111 Robert Lehman Collection, 1975. **AKG Images:** 56. **Superstock:** 124 Universal Images Group.

ISBN 978-1-80417-785-3

Printed in China | Created, Developed & Produced in the United Kingdom

Paul Gauguin

Masterpieces of Art

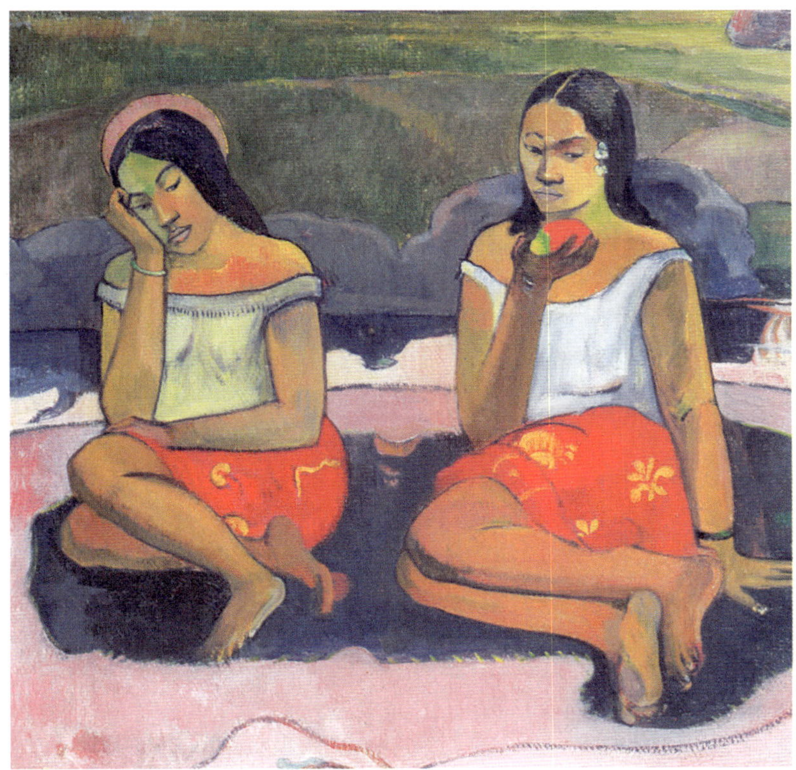

Rosalind Ormiston

FLAME TREE
PUBLISHING

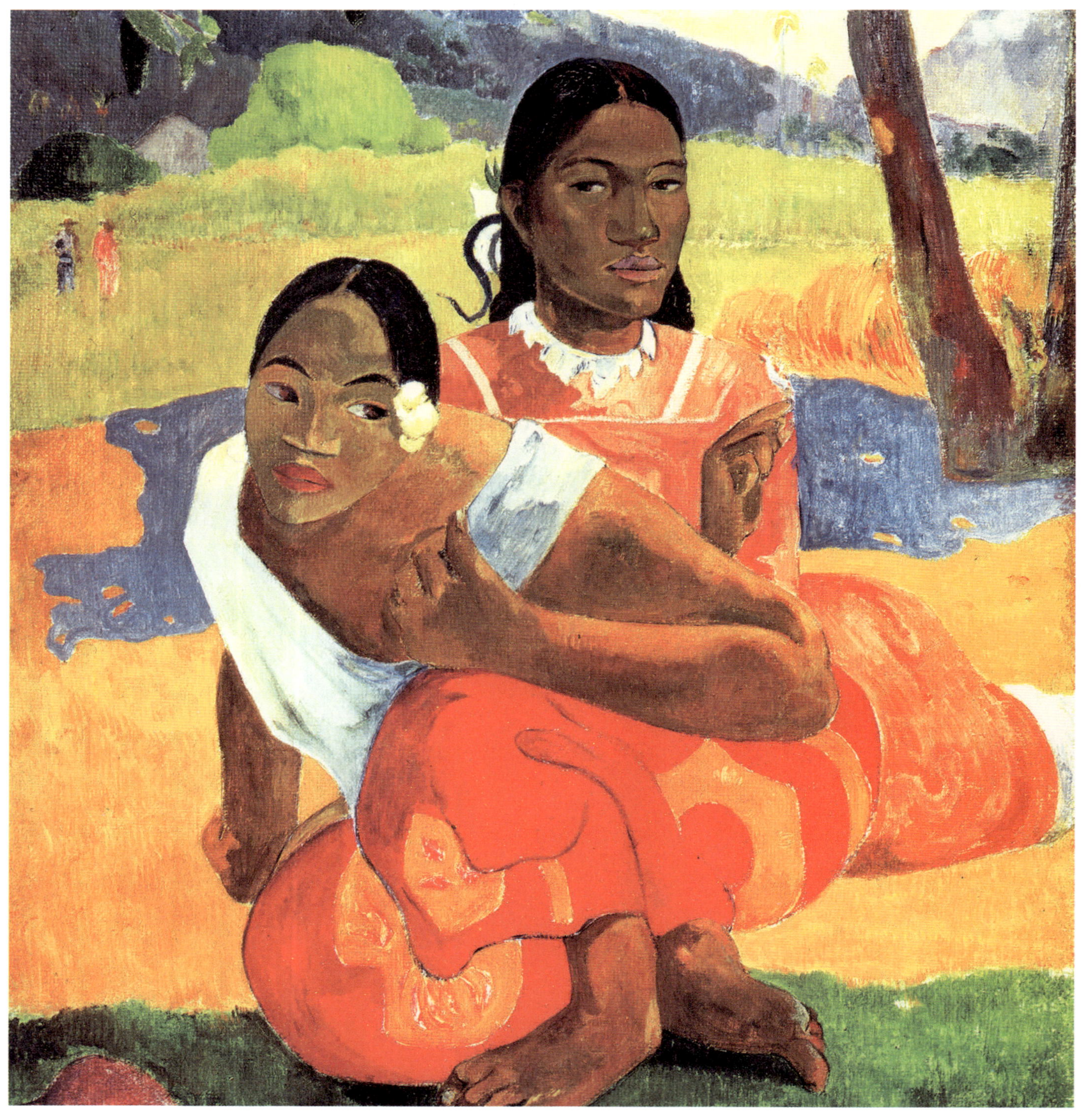

Contents

Paul Gauguin:
Innovator of Modern Art

The colour-drenched art of the remarkable French artist Paul Gauguin thrusts a twenty-first century spectator directly into the heart of late nineteenth-century France. At that time art was reaching a spectacular fin-de-siècle pinnacle in Paris, with many avant-garde experiments in art, from Impressionism to Art Nouveau, attracting new patrons. It was a heady, frenetic time for artists who could become either immensely wealthy or mired in poverty.

From Stock Exchange to Art Studio

Paul Gauguin (1848–1903), began his career as an amateur artist at the late age of 25 in 1873, and first exhibited his work in 1876. The first known painting is *Woodland Scene* (1873). It resembles a painting by the French landscape painters Jean-Baptiste-Camille Corot (1796–1875) and Camille Pissarro (1830–1903), whom Gauguin admired. It links to another Gauguin *Landscape* (1873, *see* page 30), with peasants tending a field in the foreground. Gauguin could afford to dabble in art as a Sunday painter, as he was a successful stockbroker, art collector and art dealer. With his wealth he collected art and sold it, mixing with artists and galleries, but the French stock market crash of 1882 changed Gauguin's life permanently. He lost money and the capital value of his art collection, and ignored the need to support his wife and young children. By 1883, with around 100 paintings completed, he became a professional artist.

Gaugin's Family

Eugène Henri Paul Gauguin was born in Paris on 7 June 1848, to Clovis Louis Pierre Guillaume Gauguin (1814–49), a republican political journalist, and Aline Marie Chazal (1825–67), daughter of the feminist pioneer Flora Tristan (1803–44) of Peruvian noble

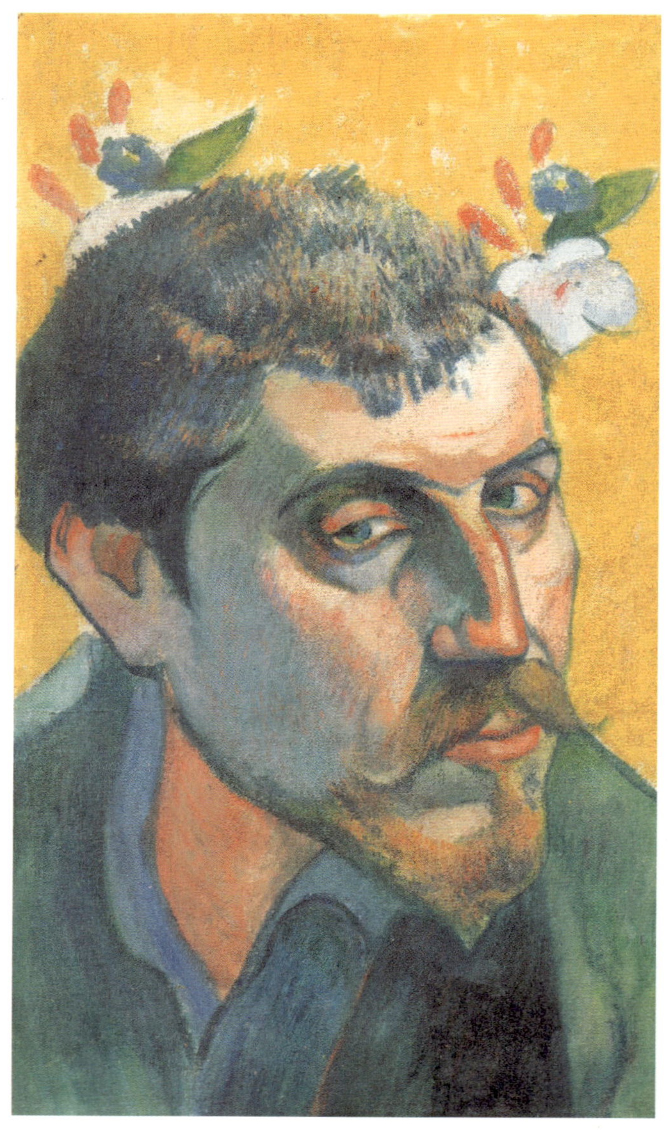

heritage. His parents had married at the *mairie* (town hall), in the 1st arrondissement in Paris on 15 June 1846. Clovis was referred to as a 'man of letters' on the marriage certificate. Their son Paul was born at his parents' home at 52 (now 56) Rue Notre Dame de Lorette, and baptised at the parish church of Notre Dame de Lorette, just over a year later, on 19 July 1849. He was the second-born child, following his sister, Fernande Marceline Marie Gauguin, born on 25 April 1847. Gauguin's paternal family came from in and around Orléans, about 110 km (68⅓ miles) south-west of Paris. Following Clovis Gauguin's decision to leave Paris with his wife and young family in 1849 (the February Revolution of 1848's upheavals led to the rise in office of Louis-Napoleon, a leader whose government was not conducive to Clovis's radical political journalism for *Le National* republican newspaper), the children would spend their early years in Lima, Peru, before returning to France to live in Orléans.

First Voyage

Thus the early years of Gauguin's life determined his future as a global traveller, a man who sought the primitivism of foreign lands. The Gauguin family left Paris on 8 August 1849, shortly after Paul's baptism. The family boarded a trading ship, the *Albert*, sailing directly to Lima. Gauguin later wrote that it was his father's intention to found a newspaper in Lima. En route, Clovis, suffering in great pain from heart disease, asked to land at Puerto del Hambre, south of Punta Arenas, in Patagonia, Chile, on the north shore of the Straits of Magellan. It was too late. He died on board and was buried in Punta Arenas, a rather desolate place. The ship's log recorded that Clovis died from a ruptured aneurism. He was 35 years old. Gauguin's mother continued the journey with the children to Lima where they lived with her wealthy uncle, Don Pio de Tristan Moscoso. Subsequently, as a young child growing up in South

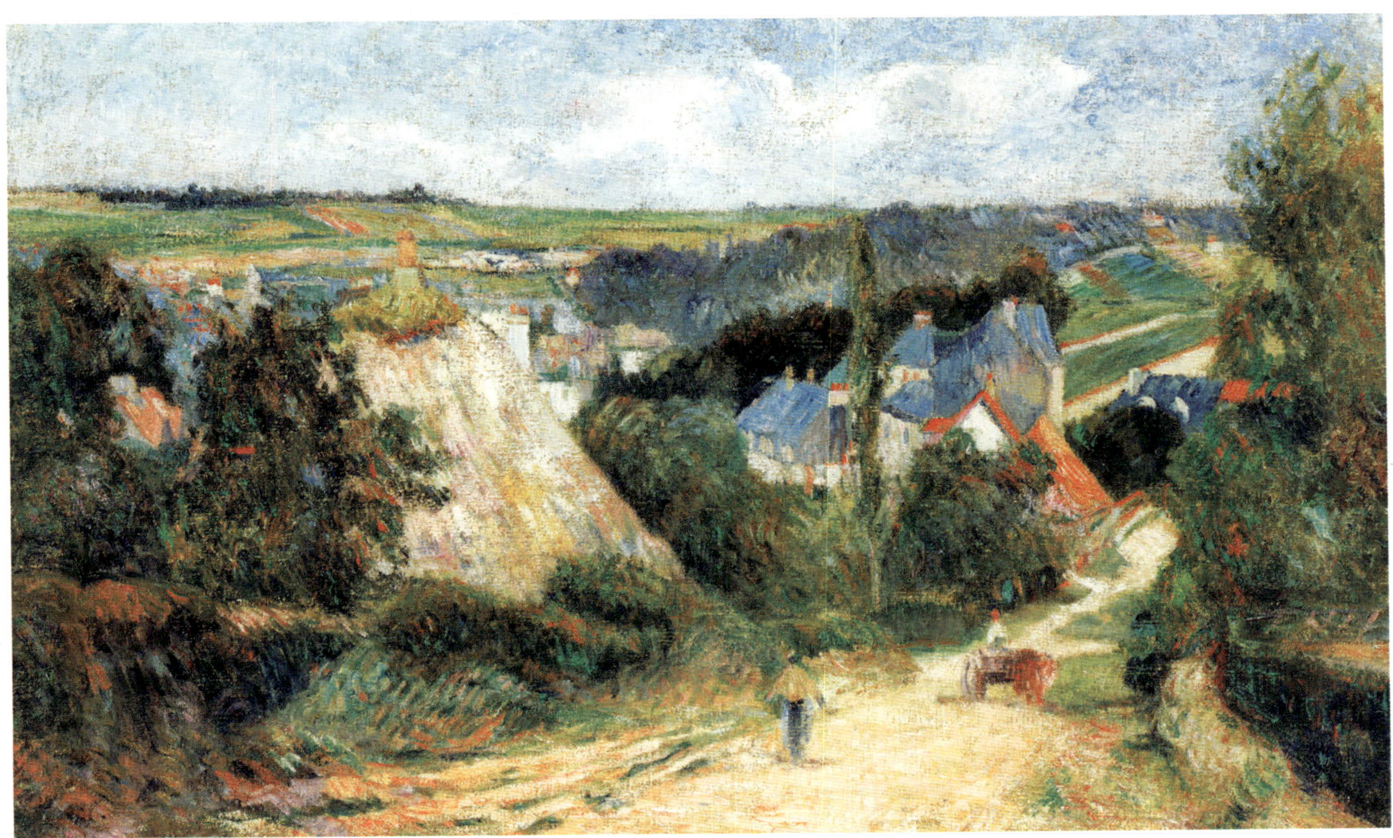

America, Gauguin lived among very wealthy Peruvian relations, cossetted by nannies and servants. He recalled memories of rich odours, intense flavours, colours and sounds, and that he spoke Spanish before he spoke French. His introduction to an exotic culture gave him the ability to adapt to different cultural customs and a different pace of life – and a longing for it.

A Return to France

Civil war in Peru was possibly the underlying factor in Aline Gauguin's decision to return to France in 1854, after five years in Lima. A contributing factor was the serious illness of the children's paternal grandfather, Guillaume Gauguin (1784–1855), who wanted to see his grandchildren. On return, the family settled in Orléans, living with the children's paternal Uncle Isidore. Gauguin was sent as a day boy to a local boarding school, the Petit Séminaire, the minor seminary of the chapel Saint-Mesmin. In his 1903 autobiography, *Avant et après*, he recalled 'At this point I was just beginning to speak French.'

Paris, 1862

Aline Gauguin returned to Paris in 1861, possibly with her daughter. Living at 33 rue de la Chaussée-d'Antin, it is recorded that she opened a workshop and worked as a dressmaker. Importantly, for her and her children, in Paris she became close friends with the wealthy Arosa family of Peruvian heritage. Gauguin joined her in Paris the following year. Official records show that Aline, with family approval, sold part of an annuity owned by Gauguin to pay for his school fees at Loriol's boarding school at 49 rue d'Enfer, a school that specialized in preparing boys for the *École navale* entry exam. Gauguin's family was immensely keen for him to gain a place at the naval school but he did not attain the required level. He returned to Orléans in 1864 to board at the *lycée* for his final year at school. Relations with his mother were perhaps strained, as her will, drawn up on 13 November 1865, was specific about his behaviour. In it she left the guardianship of her teenage children to Gustave Arosa (1818–83), and her paintings, portraits, books and other personal items to her son. She added advice to him: 'As to my dear son,

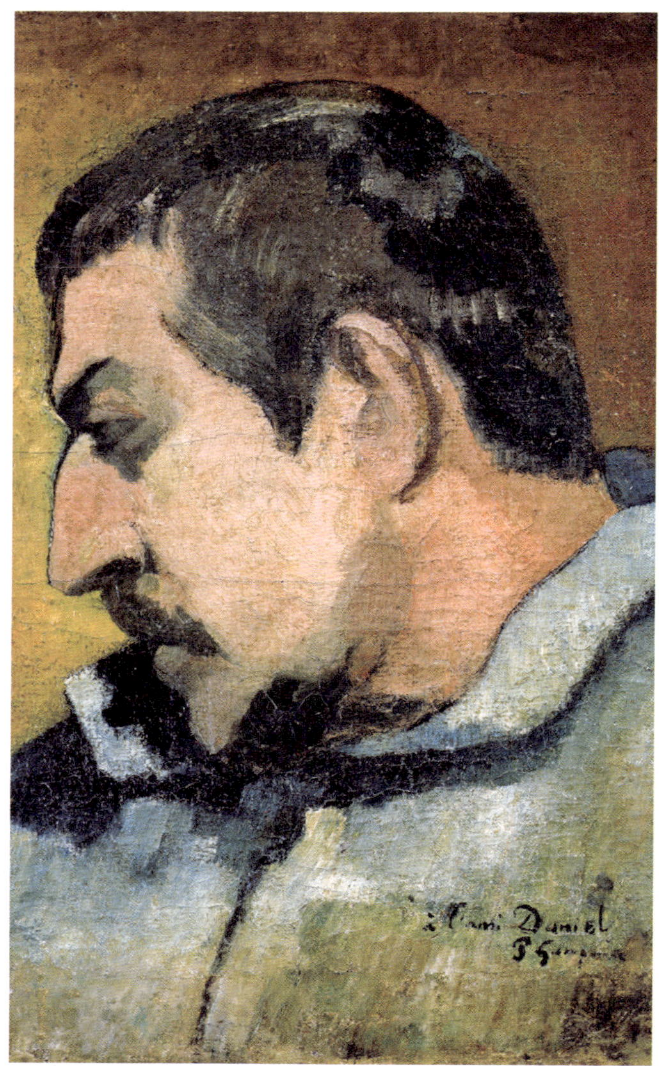

he will have to make his own career, since he has done so little to endear himself to my friends that he will one day find himself alone.' A prediction that would prove true.

Gauguin, now too old at 17 to retake the exams for the *École navale*, turned to the Merchant Navy. Employed as a trainee officer by the Union des chargeurs réunis, on 6 December he embarked on the 654 tons *Luzitano* out of Le Havre, bound for Rio de Janeiro, arriving at its destination on 11 January 1866. Aline Gauguin died on 7 July

1867 in Saint-Cloud, while her son was on the other side of the world. It can be seen from his naval record that Gauguin was not totally responsive to orders. However, by the time he was discharged from service in April 1871, he had matured and received a good conduct certificate. He returned to Saint-Cloud to find a house he and his sister owned in ruins, shelled by the Prussian army in the Franco-Prussian War of the same year.

Gustave Arosa

Gauguin was welcomed into the house of his guardian Gustave Arosa, a man of great wealth and intellect, and a cultivated collector of art. His collection included works by Delacroix, Corot, Courbet, Daubigny and painters of the Barbizon school. Arosa would prove to be Gauguin's mentor to the art world. By the end of April 1872 Gauguin's life was on track again. He had found his own apartment at 15 (now no. 21) rue la Bruyère, close to the Arosa family home at 5 rue Bréda (now rue Henri-Monnier) in the 9th arrondissement. Gauguin's parents had left him a comfortable inheritance. In October that year he was introduced to a young Danish governess, Mette-Sophie Gad (1850–1920), who would become his wife.

From Realism to Impressionism to Post-Impressionism

From the moment French artist Gustave Courbet (1819–77) decided to paint a monumental canvas depicting the local funeral of his uncle in Ornans, titled *Burial at Ornans* (1849–50), he had elevated an ordinary event to an historic occasion featuring poorer members of the French community. He broke with academic tradition in using a vast canvas, reserved for the noble genre of history painting. Courbet was making a point in his 'statement of principle', calling the work *Painting of Human Figures, the History of a Burial at Ornans*. Exhibited at the Salon in 1851, visitors disliked the 'ugliness' of the people depicted; it was too realistic. Courbet challenged the École des Beaux-Arts establishment to break with its out-dated traditions and paint real life. It led many artists to follow his radical challenge. Although still dependent on the annual Salon exhibition to attract patrons, painters felt freer to depict what they saw, however ordinary the subject: local scenes, landscapes, domestic interiors, on any size canvas they chose. The Impressionist group of painters perfected scenes of modern life in Paris, or painted Parisians at leisure along the banks of the Seine on the outskirts of the city, easily accessible by train. Further groups were formed, such as

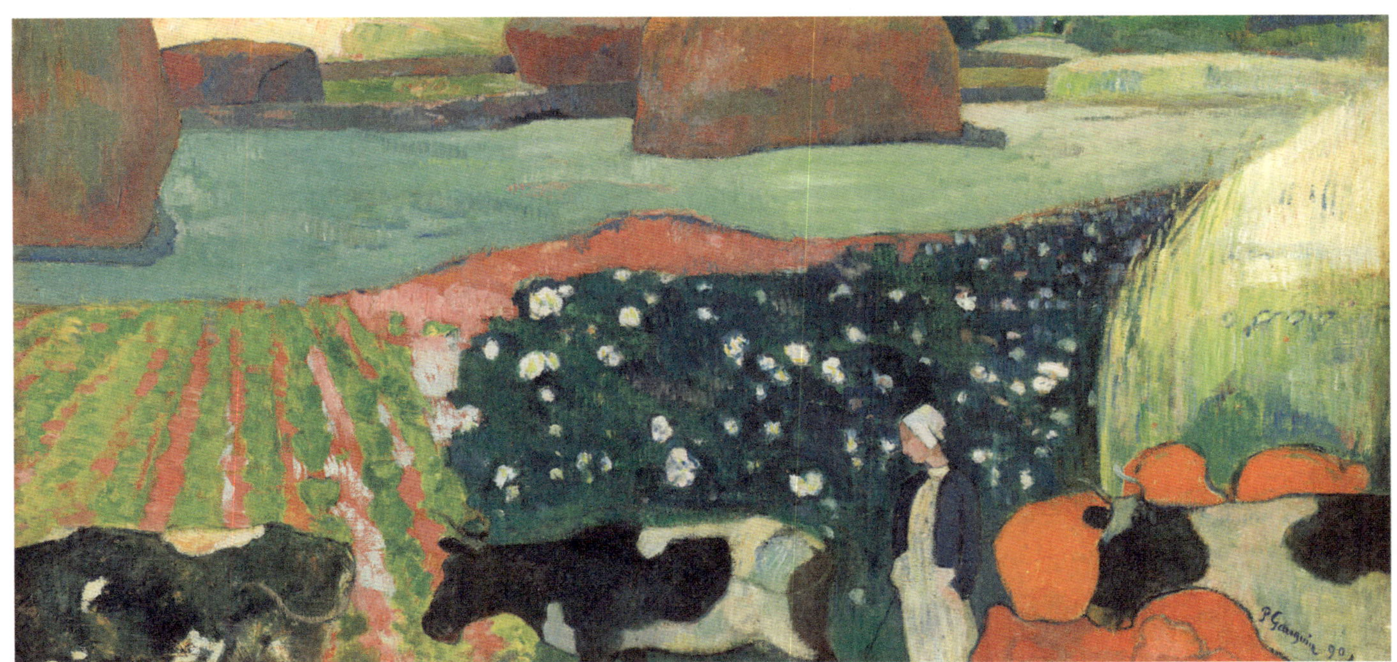

the Pont-Aven school, led by Gauguin in the 1880s, and Les Nabis, followers of Gauguin, a Post-Impressionist group formed in the 1890s, inspired by his art.

Paris, 1871

The Parisian art scene in 1871, the year Gauguin was discharged from the navy, was a pivotal moment in the birth of modern art. His time spent in the company of the Arosa family, cultured in art and collectors of contemporary art, allowed him to become part of the flourishing art movement in France. The art establishment, the École des Beaux-Arts, and its annual Salon exhibition was fighting against the liberation of artists from their academic system. Gauguin enjoyed meeting its growing group of young artists turning away from academic tradition. Perhaps it appealed to his rebellious nature. Following the early challenges made by Édouard Manet (1832–83) and Courbet, painters wanted not to depict a landscape as an ancient pastoral scene but, rather, French fields or boating and leisurely picnics on the banks of the Seine; not to paint a naked woman and title it *Venus* but, rather, a naked woman as herself, something which had not been acceptable but now gained momentum. Painters of 'modern life' flourished. Small shows exhibited new works and the first show of Impressionism in 1874 sealed this sea change that could not be stopped. Gauguin, a gentle rebel by nature, joined its group as an amateur self-taught painter.

The First Impressionist Exhibition, Paris 1874

On 15 April 1874, in the former studio of the French photographer Nadar (Gaspard-Félix Tournachon, 1820–1910) at 35 boulevard des Capucines, Paris, an exhibition of painting and sculpture was displayed, which would run until 15 May. It would become known as the First Impressionist Exhibition, of which there were eight in Paris from 1874–86. Thirty artists showed 165 works. Those involved included Paul Cézanne (1839–1906), Edgar Degas (1834–1917), Claude Monet (1840–1926), Berthe Morisot (1841–95), Pierre-Auguste Renoir (1841–1919), Alfred Sisley (1839–99) and Pissarro. Together they formed the *Société Anonyme des Peintres, Sculpteurs et Graveurs* (The Anonymous

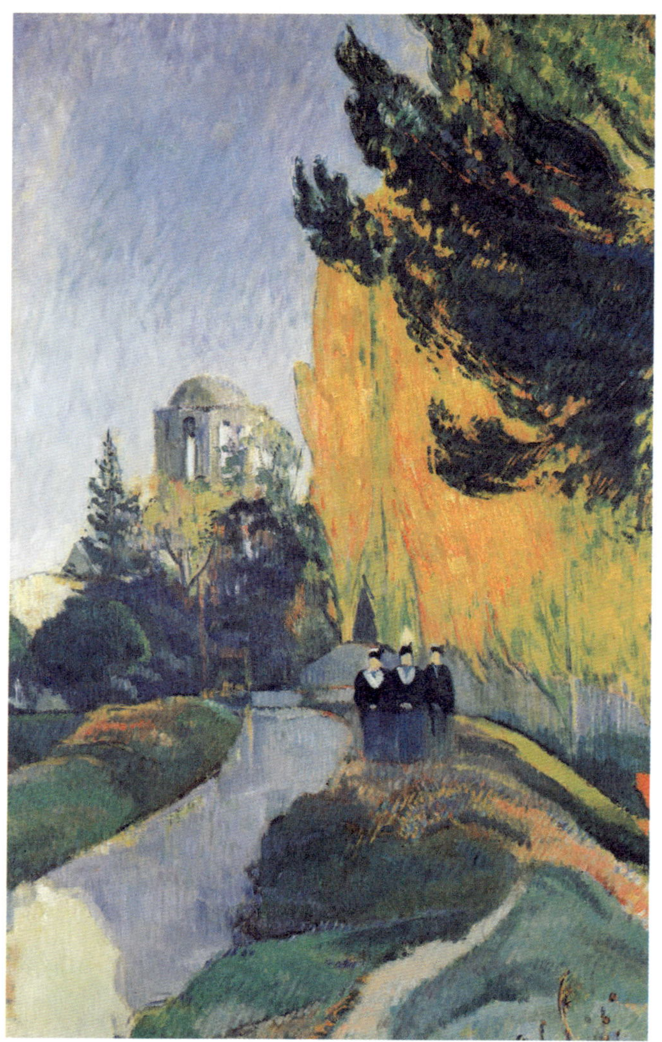

Society of Painters, Sculptors and Engravers). They would be better known as the Impressionists after one art critic, Louis Leroy, voiced a scathing, negative opinion in a review in *Charivari* titled 'Exhibition of the Impressionists' on 25 April 1874, singling out the title of Claude Monet's painting *Impression Sunrise* (1874), to sum up his opinion of the art on show. Much later, Gauguin would exhibit his work in the fourth (1879), fifth (1880) and sixth (1881) – exhibiting eight works – Impressionist Exhibitions. In 1882, the year in which he lost his stockbroker job, he exhibited 12 works at the seventh show.

From Stockbroker to Artist

With the assistance of Gustave Arosa and his banker brother Achile, and possibly son-in-law Calzado, a receiver on the Paris *Bourse*, Gauguin was given employment as a stockbroker clerk by Paul Bertin, a significant stockbroker company in Paris, with whom the Arosa family had investments. In the company's headquarters on rue Laffitte, Gauguin worked in accounts and settlements, and was clearly good at finance. It is here that he met Claude-Émile Schuffenecker (1851–1934), another young stockbroker. Their mutual interest in art, of which Emile knew much, helped to form a close friendship and they became lifelong friends. They visited the Louvre and studied fine art together at the Colarossi Academy. Gauguin's social life included dinners and parties with the Arosa family in Paris and at their country home in Saint-Cloud, where Gauguin's sister, Fernande, also had a home, which he shared. One can see from this period and into 1873 that Gauguin was dabbling in art, drawing friends' portraits, including one of Mette's Danish friend, Marie Heegaard. In a letter home in the summer of 1873, she wrote that she had sat for portraits by Margot Arosa (Gustave's daughter Marguerite) and Paul Gauguin: 'Paul and Margot again seized on me, I posed for three and a half hours for them. The portrait by Paul is a particularly good likeness.' Gauguin's artistic creativity was emerging.

The Académie Colarossi

Paris had many independent ateliers, separate to the official Academy, which welcomed art students from every country. Paris was the centre of the art world. The Académie Julian and the Académie Colarossi were two studios particularly favoured by artists interested in contemporary, avant-garde art. Gauguin joined the Académie Colarossi in 1874, the year his son Émil (1874–1955) was born. The birth of his first child led to many intimate portrait drawings of the infant by his father. In a letter to Marie Heegaard, he described Émil as '... bonny ... as white as a swan, and strong as Hercules'. In 1880 Gauguin moved to 8 rue Carcel, in the Vaugirard (15th) arrondissement. The small house with garden was big enough for his family and close enough to his financial work and the art galleries.

Pissarro and Gauguin

Gauguin's first encounter with the Impressionist painter Pissarro may have been at the Arosa family home around 1877. The artist was commissioned to create four paintings – one for each of the four seasons – as a house decoration in the home of Achile Arosa. Pissarro became a mentor to Gauguin, guiding him in the art of painting. Gauguin's painting *Mette Sewing* (1878) depicting his wife seated at a table, absorbed in her embroidery work, is informed by Impressionist technique, a subtle mix of Pissarro, Monet and Morisot. A later work in oil on canvas, *Nude Study*, also known as *Suzanne Sewing* (1880, *see* page 62), depicts a model in a similar profile pose but this time naked and seated on a bed. It reveals Gauguin's indebtedness to the Impressionists.

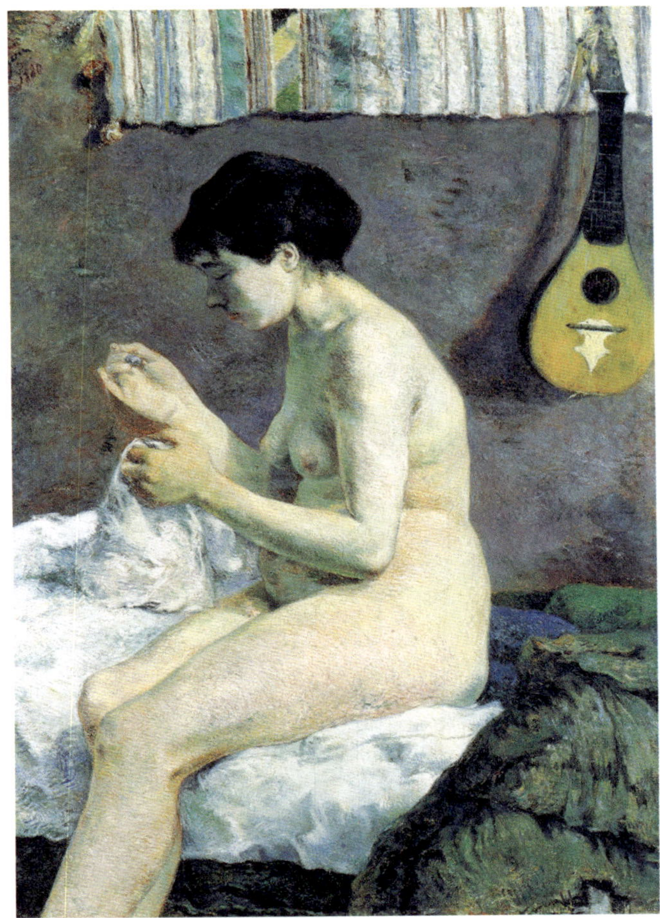

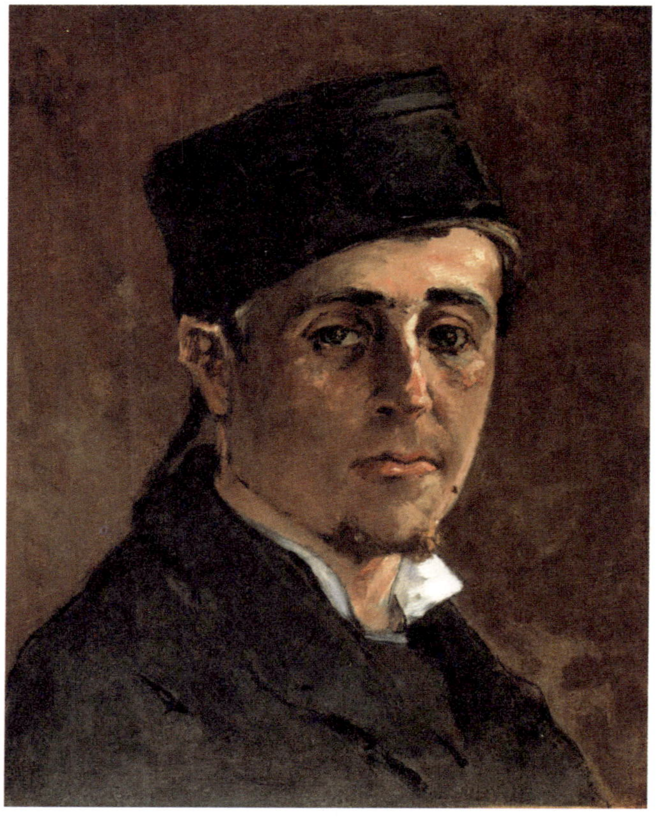

His knowledge of art, so encouraged by the Arosa family, led him to the heart of Parisian artistic circles. He was most likely introduced to the Impressionist circle through Pissarro, who was one of the Arosa family's inner circle of friends. On 3 April 1879, a week before the Fourth Impressionist exhibition opened on 10 April, his associates Pissarro and Degas had invited Gauguin to exhibit his own work. He had attended previous Impressionist exhibitions as a collector, and increasingly a dealer, and accumulated a collection of works. Now he was to attend as collector and artist. In the catalogue he is noted as the owner 'Monsieur G.' of three of Pissarro's works and himself as the creator of a small sculpture, a marble bust of his son. In the same year he exhibited his own work with the avant-garde Société des Artistes Indépendants. The marble bust illustrated his understanding and mastery of the medium. Learning from other artists, he created his first masterpiece in 1882, a wood and wax polychrome portrait of his son, which would lead him towards more dramatic 'primitive' works during his years spent in French Polynesia, particularly in wood, the local alternative to marble and ceramic. Gauguin's sculptures were sometimes used as props in his paintings, such as *Still Life with Profile of Laval* (1886, *see* page 35).

The Official Salon

In 1876 Gauguin had a painting accepted at the Salon, the official annual exhibition of art sponsored by the French government and open to all artists since the French Revolution of 1789. It was an official acceptance of Gauguin, who submitted *Landscape at Viroflay* (*Paysage à Viroflay*) (1875), a view just a few kilometres from Arosa's country home in Saint-Cloud. It was one of several accomplished works that Gauguin produced in this early period of his amateur dabbling in the art profession, including *Self-Portrait* (c. 1875, *see* above). It was at this point in their marriage that Mette may have accepted his recreational hobby as a Sunday painter. With a substantial salary Gauguin could indulge in art, buying it, selling it and creating it.

Gauguin: Artist, Sculptor, Art Collector

During his 11-year career as a stockbroker, the wealth Gauguin accumulated allowed him to indulge as an art collector and dealer.

Japonism

It is well documented that Japanese art had a dramatic effect on Western art from the late 1850s when trade resumed between Japan and Europe. The *ukiyo-e* movement of Japanese genre painting, which emerged in the sixteenth and seventeenth centuries in Japan, is recognized by its use of flat, decorative colour. Panoramic scenes of mountains and seas or city life painted without perspective had a great impact on European art, noticeable in paintings by Manet, Degas, Georges Seurat (1859–91) and many avant-garde artists, including Vincent van Gogh (1853–90) who owned copies of Utagawa Hiroshige (1797–1858) prints. Hiroshige is considered the grand master of the *ukiyo-e* art tradition, alongside Katsushika Hokusai (1760–1849), whose art was utilized by Gauguin and Degas to inform their paintings. This euphoria for Japanese art, ceramics and decorative art manifested itself in Japonism (*Japonisme*), a Westernized interpretation of Japanese art.

The Gauguin Family

Gauguin fathered nine children: five legitimate and four illegitimate. His wife Mette gave birth to Émil, nine months after their marriage, and there followed Aline (1877–97), Clovis (1879–1900), Jean René (1881–1961), and Paul Rollon 'Pola' (1883–1961). The first of his four illegitimate children was Germaine Huet (b. 1891), daughter of a Parisian seamstress Juliette Huet/Huret. Following his sojourns in Polynesia, in December 1896 Pahura (Pau'ura) a Tai, a 14-year-old Tahitian girl, became Gauguin's live-in housekeeper and mistress. She gave birth to a daughter, but the baby died soon after birth. Their son, Émile Marae a Tai (1899–1980), was born in a few years later. Another child, a daughter Vaa'oho, was born in 1902 to 14-year old Vaeoho, also known as Marie-Rose, a Tahitian girl, rumoured to have been sold to Gauguin by her father, a local chief, in exchange for 200 francs of ribbons and cloth from a local store.

Gauguin the Art Dealer

Paul Durand-Ruel (1831–1922), the most prolific collector and dealer of Impressionist art in France, sold Gauguin a Monet marine painting and two Renoir paintings on 27 April 1881. Gauguin collected but he also invested to sell. He frequented galleries such as those of the art suppliers and dealers Julien Tanguy and Madame Latouche, to invest or to barter. Durand-Ruel, possibly encouraged by Degas, purchased paintings by Gauguin. The appalling financial crash of January 1882, with the devastating collapse of the Union Générale, affected almost every French citizen. Émile Zola (1840–1902), created a fictional account of the financial catastrophe in *L'argent*, the eighteenth volume of the Rougon-Macquart series, published in 1891. The crash created a slump on the Paris *Bourse*, sending businesses,

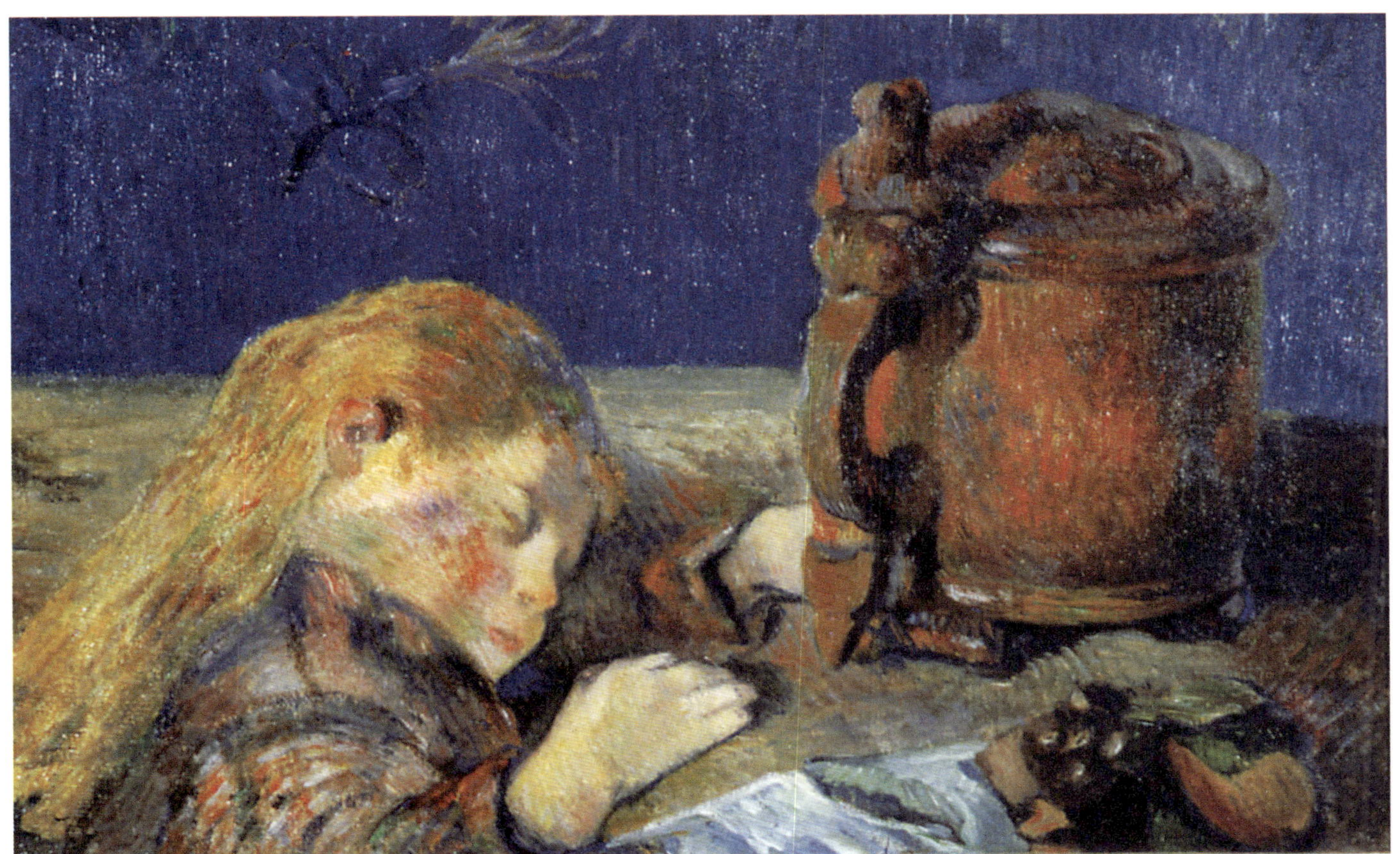

including Durand-Ruel's, who had been financed by a partner in the bank, into meltdown. His collection of Impressionist works became near impossible to sell. Gauguin also found it difficult to sell the paintings in which he had invested. One highlight for Gauguin was that his painting, *Still Life with Danish Schnapps Carafe* (1882), sold to Mette's Danish friend, Marie Heegaard, and her husband, Bjorn Stephensen, during a visit to Paris. It gave Gauguin serious thought that there could be a market for his work in Scandinavia. From the summer of 1882, and decisively by the autumn of 1883, Gauguin adjusted his career ambition to full-time professional painter. He wrote in a letter to Pissarro in June 1882: 'I cannot resign myself to spending the rest of my life in finance and amateur painting. I have got it into my head that I shall become a painter.'

Rouen, 1884

The omission of an Impressionist group exhibition in 1883 – Durand-Ruel gave Degas, Monet, Renoir, Eugène Boudin (1824–98), Pissarro and Sisley solo shows (with Gauguin not included) – illustrated the uncertain mood of the art market and artists. Gauguin was not a professional full-time artist, rather a Sunday painter who bought art. It made him consider his position, writing to Pissarro on 11 October 1883 for help and guidance: 'Love of my art is preoccupying me too much for me to be a good employee in the business world where dreamers are of no use, and on the other hand I have too large a family, and a wife incapable of living in poverty…. In a word, I absolutely have to make a living as a painter.'

Gauguin visited Pissarro in Rouen during the artist's stay in the prosperous city. Having met prospective dealers and art collectors there as well, some with Scandinavian connections, Gauguin vacated his Paris home in January 1884 and moved Mette and the children to Rouen. The lower cost of living outside Paris gave him a chance to establish himself as a full-time painter. He had enough money for them to live there for six months, and Mette worried that Gauguin working as a professional painter would not earn enough for the family to live on. The market was slow and sales were poor. They would have to move again.

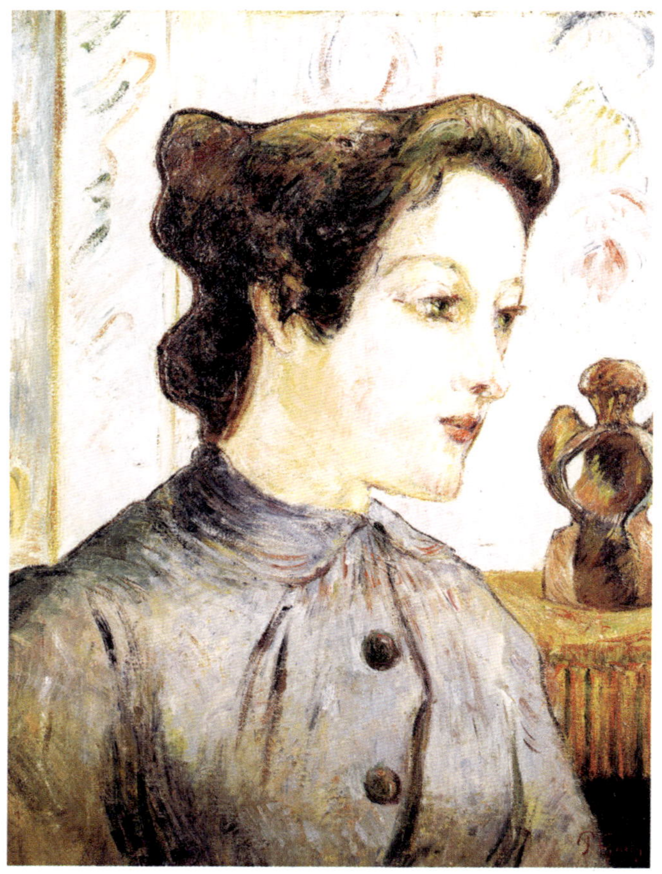

Copenhagen

Much like his father's decision to leave France when he lost his editorial role on *Le National*, Gauguin, after losing his stockbroker job, decided in November 1884 to move from Rouen to Copenhagen, the home-city of his wife Mette. He took with him his collection of paintings, which he hoped to sell or exhibit. His original plan was for Mette to go to Copenhagen in July 1884, while he remained in Rouen; she would get a job to support the family and then Gauguin would join her to sell his paintings in the Danish art market. In a letter of late 1884 to Pissarro, Gauguin damns the popular art of Denmark: '… what there is here is so bad, in such bad taste that the slightest work of art shines like a beacon in the middle of all that rubbish…. It's difficult because this bad taste is so much part of the national character that it is almost impolite to produce anything else.' He was not successful, and his Danish in-laws and extended relations did not approve of his lack of a job and poor treatment of Mette.

At first, the family lived with Mette's mother and then moved to 105 Gammel Kongevej. Mette worked as a language tutor, teaching French. To make an income Gauguin took a job as a tarpaulin salesman for Dillies and Co. In a letter written to Pissarro at the end of May 1885, he wrote: 'The most terrible cannibal is nothing compared to a Danish property owner.' His words sum up the uneasy, unhappy life he was leading in Copenhagen. His life had altered dramatically.

Return to Paris

Gauguin tried to make a success of his new profession as a painter in Copenhagen. From 1–6 May 1885 he exhibited his work at the Society of the Friends of Art. However, he moved back to Paris in June 1885, leaving his wife and four of his children in Copenhagen and taking Clovis with him as a threat to Mette that by right he could take all the children from her. When he made this life-changing decision to return to an artist's existence in Paris, Gauguin found that the art world had changed. Many who knew him shunned association with him due to his abandonment of his family, including the wilful removal of his six-year-old son from his mother, and subsequent neglect of Clovis while in his care.

Summer 1886

In the summer of 1886, Gauguin returned Clovis to Mette in Denmark – the boy's presence was not conducive to his plans. He moved to an artists' colony in Pont-Aven, over 500 km (310 miles) south-west of Paris, a beautiful location on the shores of the Atlantic coast of Brittany. Gauguin found a creative energy during his time there, writing: 'I love Brittany. I find wildness and primitiveness there. When my wooden shoes ring on the granite, I hear the muffled, dull, powerful tone I seek in my painting.' He took up residence at Madame Marie-Jeanne Gloanec's auberge alongside other artists, living cheaply. Pension Gloanec, at the centre of the village, was home to the Pont-Aven school of painters. A feature in the British journal *Magazine of Art*, of 1889,

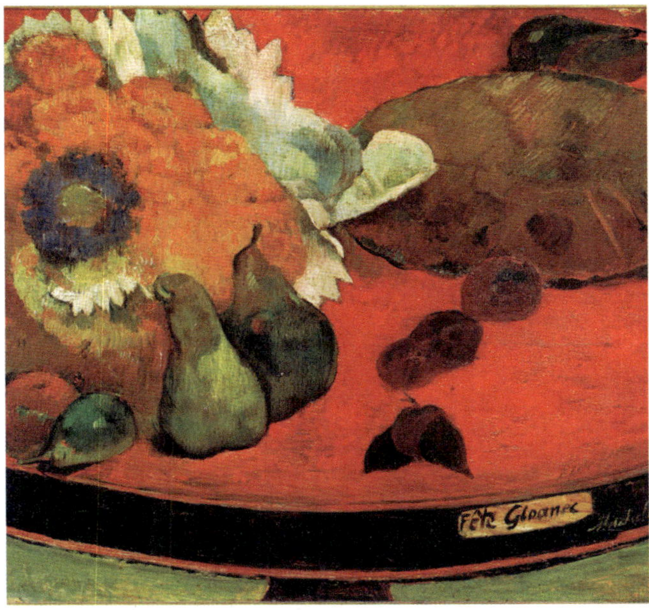

including sketches by Randolph Caldecott (1846–86), described the 'Bohemian' setting of the inexpensive inn and artists at leisure, seated around a table outside the building, morning and evening. Madame Gloanec, affectionately called 'Mother Gloanec' by her residents, was celebrated by Gauguin in a still-life, *Fête Gloanec* (1888, *see* above), a birthday present to her.

Breton Costumes and Customs

Gauguin and the Pont-Aven group of artists, such as Paul Sérusier (1864–1927) and Émile Bernard (1868–1941), utilized their location and the traditions of south-west Brittany, its work, leisure and religious customs, to create remarkable paintings. Gauguin produced many works of simple scenes, of the landscape featuring Pont-Aven or Lézavan in the distance, or farmworkers in the fields, or turkeys, or a cow under trees or by the sea, or of local boys wrestling or playing by the riverbank, or a clog maker at work. He made many drawings on site in his sketchbooks, often to create a painting from sketches and memory later, wherever his studio was, in Paris, Arles or Tahiti. He captured the distinguishing characteristic of Breton women in their traditional dress with bonnet (the *coiffe*), often worn with long white tails to denote craftswomen. Gauguin, informed by Pissarro and Degas, depicted them in *Four Breton Women* (1886, *see* page 92) and *The Breton Shepherdess* (1886, *see* page 93). On a subsequent stay, his technique altered in *Vision after the Sermon (Jacob Wrestling with the Angel)* (1888, *see* page 95), full of religious symbolism, and its antidote *Breton Girls Dancing, Pont-Aven* (1888, *see* page 96), capturing the joy of summer and happy children in Lollichon field. A later work, *Haymaking* (1889, *see* page 100), exhibits Gauguin's move away from the picturesque to the symbolic in its striking anti-natural colours and flat Japanese plane, first practised in *Vision after the Sermon*.

Bernard and Gauguin

Gauguin began *Vision after the Sermon (Jacob Wrestling with the Angel)* in August 1888 in Pont-Aven. A gifted young artist, Bernard, a pioneer of cloisonnism whom Gauguin had briefly met in Pont-Aven in 1886, had joined him. Bernard brought his painting *Breton Women in the Meadow* (1888), depicting Breton women attending a religious rite called a 'Pardon', festival celebrations for each of four Breton saints, for whom the cow is a symbolic attribute. Was the cow in Gauguin's *Vision after the Sermon* depiction a symbol of the Breton saints and the service? The symbolism of Bernard's subject, its striking cloisonné jewel-rich colours and subject, are said to have inspired Gauguin's *Vision after the Sermon*. Japanese prints were also primary sources. Gauguin wrote to Pissarro about the work, that its timing followed a church service and a sermon, with the congregation witnessing the angel and Jacob wrestling. Reading the Bible extract, Genesis 32: 22-31, with its depiction of the location where the angel wrestles with Jacob, one can see Gauguin's symbolic use of the textual context. The style of the wrestle scene is possibly informed by Hokusai's wrestlers in his *Manga* (from 1814), the French edition of which was published in 1888–89. Gauguin's time spent with the École de Pont-Aven art movement in 1886, 1888, 1889 and 1890 undoubtedly launched the phenomenal body of bold work that he would create in Martinique, Tahiti and the Marquesas Islands, such as *Seashore, Martinique Island* (1887, *see* page 94).

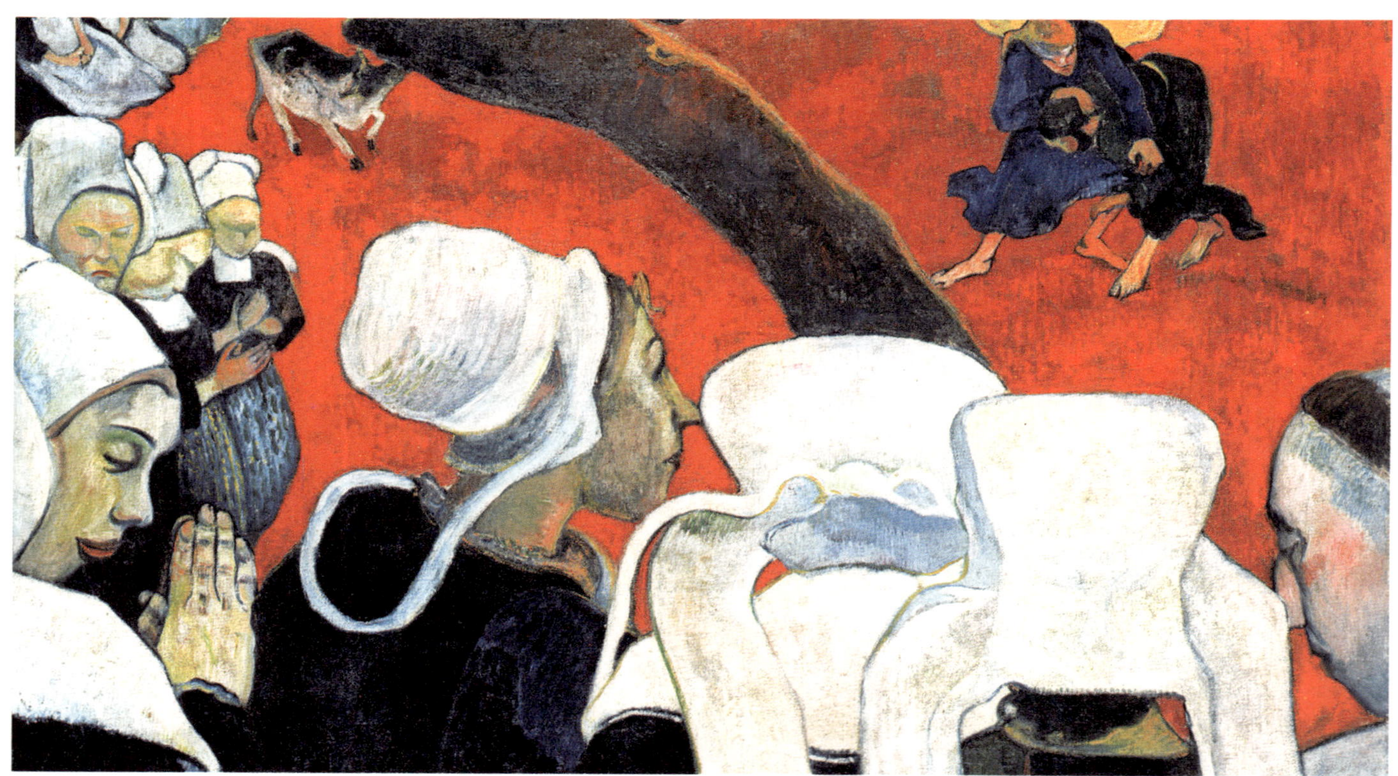

Complementary Colours

The immediate difference one notices in Gauguin after Impressionism, coming to fruition during his Pont-Aven stay in July–October 1888, was his bold use of complementary colours, red/green, blue/orange, yellow/violet. It was a technique used by Van Gogh and Gauguin to great effect, creating a vivid intensity of colour to focus attention on a painting's subject. Gauguin used it, with remarkable results, in *Fête Gloanec* (1888), *Still Life with Profile of Laval* (1886), *Breton Girls Dancing* (1888), *Vision after the Sermon* (*Jacob Wrestling with an Angel*) (1888) and *Self-portrait* (1889, *see* page 69).

Sérusier: Gauguin Disciple

In 1888 Sérusier joined the Pont-Aven art colony, and looked to Gauguin for help with his painting style. In a now-famous text, written by artist Maurice Denis (1870–1943), he recalled a conversation at a forest's edge between Gauguin and the young artist. Gauguin offered advice: 'How do you see these trees? They are yellow. So, put in yellow; this shadow, rather blue, paint it with pure ultramarine; these red leaves? Put in vermilion.' The resulting work was *The Talisman, the Aven River at the Bois d'Amour* (1888), painted on a cigar box. When Sérusier returned to Paris and showed it to his friends, Gauguin's reputation as an artist soared.

Panama and Martinique

In a letter to his wife Mette, written from Paris, Gauguin wrote that his intention was to go to Panama 'to live the life of a native' on the then-uninhabited island, Taboga, to 'reinvigorate myself far from the company of men'. Mette would have to continue to work to support herself and the children. An inheritance that Gauguin had received from his Uncle Isidore had given him 13,000 francs but letters to Mette show that he was reluctant to share it with her for the children. After she pleaded, he sent 1,500 francs and kept the rest for his travels. He left for Panama with fellow-painter Charles Laval (1861–94) – whom he had first met in Pont-Aven during his three-month stay in the summer of 1886 – arriving in Panama City in April 1887. They were employed briefly as workers building the Panama Canal before moving

on to Martinique in May 1887 (it seems Gauguin never achieved his aim of visiting Taboga). The Caribbean island of Martinique, a French overseas territory since 1815, was Gauguin's 'primitive, native life' destination but both he and Laval became extremely ill with dysentery and returned to Paris by the end of the year. However, during their time on the island each painted remarkable works, as Gauguin's *Martinique Landscape* (1887, *see* page 36) and *Seashore, Martinique Island*, reveal. Away from the Parisian art scene and influence of other art forms, Gauguin further developed his own technique, building on rich, vibrant colours and Japanese painting.

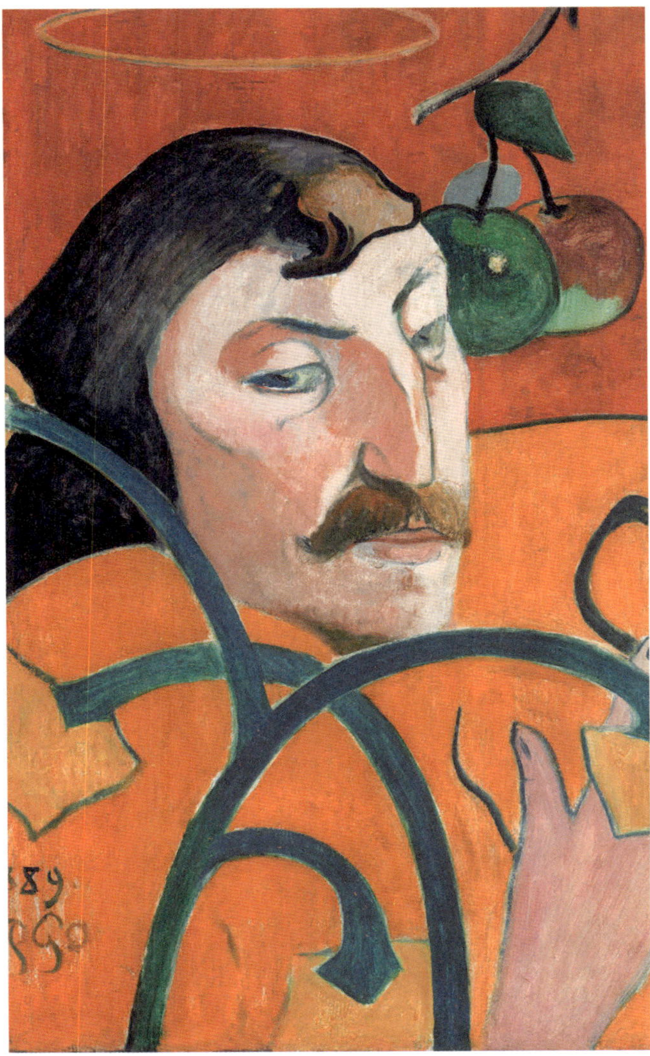

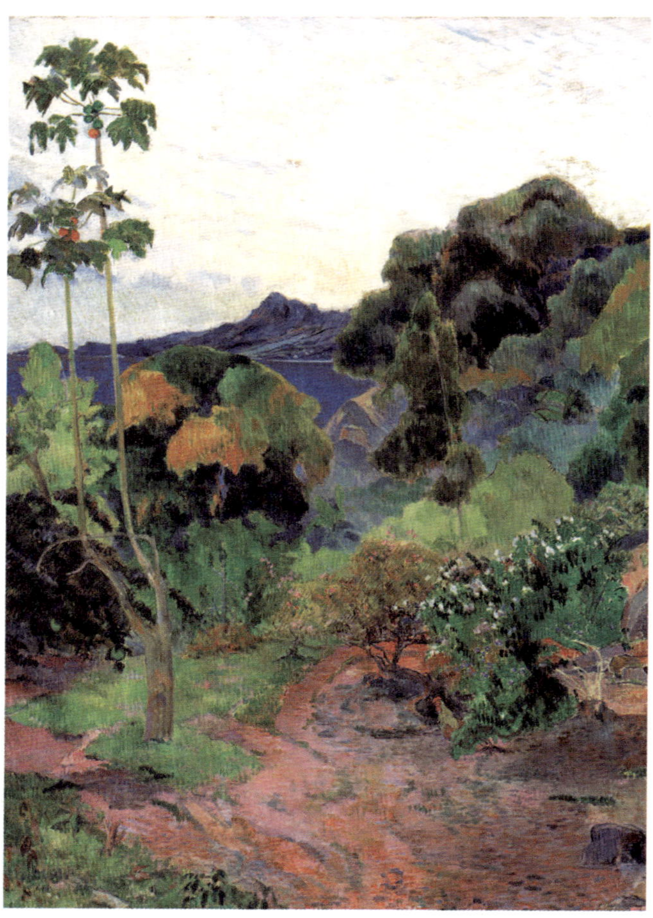

Arles, 1888

It was Van Gogh's idea to start an art colony in the South of France.
He moved to Arles in February 1888 and lived there for 15 months,
producing around 200 paintings. He asked artists to join him, including
Bernard and Laval, but only Gauguin responded, after months of letters
of invitation. Gauguin employed Theo van Gogh (1857–91), Vincent's
brother, as his art agent. Gauguin arrived in Arles around 5.00 a.m.
on 23 October 1888, at the end of a two-day journey from Pont-Aven,
nearly 700 miles away. When he walked into the Café de la Gare, the
owner Monsieur Joseph Ginoux recognized him, as each artist had
agreed to send a self-portrait in character. Gauguin painted himself
as the fictitious hero Jean Valjean from Victor Hugo's 1862 novel *Les
Misérables*: 'It is the face of an outlaw…. The lusty blood spreads over

the face and the hues of a furnace fire around the eyes indicates the
fiery lava that engulfs our painters' souls.'

Van Gogh had sent Gauguin a self-portrait as a Japanese missionary.
It would be an interesting experience living together. During the nine
weeks spent in Arles, Gauguin painted Van Gogh's portrait, presenting
the artist painting sunflowers. It was an intimate portrayal of the artist,
from the confined space that he worked in to his mode of dress and
intense concentration when painting, his manner of holding the palette
and its colour-scheme: ochre yellows, blues and greens, the paintbrush
held at arm's length. *Van Gogh Painting Sunflowers* (1888, *see* page
68) was sent to Theo as a gift. Gauguin wrote to him from Arles on 20
December 1888, '… perhaps, it is not a very good likeness, I think it
does convey some of his inner character and if you have no objection
keep it, unless you do not like it'.

Painting Life

Gauguin and Van Gogh had shared interests and they both enjoyed
painting en plein-air, but there were also many differences of opinion.
Gauguin, writing to his painter-friend Bernard in early December 1888,
cited '… in general, Vincent and I do not see eye to eye, particularly on
painting. He admires Daumier, Daubigny, Ziem and the great Rousseau,
all of whom I cannot bear. And he hates Ingres, Raphael, Degas, all of
whom I admire'. After settling in, Gauguin organized a proper procedure
to allot finances for their necessities: painting materials, as well as eating,
drinking and socializing with women from the local brothel. On good
weather days both painted the same locations quite differently. Gauguin
created dramatic, symbolic paintings from local characters, motifs and
activities to intense effect, as in *Arlésiennes (Mistral)* (1888, *see* page
97) and *Grape Harvest at Arles (Les Misères humaines)* (1888, *see* page
98). Gauguin wrote to Theo in Paris about the latter in November 1888:
'I have done a painting from memory of a really bewitched poor wretch
in the middle of a red vineyard.' Gauguin had placed women in Breton
costumes in an Arlésienne landscape. The figure to the left in black
represents death, a precursor to the figure of death in his monumental
work *The Spirit of the Dead Watching (Manao Tupapau)* (1892, *see* page
113). The seated figure, based on a Peruvian mummy that Gauguin had
seen in Paris, represents human misery.

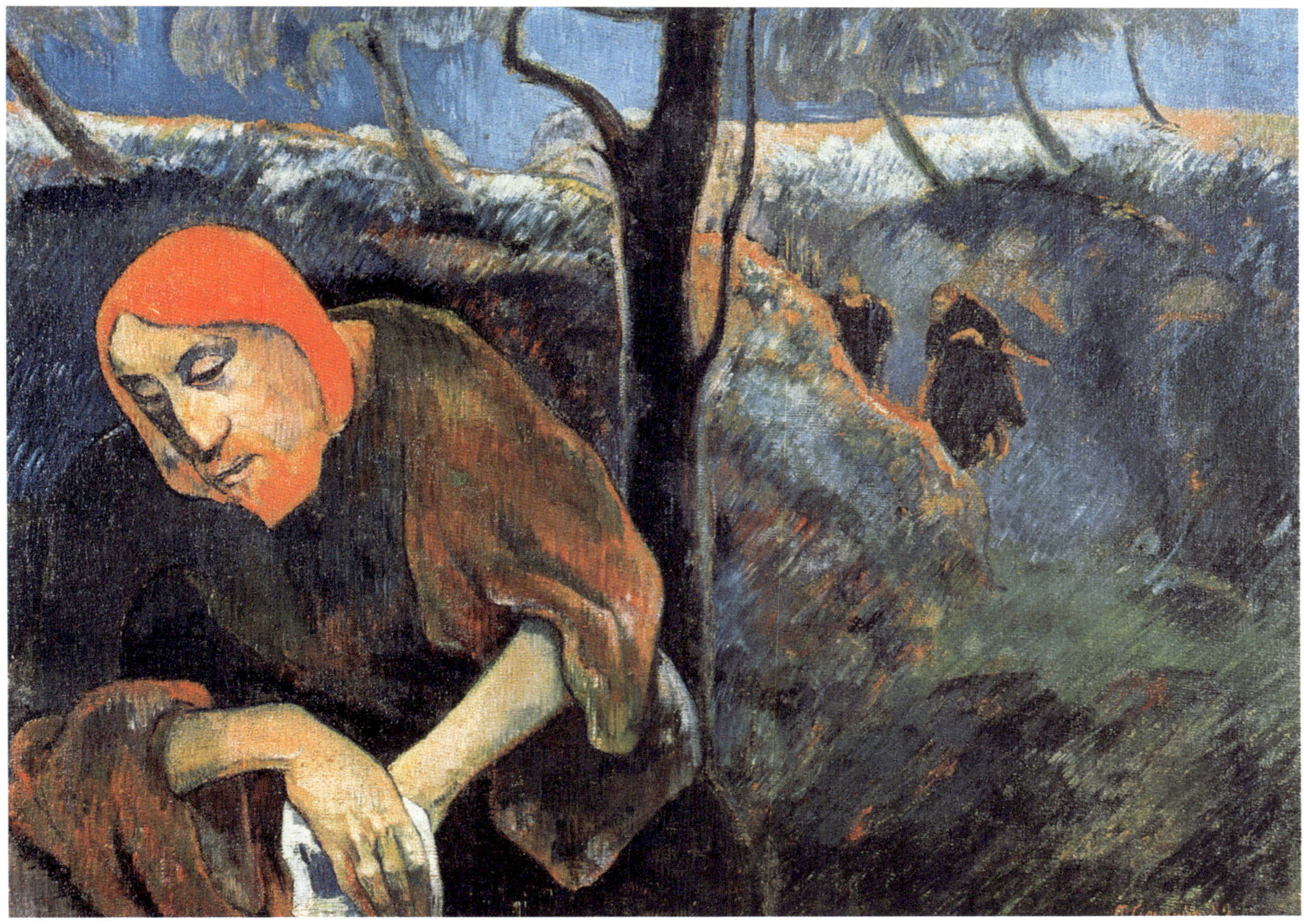

Simmering Tensions

Tension rose in the winter spell of continuous rain, for days on end, which left Gauguin and Van Gogh working in a small studio space. Gauguin's bedroom could only be accessed through Van Gogh's bedroom, which would have made privacy difficult. The cafés and bars were a release. Living day to day in Van Gogh's Yellow House may have pressured them to produce remarkable art, but local young women were reluctant to pose, so models were scarce. They used the same model, such as the older woman Madame Ginoux in Gauguin's *Café at Arles* (1888, *see* page 67), which shows the pool table of Van Gogh's *The Night Café (Café de nuit) in Arles* (1888). Gauguin wrote to Theo, on 12 December 1888, 'Vincent and I find it absolutely impossible to live peacefully in each other's company; our temperaments are incompatible'.

Gauguin returned to Paris and the artists would never again see each other. However, they continued to correspond. Gauguin wrote from Le Pouldu in early November 1889, referring to one of his paintings, *Christ in the Garden of Olives* (1889, *see* above): 'A greenish-blue twilight sky, trees all leaning together in a crimsonish mass, purply earth and the figure of Christ, enveloped in dark ochre clothing and with bright red hair.' He enclosed a sketch for Vincent. Gauguin had much admired the paintings of sunflowers that Van Gogh had created to decorate his Yellow House bedroom.

In February 1890 Gauguin sent him a painting in exchange for two paintings of sunflowers, copies of the originals. On 29 July 1890, Van Gogh died at Auvers-sur-Oise.

Yellow Christ, 1889

Fifteen paintings by Gauguin relate to the image of Christ. Near Pont-Aven in the Bois d'Amour is a small seventeenth-century church. Within its interior is a yellow polychrome wooden Christ, the source for Gauguin's remarkable work the *Yellow Christ* (1889, *see* page 102). Many speculated that it was a self-portrait – Gauguin punished for the abandonment of his family. *Yellow Christ* and *Self-Portrait with Yellow Christ* (1889) are rich in literary symbolism. The same wooden Christ informed Gauguin's *Green Christ* (*Breton Calvary*) (1889, *see* page 99) as well.

Journey to Tahiti

Tahiti in French Polynesia, in the central South Pacific Ocean, has 118 islands, extending 2,000 km. There are five groups of islands, of which Tahiti, the largest island and its cultural capital Papeete, became a protectorate of France in 1842. Like other French overseas domains, French citizens owned properties and plantations, and lived on the islands. Gauguin sailed from France in April 1891 via the Suez Canal to Australia and New Caledonia before arriving in Tahiti. He must have felt a long way from home. Letters to and from friends, art dealers and his wife took four months to arrive. His career as a professional artist was approaching its tenth year, and he felt assured that artwork reflecting primitive local people and customs, produced in Tahiti, would sell to French audiences. He needed money and a change of direction. He wanted a low-cost way of living while leading a primitive life.

Gauguin in Tahiti

The first sojourn in Tahiti, a stay of two years, took place from June 1891 to June 1893. On arrival, Gauguin was disappointed to find that Tahiti was fast losing its Polynesian identity, becoming an outpost of Europe:

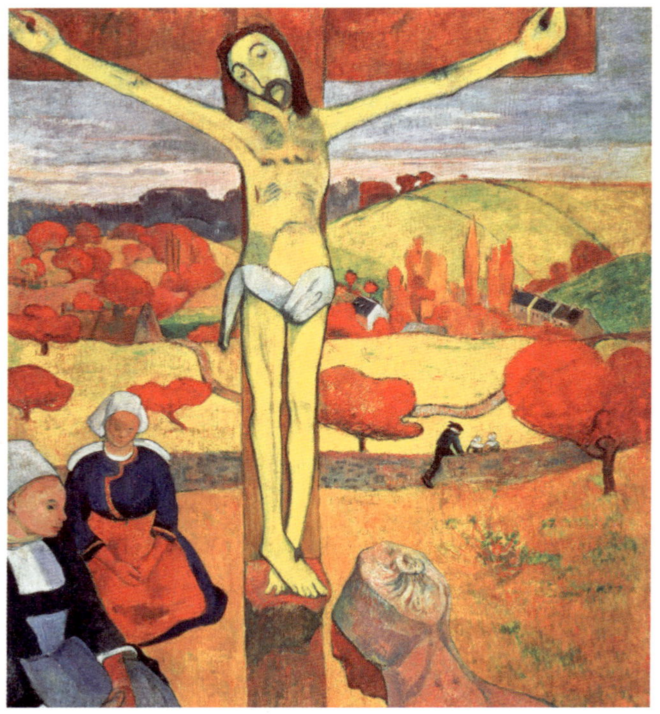

It was Europe – the Europe which I had thought to shake off – and that under the aggravating circumstances of colonial snobbism, and the imitation, grotesque even to the point of caricature, of our customs, fashions, vices, and absurdities of civilization. Was I to have made this far journey, only to find the very things which I had fled?

Under French colonial rule, Tahiti was cultivating a tourist industry. With dual languages of French and Tahitian, visitors felt at home among the native population of around 10,000 inhabitants. It was not in keeping with Gauguin's fantasy of a primitive, savage nation. In an interview in *L'Écho de Paris* on 13 May 1895, he considered primitivism the 'childhood of humanity rediscovered'. Only in areas outside the colonial cities did Maori traditions continue. He moved to Mataiea in late September, a quieter place, about 80 km from the city. It was a beautiful coastal location with a coral reef, lagoons and lush vegetation. However, through his paintings Gauguin substantiated a Western myth of the South Sea islanders, exploiting and exploring their local customs, superstitions and, in younger women and boys, their trusting naïvety to pose for his art. His first impression of the island was that it was not a magical sight. But for him, permissible sex with adolescent girls was an invitation to behave immorally, without thought for his wife, his children or Tahitian women.

Tehamana

A 13-year-old girl, Tehamana, living in a rural area of the island, was invited to live with Gauguin as his *vahine*, to keep house for him and to be his mistress. Many of his most famous paintings and his manuscript *Noa Noa* (as Tehura), feature Tehamana. To Gauguin she embodied an earlier Tahitian way of life: its respect of ancestors; its gentle, naïve, trusting, primitive existence. In his first stay of 1891–93, Tehamana was the model for drawings and paintings including *Woman with Mango* (1893, *see* page 76), *The Spirit of the Dead Watching* (*Manao Tupapau*), and *The Ancestors of Tehamana* (*Merahi Metua no Tehamana*) (1893, *see* page 75).

An Idyllic Paradise

Gauguin painted an island that barely existed beyond his mind. Tahiti was pleasant but he exaggerated its beauty, creating richer vegetation, sands and sea in anti-naturalistic colour forms, heightening its charisma and temptations. Native women were depicted as objects, as in *Women of Tahiti, On the Beach* (1891, *see* page 105) or *And the Gold of their Bodies* (1901, *see* page 87), and *Are You Jealous? (Aha Oe Feii?)* (1892, *see* page 112) and *The Spirit of the Dead Watching* (*Manao Tupapau*). Was Gauguin creating a fantasy island of desirable young women for the male gaze? His two-year stay on the island was productive, creating masterpieces of colour and form, but would his paintings sell in Europe?

A Return to Paris

Returning to France via Marseille on 30 August 1893, with only four francs on him, Gauguin needed to make money and re-establish his reputation as an artist. During his two-year absence, younger artists had gained public attention. With his agent Theo van Gogh dead, he needed to renew contacts in order to exhibit his Tahitian paintings. Sérusier sent Gauguin 250 francs for the train journey to Paris, so that he could start work. Gauguin wrote to Mette, asking her to return him the paintings he had sent her in 1892 for a Danish exhibition. Her animosity towards Gauguin was evident in a letter of 15 September 1893 to their mutual friend Schuffenecker: 'he seems just as he was when he departed, steeped in the most brutal egoism', without a thought for her or their children's welfare.

Gauguin's Solo Show

Contact with the Durand-Ruel Gallery instigated a prestigious solo show, an 'exhibition of recent works by Paul Gauguin', organized by Paul Durand-Ruel's sons. Years earlier, Gauguin had made a caustic remark that artists should only ever have a solo show after their deaths. He had changed his mind. The show was held from 10–25 November 1893, with dealers, collectors, artists, art critics, poets, writers and friends invited. The catalogue preface was written by the Symbolist poet Charles Morice (1860–1919). The exhibition included 41 new paintings created in Tahiti, which are today recognized as Gauguin's finest works. Prices were high – between 1,000 and 4,000 francs – and a total of 11 paintings were sold. Alongside a few sculptures and three paintings from Brittany, there were exceptional masterpieces, such as *When Are You Getting Married? (Nafea Faa Ipoipo?)* (1892, *see* page 109), which commanded a price of 1,500 francs, *Hail Mary*

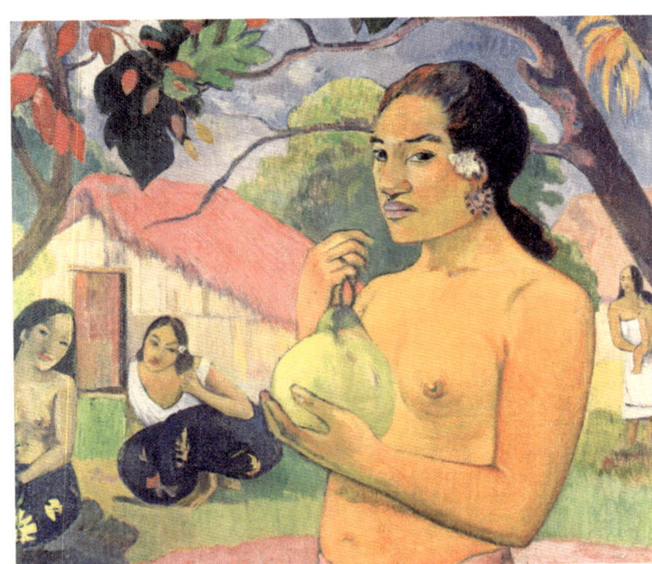

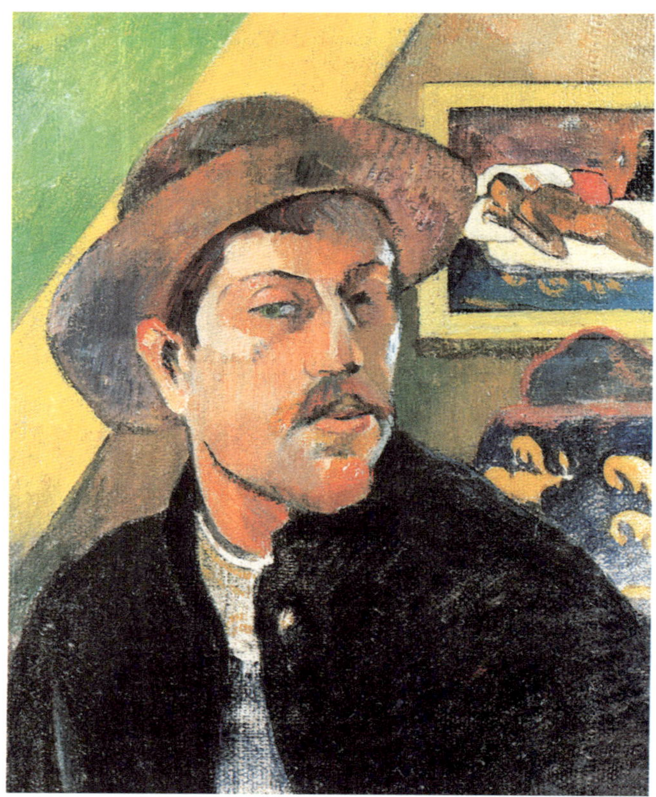

painted the studio in Tahitian island colours of olive green and yellow, and held another show at the studio in January 1894. At this time Gauguin painted *Self-Portrait in a Hat* (1893–94, *see* page 74). In a favourite hat and jacket, he placed himself among Tahitian mementoes brought back from Polynesia. In the background was his controversial *The Spirit of the Dead Watching* (*Manao Tupapau*) in mirror reverse, which had received adverse criticism at the show for its erotic content. Was Gauguin making a point by its inclusion in this self-portrait, which is similar to Manet's earlier *Portrait of Émile Zola* (1868), which had within it a copy of Manet's controversial painting *Olympia* (1863), criticized by French society but praised by Zola? On the reverse side of Gauguin's painting is another work, *Portrait of William Mollard* (1894), a musician and Gauguin's neighbour.

Hail Mary (*Ia Orana Maria*), 1891

Hail Mary (*Ia Orana Maria*) was Gauguin's first major work in Tahiti. He based its layout on a photograph he owned of a bas-relief in the Javanese temple of Borobudur, Indonesia. In his work he depicts Christian – rather than Tahitian – religious iconography. In a letter dated 11 March 1892, he described its content and meaning to the American-born French painter, art collector, and Gauguin's first biographer, George-Daniel de Monfreid (1856–1929), based in Paris:

> *An angel with yellow wings reveals Mary and Jesus, both Tahitians, to two Tahitian women, nudes dressed in pareus, a sort of cotton cloth printed with flowers that can be draped from the waist. Very sombre, mountainous background and flowering trees … a dark violet path and an emerald green foreground, with bananas on the left. I'm rather happy with it.*

A Return to Tahiti

Without seeing his wife or children, Gauguin left Paris after a small farewell party in late June 1895, to arrive in Papeete on board the *Richmond* on 9 September. He had written to Durand-Ruel in early January: 'I am absolutely determined to go back to the islands of Oceania for many years so I can study there seriously in peace.' His first reaction on landing was to leave, due to the increased colonialism

(*Ia Orana Maria*) (1891, *see* page 103), and *By the Sea (Fatata Te Miti)* (1892, *see* page 46), plus the eerie *The Spirit of the Dead Watching (Manao Tupapau)* and *Joyousness (Arearea)* or *The Red Dog* (1892, *see* page 110), which produced some sarcastic comments as to whom the red dog represented. Gauguin liked this painting so much, considering it one of his finest, that after it was sold he bought it back in 1895. *The Moon and the Earth (Hina te Fatou)* (1893), Gauguin's depiction of a Polynesian myth, was purchased by Degas. In December 1893, Gauguin wrote to Mette, 'the most important thing is that my exhibition has had a very great artistic success … for the moment I am considered by many people to be the greatest modern painter'.

Mixed Reviews

The show received diverse press publicity, which increased interest in Gauguin's Tahitian art. Sales from the show allowed him to move into an apartment at 6 rue Vercingétorix, close to Montparnasse. He

of the island, but he took lodging in a bungalow owned by a local, Madame Charbonnier. His time would be spent increasingly in hospital, suffering from syphilis, severe eczema, alcohol dependency and terrible leg pain from a fracture he had received during an altercation in Pont-Aven. He sent for his 'wife' Tehamana. She had married during his absence but that did not stop Gauguin. She stayed for a week before returning to her home.

A Move to Punaauia

After two months Gauguin moved to a village, Punaauia, on the Tahitian west coast. He rented land and built a house. 'Imagine a sparrow cage made of bamboo and divided in two by my old studio curtains, the roof thatched and coconut eaves', he wrote to his friend de Monfreid. He lived as a resident in Punaauia, among the French colonials and locals, and took another *vahine*, Pahura (Pau'ura a Tai), who was 14 years old, to be his mistress, keep house for him and pose as his model. Whatever she thought of him – and local families were keen for their daughters to engage with wealthy Europeans – he viewed her as little more than an employee. Her baby, a daughter, conceived with Gauguin, only lived a few days.

Cahier pour Aline

In her infancy Gauguin doted on his legitimate daughter Aline, born in 1877. He was besotted with her charms. His chosen life, in Pont-Aven and the South Sea islands, meant that he did not see her or his other children living in Copenhagen. Mette, angry at his abandonment as husband and father, strained family relations but he felt a 'savage' bond between himself and Aline. Mette wrote to him only when necessary. It was thus a great shock to receive a letter from her in 1897, abruptly informing him of the sudden death of Aline from pneumonia. Gauguin wrote that at first he had no reaction to the news, perhaps hardened to his life alienated from his family, and then the reality of his loss hit him. He was bereft. He wrote back to Mette, 'I have just lost my daughter; I no longer love God'. He had kept a journal dedicated to Aline, *Cahier pour Aline*, meaning to give it to her, which he described as meditations, 'a reflection of myself', that he wanted to share with her. Reflections, for example, on the Tahitians' fear of ghosts, which made the reading of *The*

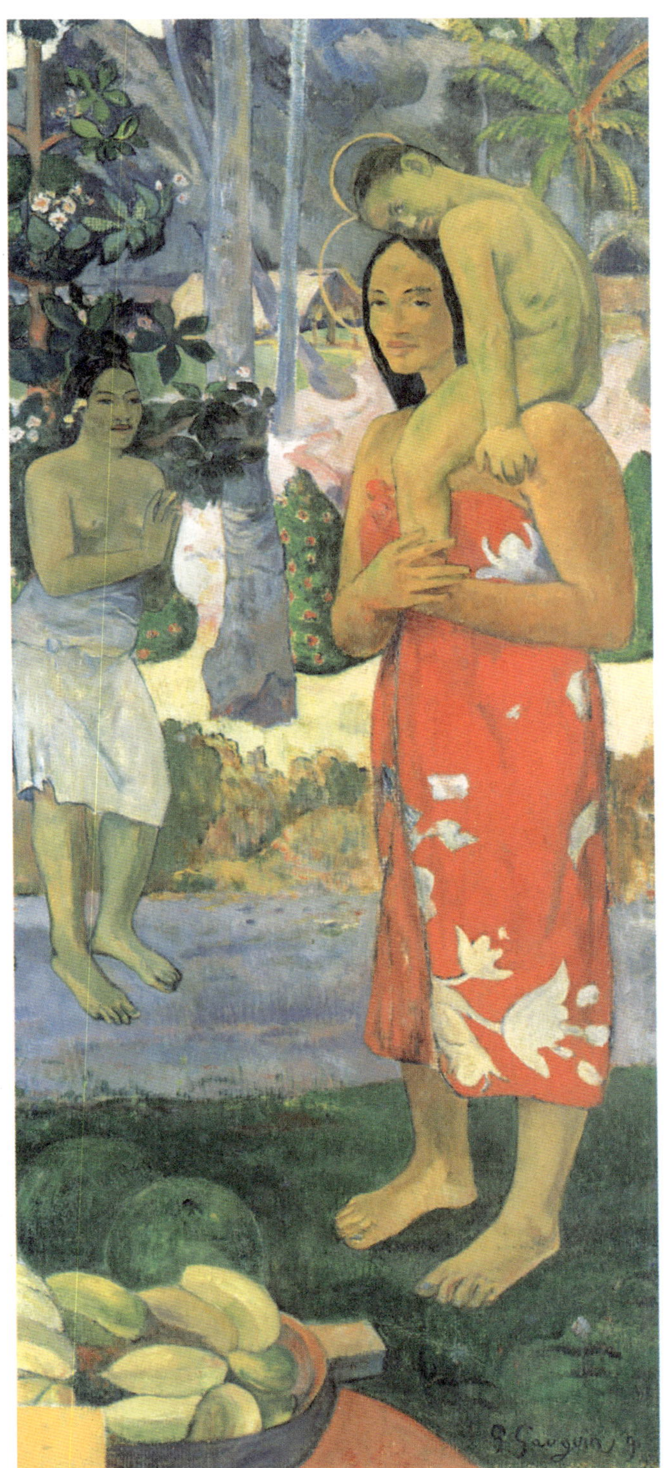

Spirit of the Dead Watching (*Manao Tupapau*) more understandable to a Western audience. Descriptions of works would allow her to discuss them confidently in company, if people wanted to know the 'whys and the wherefores'. It was not to be. Gauguin's bereavement over Aline's death may have led him to attempt suicide.

Where Do We Come From? What Are We? Where Are We Going?, 1897

For Gauguin, of all his paintings – which numbered over 300 created during his professional career – *Where Do We Come From? What Are We? Where Are We Going?* (1897, *see* page 118), painted in Tahiti in December, was his greatest masterpiece. It was his most ambitious work, with the largest number of figures, its content complex in its layered meaning. In February 1898, he wrote to his friend de Monfreid. The letter had a sketch of the work and a description of why and how it was created:

Before I died I wanted to paint a large canvas that I had worked out in my head, and all month long I worked at it at fever pitch…. It's all done without a model, feeling my way with the tip of a brush on a piece of sackcloth that is full of knots, and rough patches so it looks terribly unpolished…. People will say it's slipshod, unfinished … but even so I do believe that not only is this painting worth more than all the previous ones but also that I will never do a better one.

The painting was created at a vulnerable moment in Gauguin's life, which must have added to his engagement with it. Prior to painting the vast canvas, he had experienced the severe loss of his beloved daughter Aline. He wrote about his heartache in April 1897, saying 'each day, as thoughts kept piling in, the wound opened up, becoming deeper and deeper, until now I am completely overwhelmed'. He was dangerously ill, suffering from pain, lack of food and lack of money. He was in despair, contemplated suicide and tried to kill himself. In the

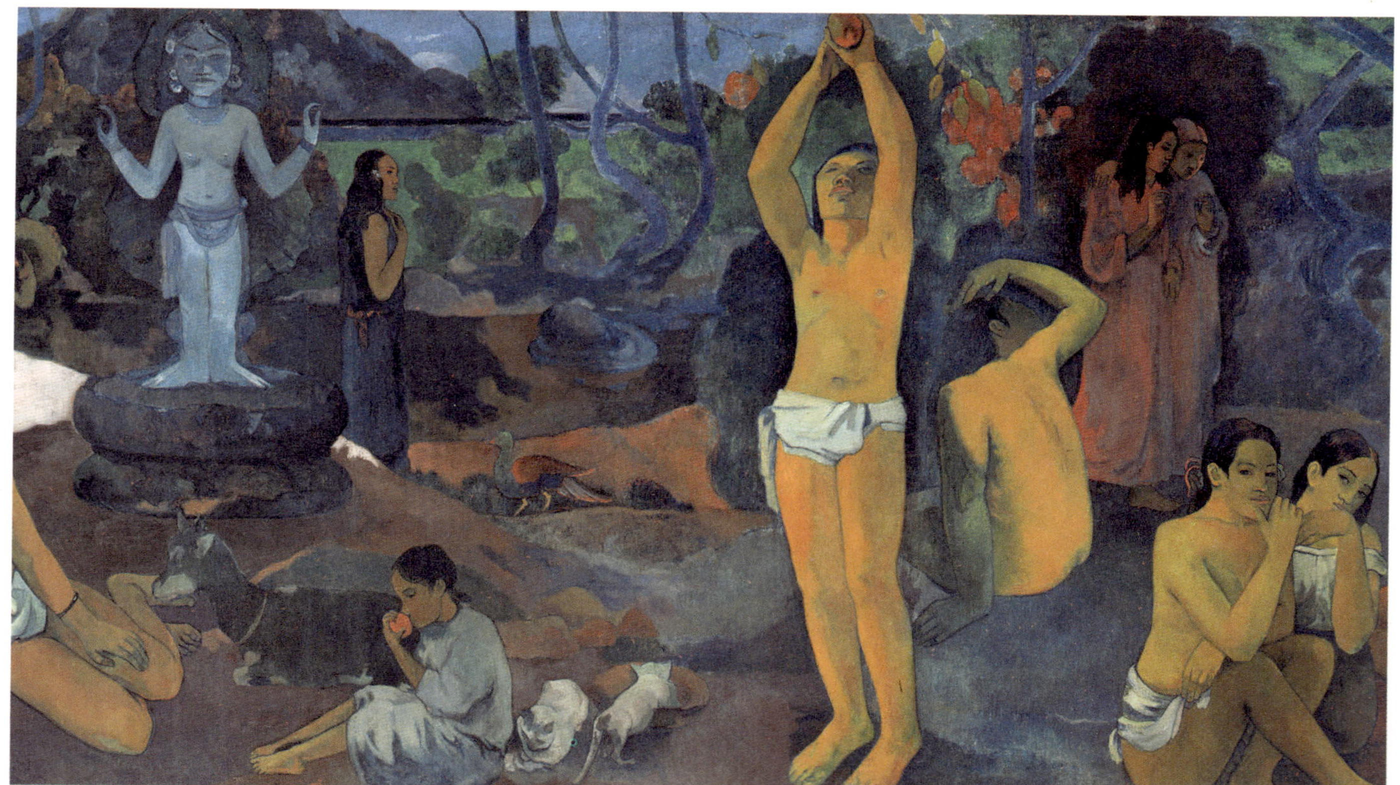

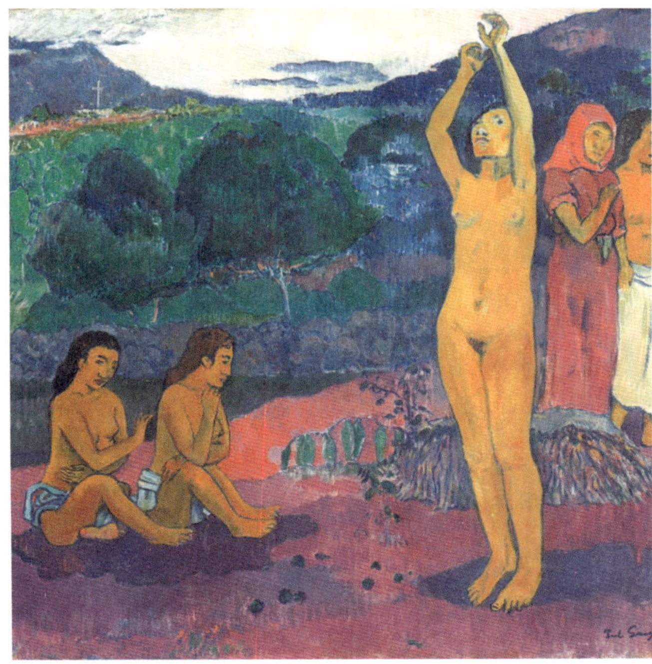

same letter to de Monfreid of February 1898, he voiced his suicidal feelings. He did not have a revolver but he did have a large amount of arsenic saved up from his eczema treatment. However, he explained that perhaps the dose had been too large because he vomited and thus saved his own life. The painting's title may suggest questions that were going through his mind. In the same letter to de Monfreid he gave a long description of the work in every detail.

Iconography

The painting content reads from right to left as in Japanese art, which informed Gauguin's work. It begins with birth, and a small baby, and ends with death. At the centre, the idol with arms uplifted may indicate the world to come. As life moves towards death, the blue idol represents 'the Beyond'; and the elderly woman seated far left, close to death, accepts her end of life. The stages of life continue through the complex visual narrative. Gauguin described the different stages with various figures pondering the questions posed in the title in relation to human existence. In the upper left corner Gauguin painted in its title in French, without question marks, 'D'où Venons Nous / Que Sommes Nous / Où Allons Nous'.

An Exhibition Arranged

When the painting was sent by ship to de Monfreid in July 1898, to arrange its sale with other new works, Gauguin wrote a list of who should be invited to the preview. Among the guests were Degas, Pierre Puvis de Chavannes (1824–98), Renoir and Odilon Redon (1840–1916). The painting was exhibited at the Gallerie Ambroise Vollard from 17 November–10 December 1898. *Where Do We Come From? What Are We? Where Are We Going?* inspired other works which carry part of the narrative, including *Delectable Waters* (*Te Pape Nave Nave*) (1898, *see* page 121), and one of Gauguin's very last works, *The Invocation* (1903, *see* page 125).

The Marquesas Islands

Gauguin's existence in Punaauia deteriorated when a new landlord made him pull down his house. News of the death of his son Clovis, from blood poisoning, increased his anxieties and poor health. He decided to move to the Marquesas Islands, considered the most exotic of all the South Pacific islands, on 1 September 1901. He wanted to

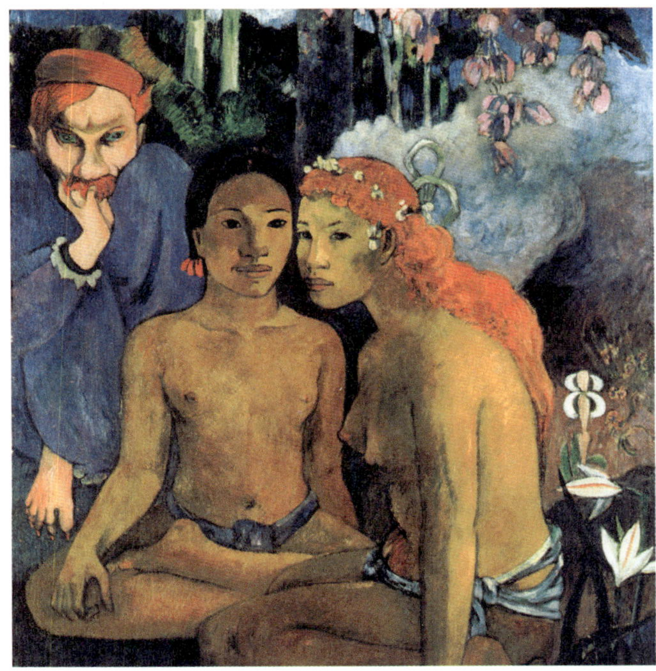

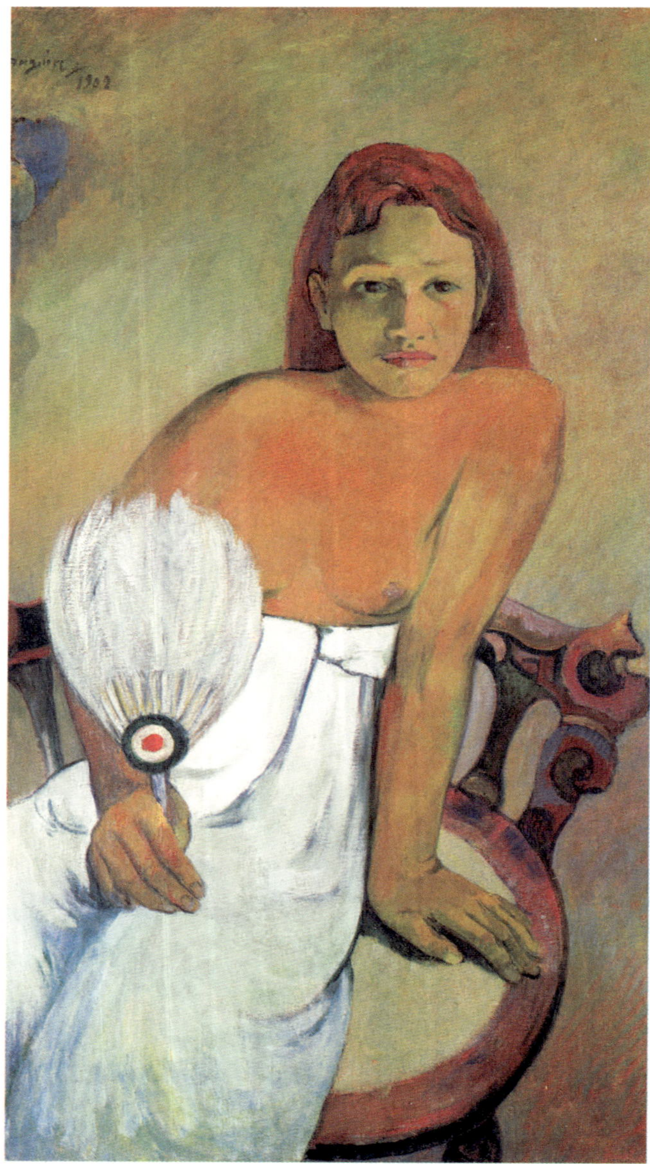

(*Maison du Jouir*), creating Maori-influenced wood carvings to name his home. It was a complete work of art. Gauguin was happy, and wrote to de Monfreid, 'I am more and more pleased with my choice [location] … from the point of view of painting it is admirable. What models! A wonder; I have begun to work already.' His hut-house, situated between the Protestant missionary school and Catholic bishop's residence, meant many young girls passed his door, and he encouraged them to pose for him. From this period, he created some of his most memorable masterpieces, such as *Barbarian Tales* (*Contes barbares*) (1902, *see* page 88), *Girl with a Fan* (1902, *see* page 89) and *Riders on the Beach* (1902, *see* page 123). With a few exceptions, the local people liked him, and in turn he helped them in matters of law, standing up for their rights. Animosity towards him came after he paid for a tribal chief's young daughter, Marie-Rose, to live with him as a *vahine*. She gave birth to a daughter soon afterwards. The missionaries were angered by his immoral behaviour, and his former good relationship with the religious authorities was destroyed.

Journey's End

Did Gauguin know that he would die in his 'savage' paradise, created from his imagination? Within 20 months of his arrival in Atuona, Hiva Oa, Gauguin was dead, his severely poor health deteriorating beyond help. He had spent nearly all his 54 years seeking the 'other', a 'primitive', 'savage', alternative existence. Surrounded by artists in Pont-Aven producing works informed by his own art, or similar, he needed to get away, to produce original work, not inspired by or copied by them. His nine-week stay in Arles had produced exciting work; he had considered returning to stay with Van Gogh again but it was not to be, through Vincent's ill health and then unfortunate death. Martinique and Tahiti, and finally the Marquesas Islands, were his alternative life choices. But his health failed. Despite a regular income in return for paintings from the French art dealer Ambroise Vollard (1866–1939), one of the most important dealers in French contemporary art, making life bearable, his body and his eyesight were weak. He was reliant on morphine. Living a distant life from family, friends and medical treatment that might have helped him recover, took its toll as Gauguin remained in Atuona. He died in his house on 8 May

find a new location, a primitive, remote, sparsely populated habitation – the Marquesas Islands' distant history included cannibalism – 'where life is simple and cheap', he wrote, but found it home to French colonials. However, in the relatively unspoilt Atuona, he began attendance at the Catholic church, bought a plot of land from the local bishop for 650 francs and proceeded to build a thatched hut on it with the help of the local people. He called it the 'House of Pleasure'

1903, possibly of a heart attack. He was buried in the Catholic Calvary Cemetery in Atuona, Hiva Oa, Marquesas Islands.

Gauguin's Writings

Gauguin was such a phenomenal painter that his writing – and sculptures – are often overlooked. On his sojourns in Polynesia he kept regular journals and wrote many letters. In Tahiti he began *Noa Noa*, a journal of his life in Tahiti. It translates as 'more fragrant' in the Maori language, and was the name Gauguin gave to his handwritten manuscript, which he began in 1894, with illustrations added in 1896. He also, of course, had kept the journal *Cahier pour Aline*. An autobiography *Avant et après* (*Before and After*), a handwritten manuscript, was written between January and February 1903, in Atuona. On his death, the autobiography became the property of his family, who sold it to the publisher Kurt Wolff in 1913. It was finally published in 1918.

Gauguin's Legacy

After his death, Gauguin gained public recognition and great acclaim for his work following a retrospective exhibition held in 1906 in Paris. The artist's intensely emotional experimental Synthetist–Symbolist art inspired many artists among his peer group, as well as others, such as Les Fauves (wild beasts), an informal group led by Henri Matisse (1869–1954), André Derain (1880–1954) and Maurice de Vlaminck (1876–1958), whose style would become known as Fauvism (1904–07). In an essay of 1908, Matisse commented:

What I am after, above all, is expression…. I am unable to distinguish between the feeling I have for life and my way of expressing it…. The chief aim of colour should be to serve expression as well as possible….

One only has to look at Derain, Matisse and Vlaminck's art to see the legacy of Gauguin's Synthetism. Later generations of artists, inspired by Gauguin's emotional, expressionist use of colour and figurative primitivism, were reflected in the Expressionism and Cubism art movements.

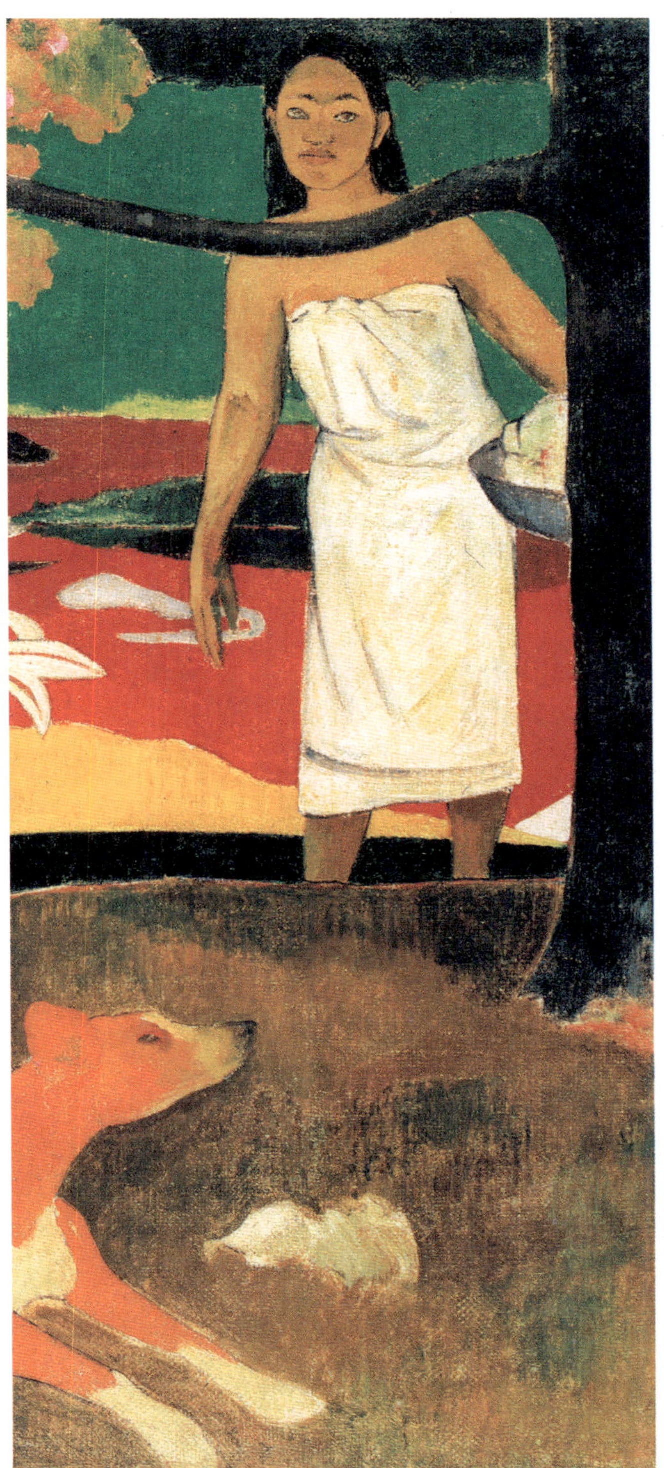

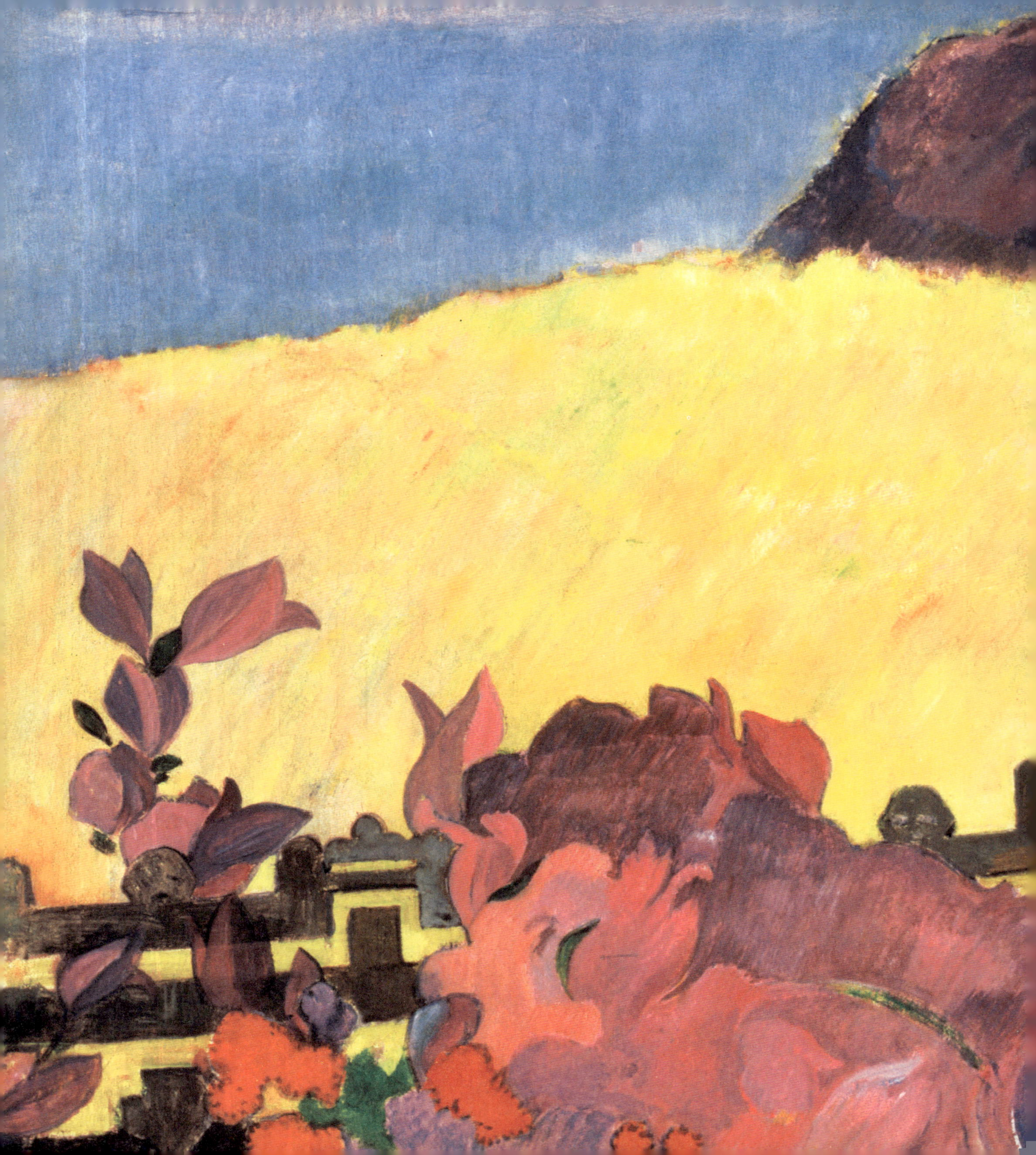

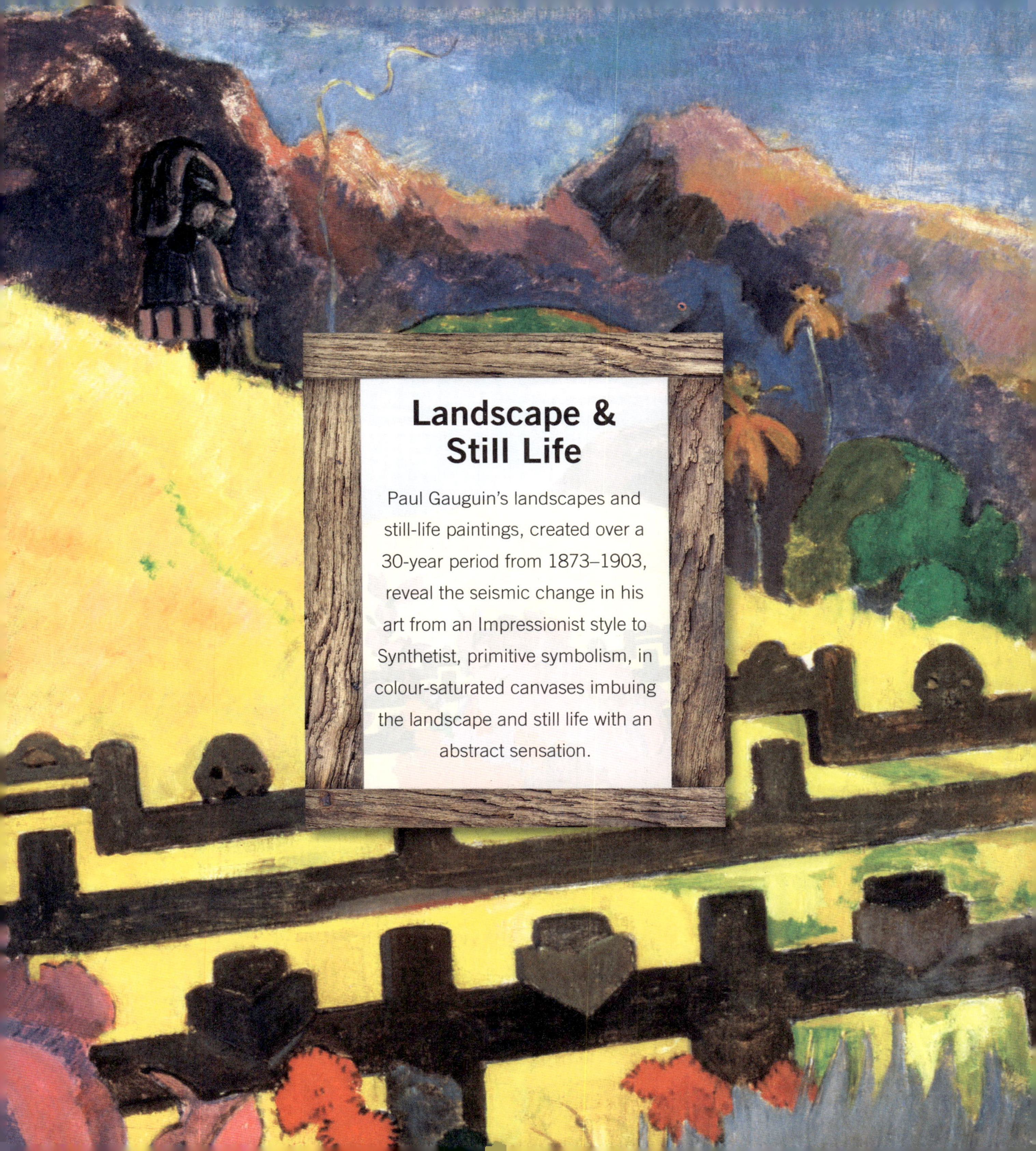

Landscape & Still Life

Paul Gauguin's landscapes and still-life paintings, created over a 30-year period from 1873–1903, reveal the seismic change in his art from an Impressionist style to Synthetist, primitive symbolism, in colour-saturated canvases imbuing the landscape and still life with an abstract sensation.

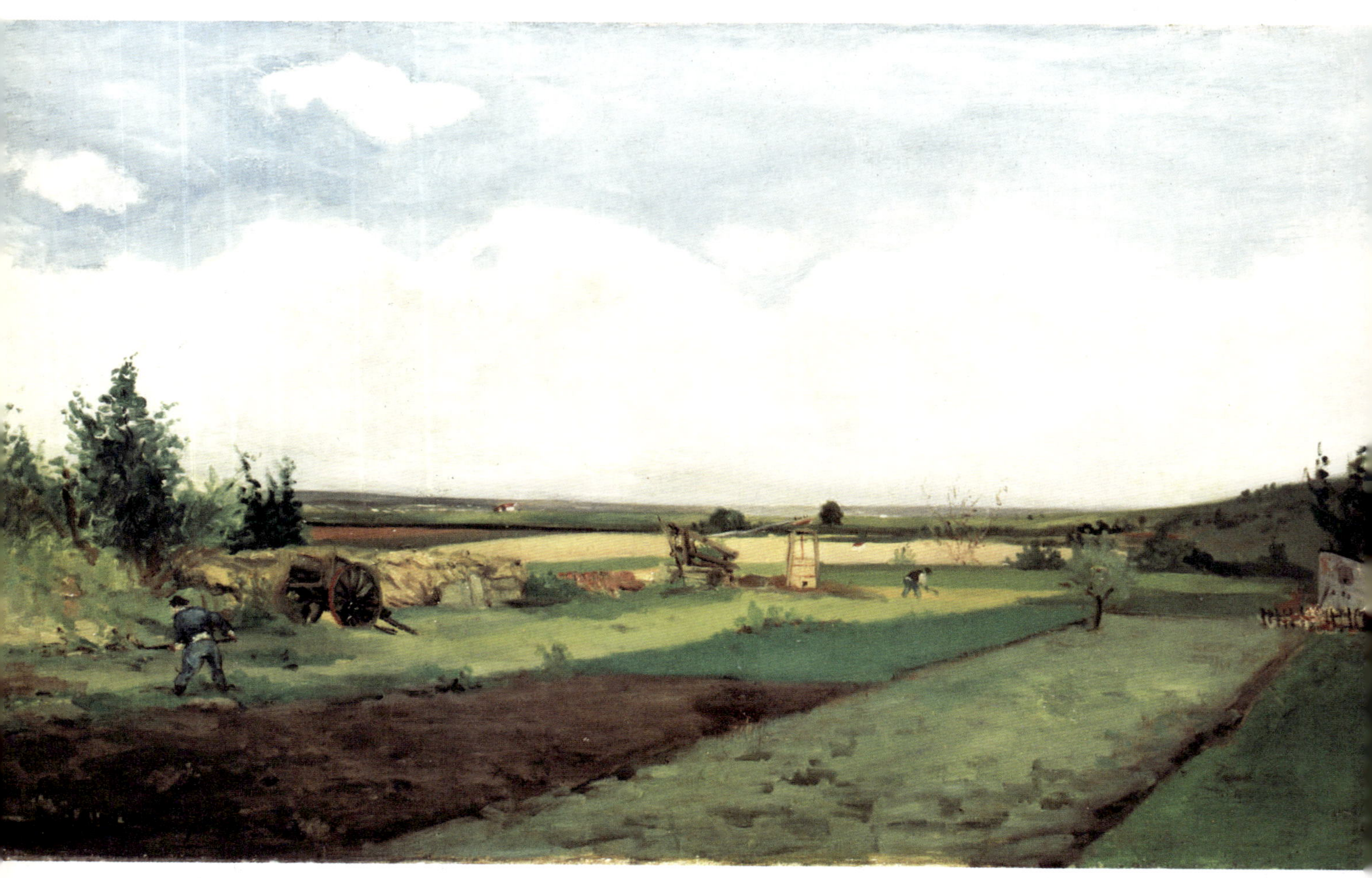

Landscape, 1873
Oil on canvas, 50.5 x 81.5 cm (19⅞ x 32 in)
• Fitzwilliam Museum, Cambridge

Gauguin's first large-format work, it was informed by the paintings of Jean-Baptiste-Camille Corot and Johan Jongkind (1819–91). Gauguin portrays an open sky, thick with white cloud. Fields stretch as far as the distant horizon, while in the foreground peasants work the land.

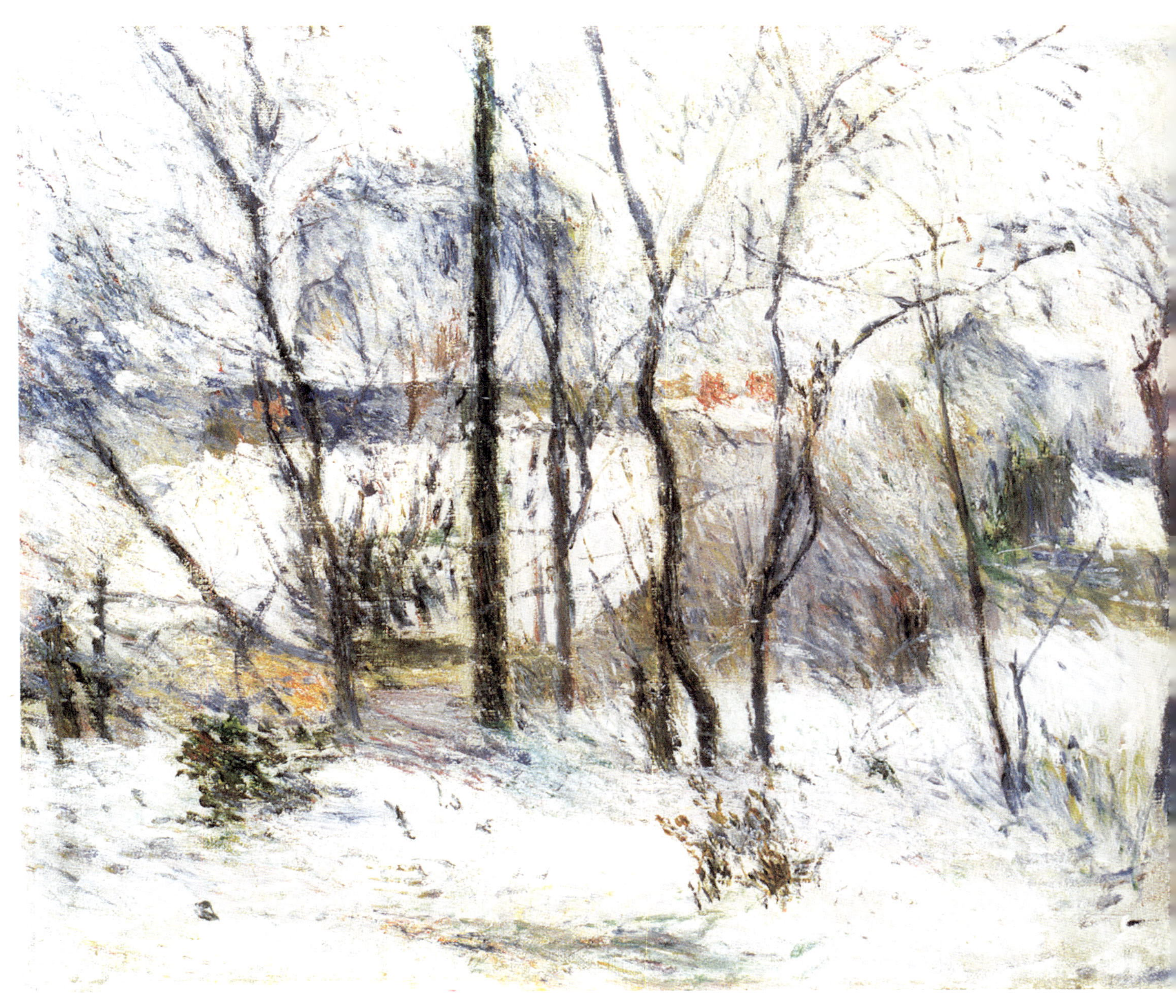

Garden under Snow, 1879
Oil on canvas, 60.5 x 80.5 cm (23⅞ x 31⅔ in)
• Museum of Fine Arts (Szépmüvészeti), Budapest

In this snowy landscape, created during one of the harshest winters in France, Gauguin uses colour sparely and captures the view from his window in the style of Camille Pissarro, with whom he had spent the summer in Pontoise.

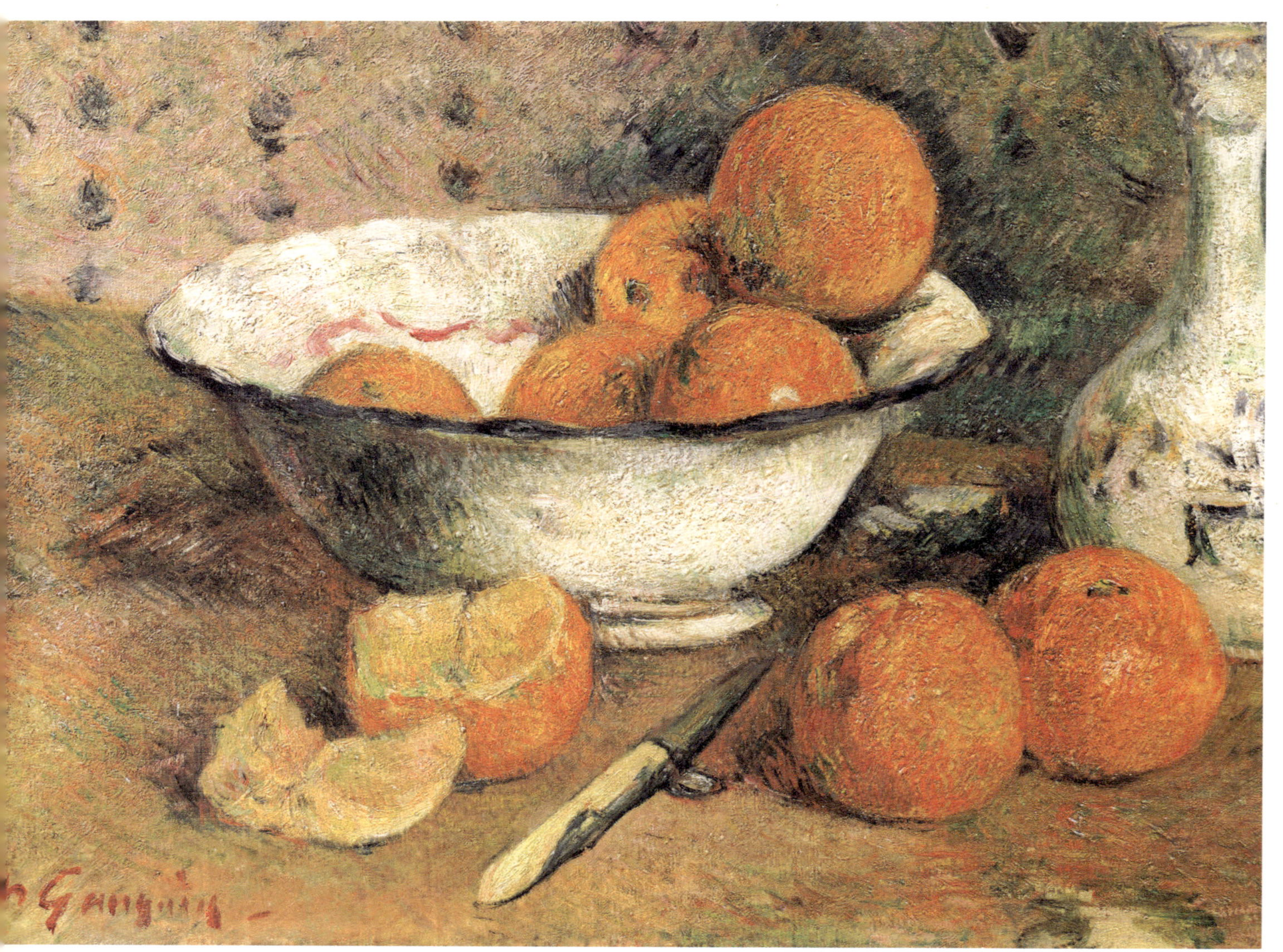

Still Life with Oranges, 1881
Oil on canvas, 33 x 46 cm (13 x 18⅛ in)
• Musée des Beaux-Arts de Rennes, France

Gauguin creates a sumptuous depiction of orange fruit. The artist dabbled with Impressionism, following his painter friends, learning from them, but it was not his favoured method of painting. He soon adapted and changed his technique.

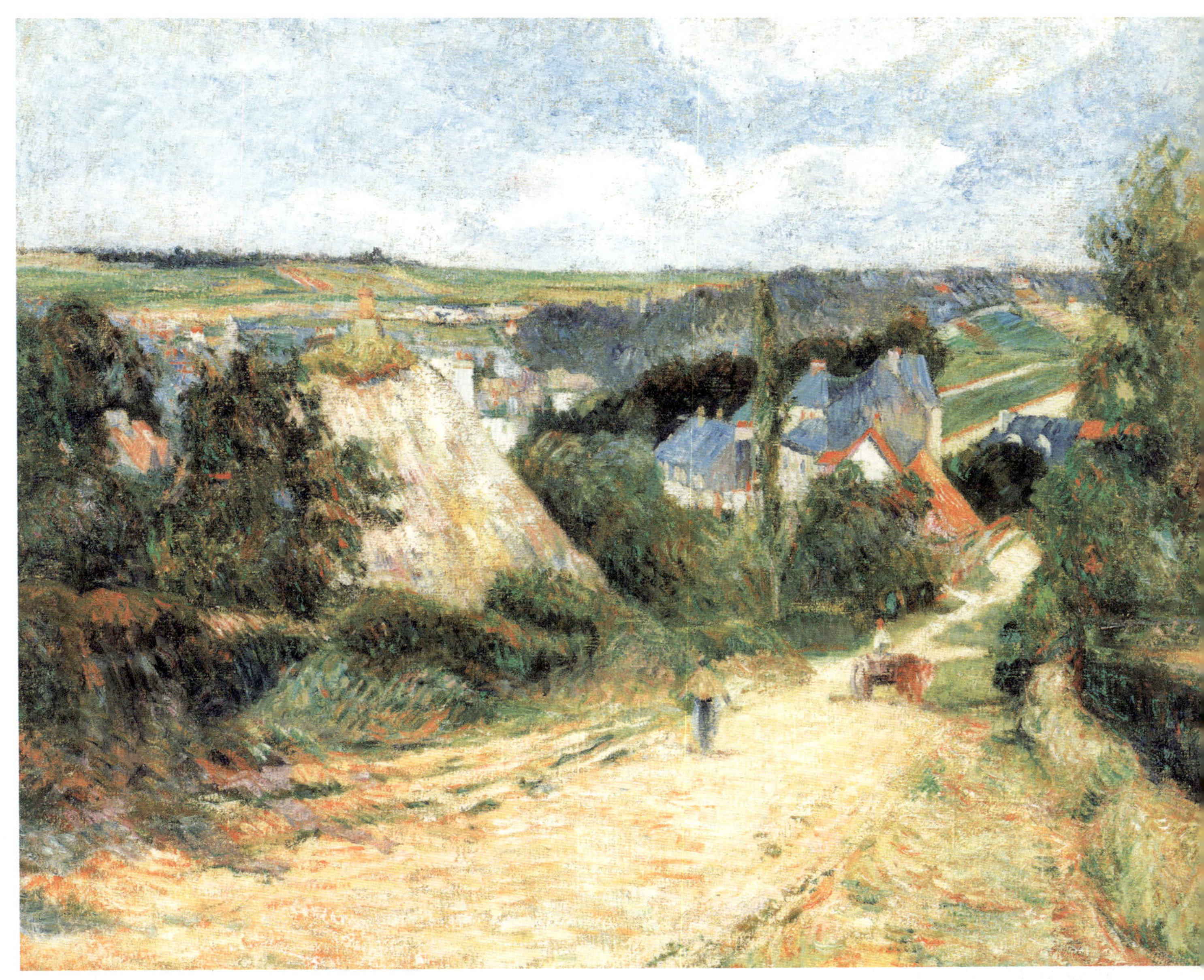

Entrance to the Village of Osny, 1882–83
Oil on canvas, 60 x 72.7 cm (23⅝ x 28⅝ in)
• Museum of Fine Arts, Boston

The landscape painter Pissarro lived in Osny, on the north-west outskirts of Paris, from 1882–84.
Gauguin stayed with him and created this painting in the style of Pissarro. He gave it as a gift to his host
and mentor.

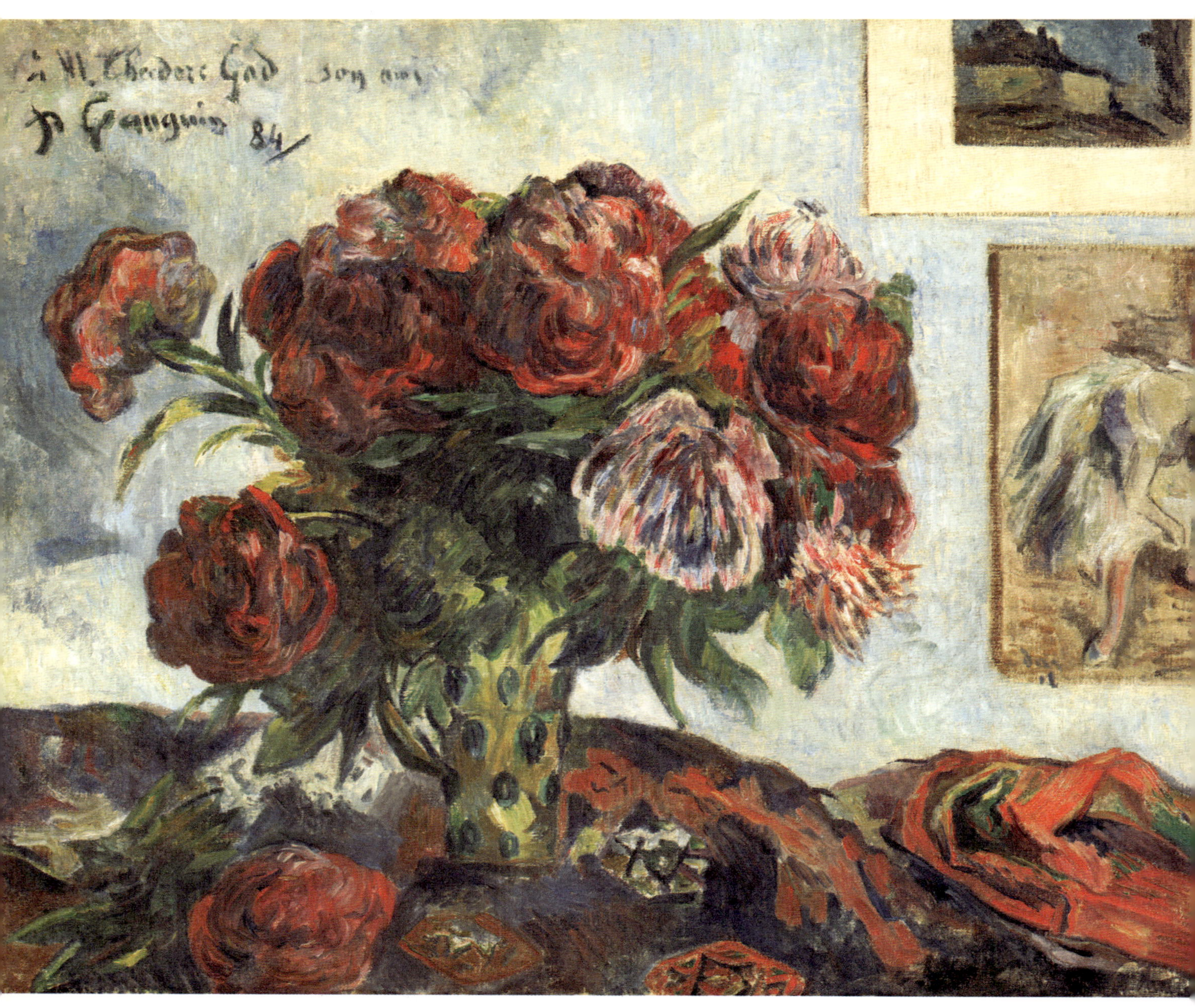

Still Life with Peonies, 1884
Oil on canvas, 59.7 x 73 cm (23½ x 28¾ in)
• National Gallery of Art, Washington D.C.

Gauguin had seen Pierre-Auguste Renoir's painting *Peonies* (*c.* 1880) at the 1882 Impressionist exhibition. He then painted his own versions, including this one, dedicated to his brother-in-law Theodore Gad. The vase sits on a brightly coloured cloth in a domestic interior.

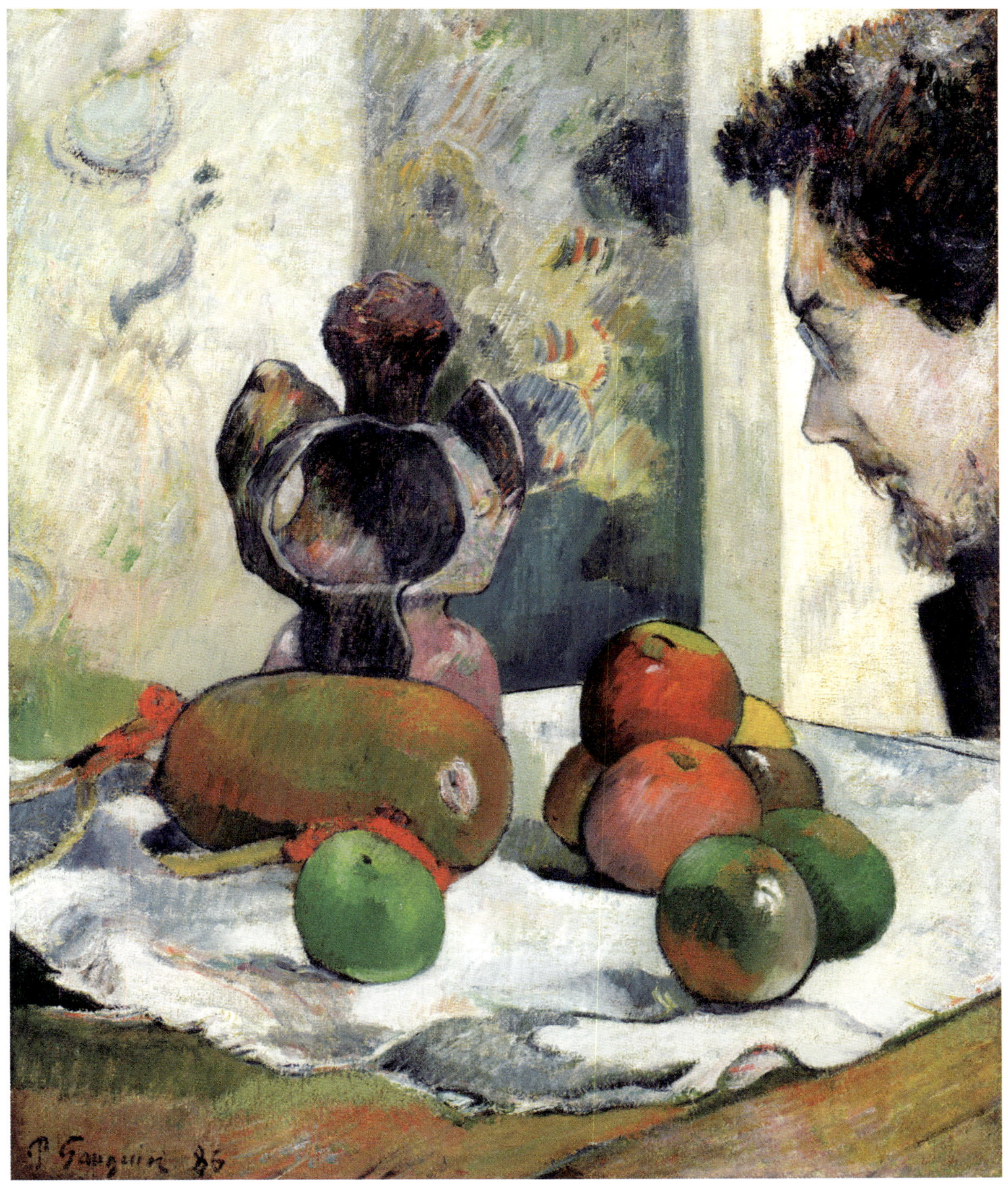

Still Life with Profile of Laval, 1886
Oil on canvas, 46 x 38.1 cm (18⅛ x 15 in)
• Indianapolis Museum of Art, Indiana

Charles Laval was a painter-friend of the artist. The style of painting owes a debt to Edgar Degas, and follows Gauguin's interest in mixing still life with portraiture. Laval stares closely at a ceramic sculpture created by Gauguin.

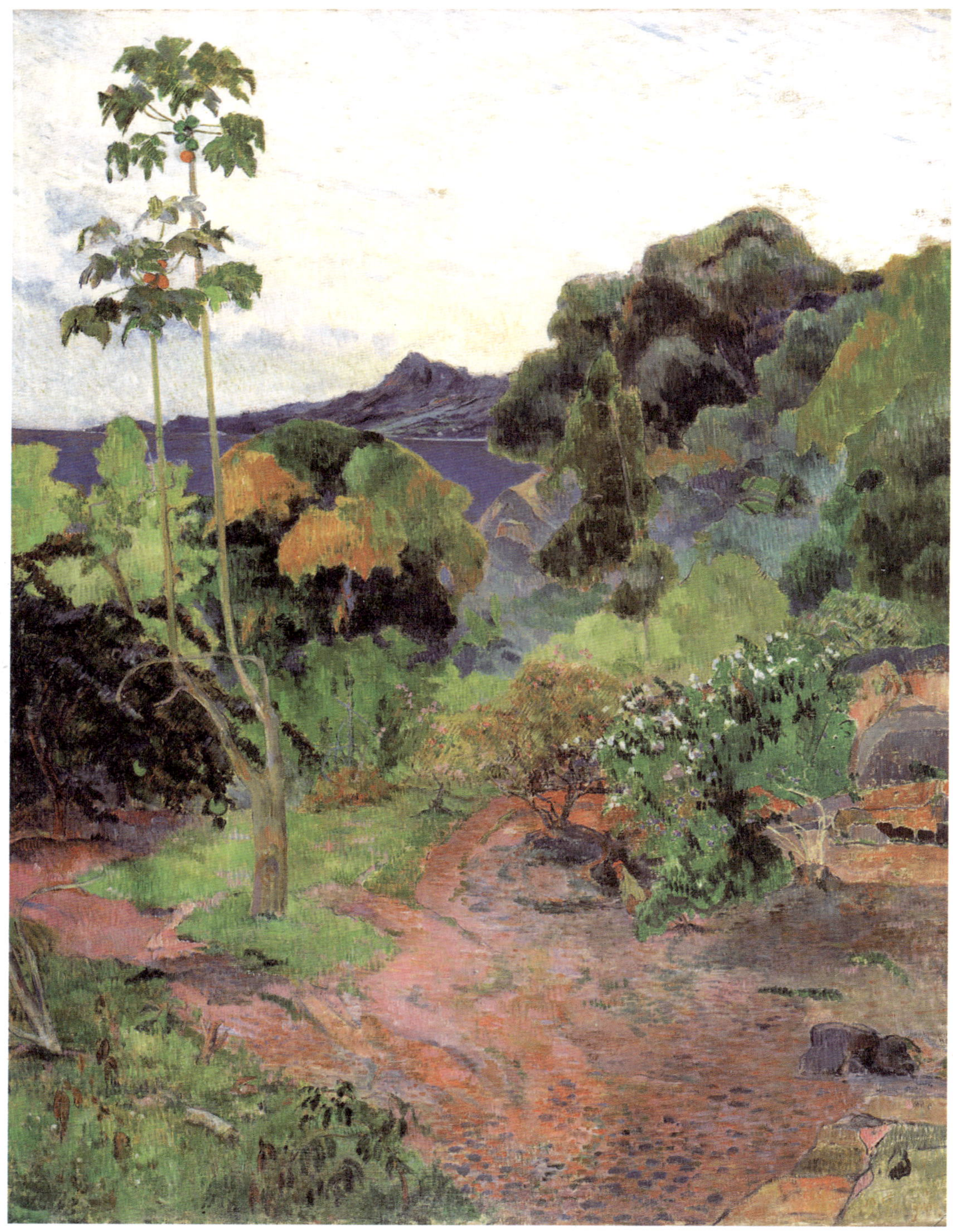

Martinique Landscape, 1887
Oil on canvas, 116 x 89 cm (45⅔ x 35 in)
• National Galleries of Scotland, Edinburgh

Gauguin portrays Martinique as an idyllic island, rich in colour with deep blue seas, luxuriant trees and shrubs. But for Gauguin his time on the island was short, because of illness and lack of money. He returned to Paris.

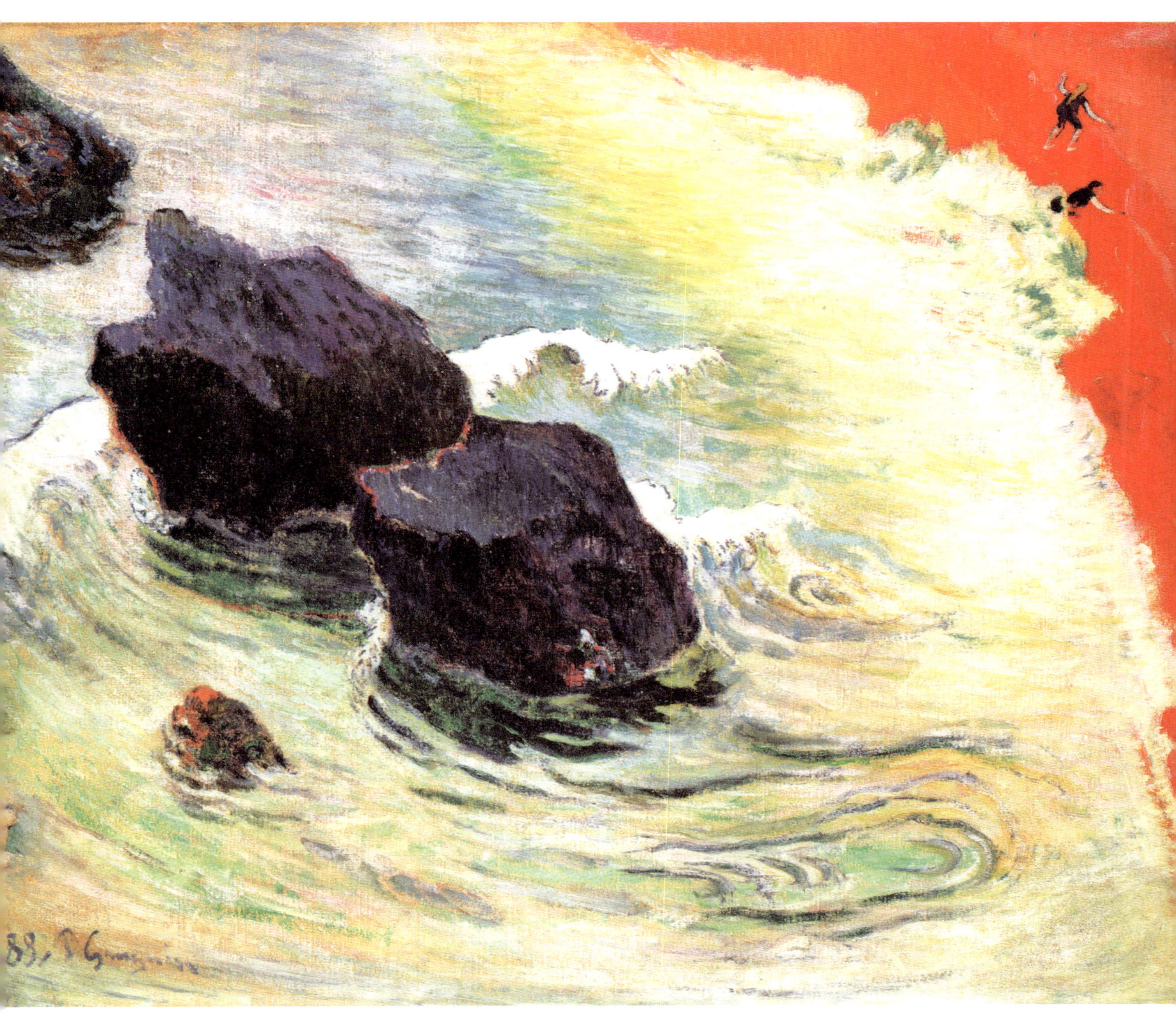

The Wave, 1888
Oil on canvas, 49 x 58 cm (19⁵⁄₁₆ x 22¹³⁄₁₆ in) • Private Collection

An overview of rocks by the seashore, their size accentuated by small figures dashing from giant waves, Gauguin painted the work from the top of a cliff at Le Pouldu, Brittany. The rocks appeared in several of his paintings.

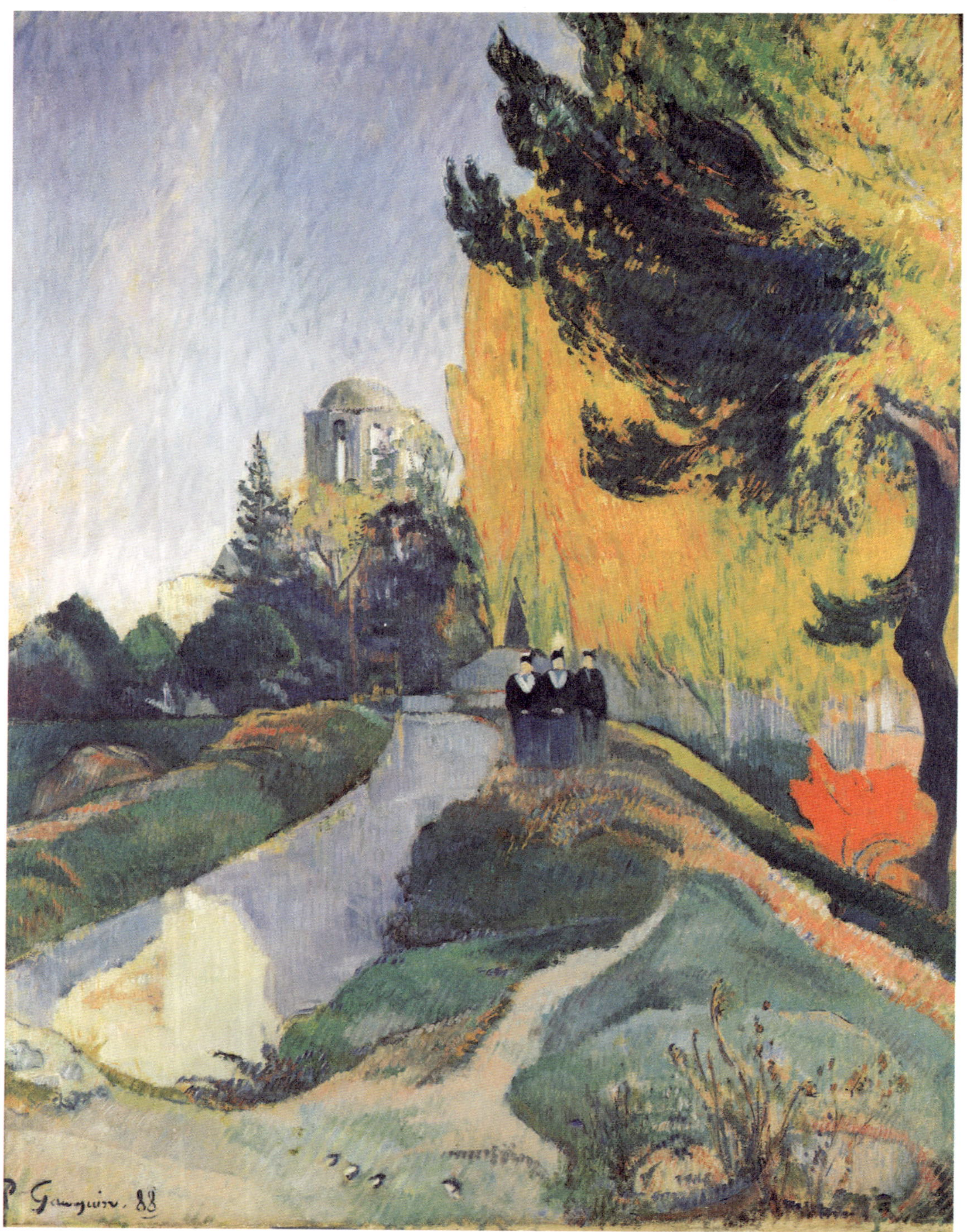

The Alyscamps, Arles, 1888
Oil on canvas, 91 x 72 cm (35⅞ x 28⅓ in) • Musée d'Orsay, Paris

One of Gauguin's first paintings in Arles, depicting the late autumn of the Alyscamps in rich-jewel tones. A favourite location of Vincent van Gogh, it was a Roman necropolis still used in medieval times, with tombs scattered among wooded glades.

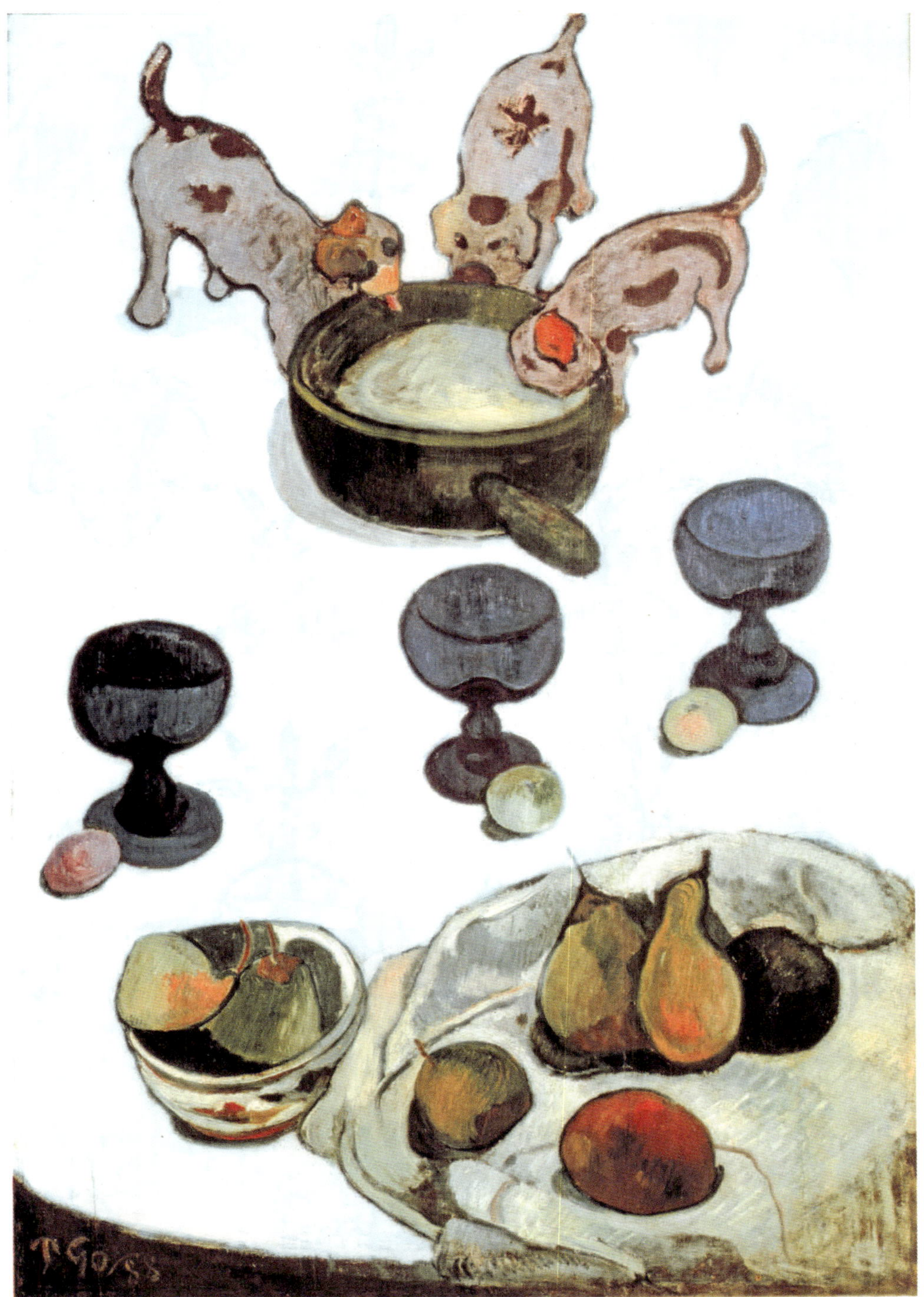

Still Life with Three Puppies, 1888
Oil on wood, 91.8 x 62.6 cm (36⅛ x 24⅝ in)
• Museum of Modern Art, New York

Painted in oil on wood, inspired by children's book illustrations and Japanese prints, the content is divided into three. Above, puppies are outlined in blue paint, with patterned coats that mirror the fruit in the foreground, separated by three blue goblets.

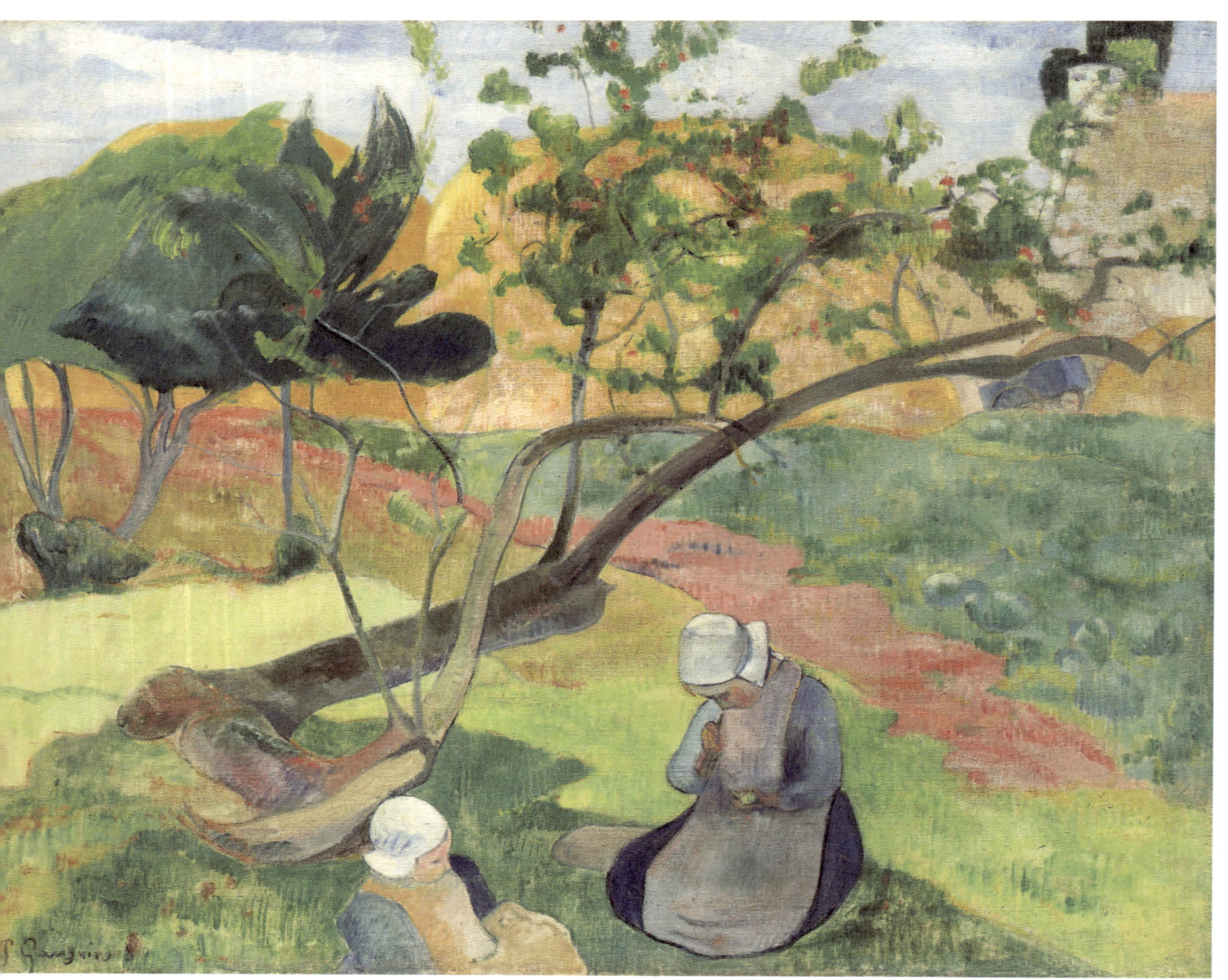

Landscape with Two Breton Women, 1889
Oil on canvas, 72.4 x 91.4 cm (28½ x 36 in)
• Museum of Fine Arts, Boston

The Breton landscape is divided into blocks of rich colour banding. At the forefront of the picture two Breton women in traditional dress are seated in the shade of a tree.

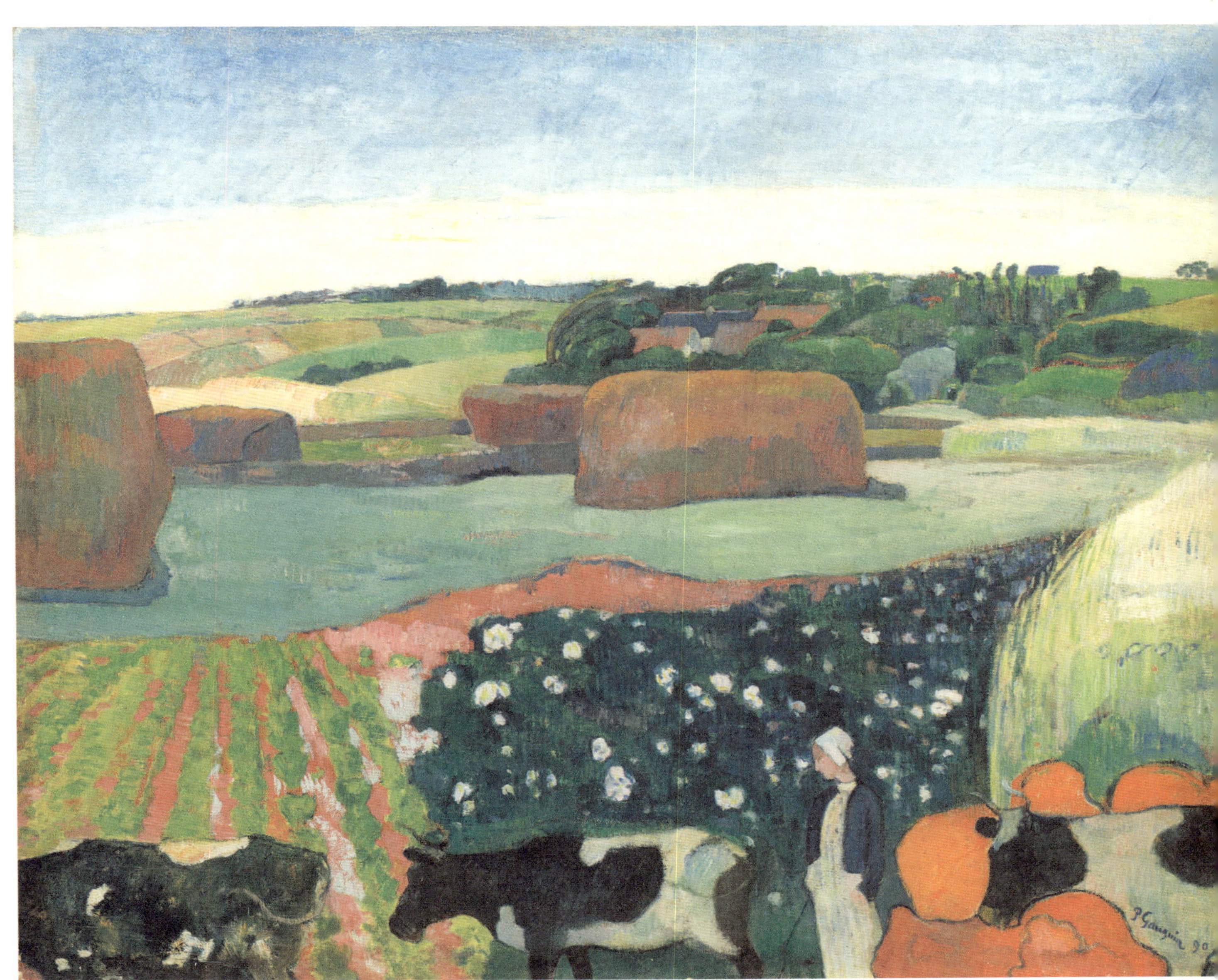

Haystacks in Brittany, 1890
Oil on canvas, 74.3 x 93.6 cm (29¼ x 36⅞ in)
• National Gallery of Art, Washington D.C.

Possibly informed by Paul Cézanne and Claude Monet's haystacks, the Breton landscape is transformed into a patchwork of colour. Gauguin stated that 'art is abstraction', and here one can see his intention, reducing landscape, people and animals to form, colour and light.

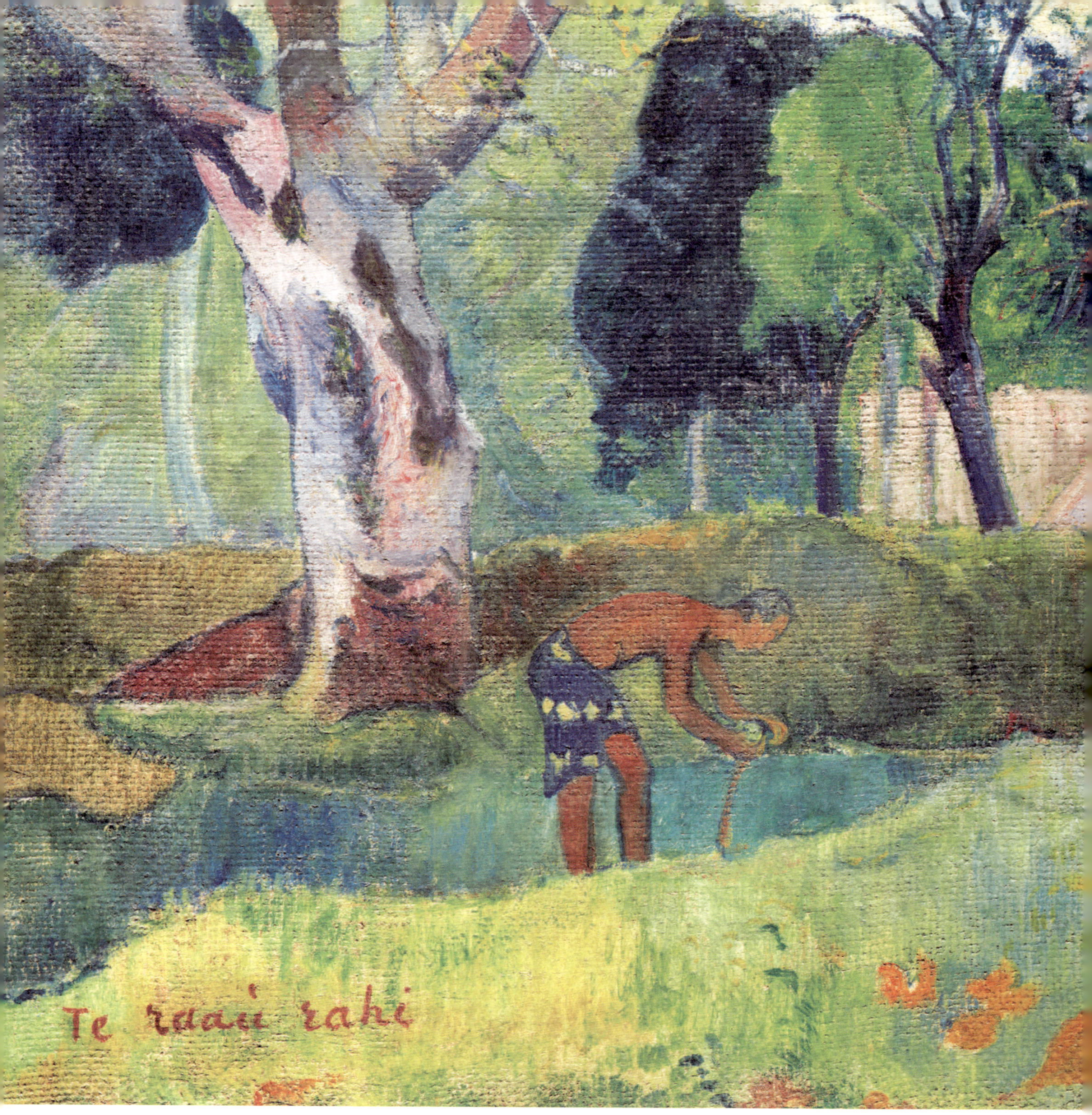

The Big Tree (Te Raau Rahi), 1891
Oil on jute canvas, 73 x 91.5 cm (28¾ x 36 in)
• The Art Institute of Chicago

In 1891 Gauguin left his wife and children in Copenhagen and friends in Paris, and departed for Tahiti, arriving in June 1891. Setting to work, he chose to paint the magnificent trees that stand tall in the Tahitian landscape.

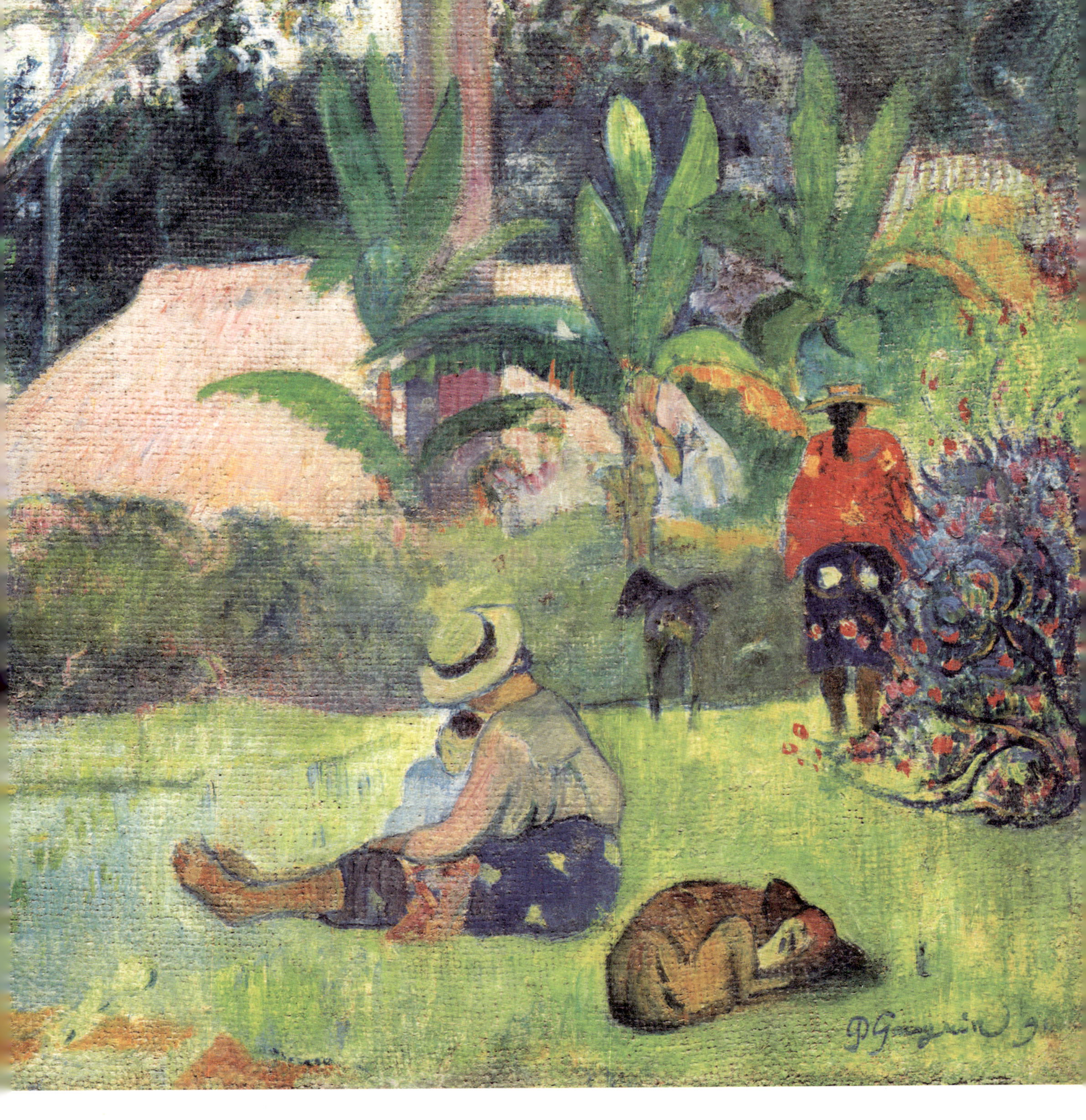

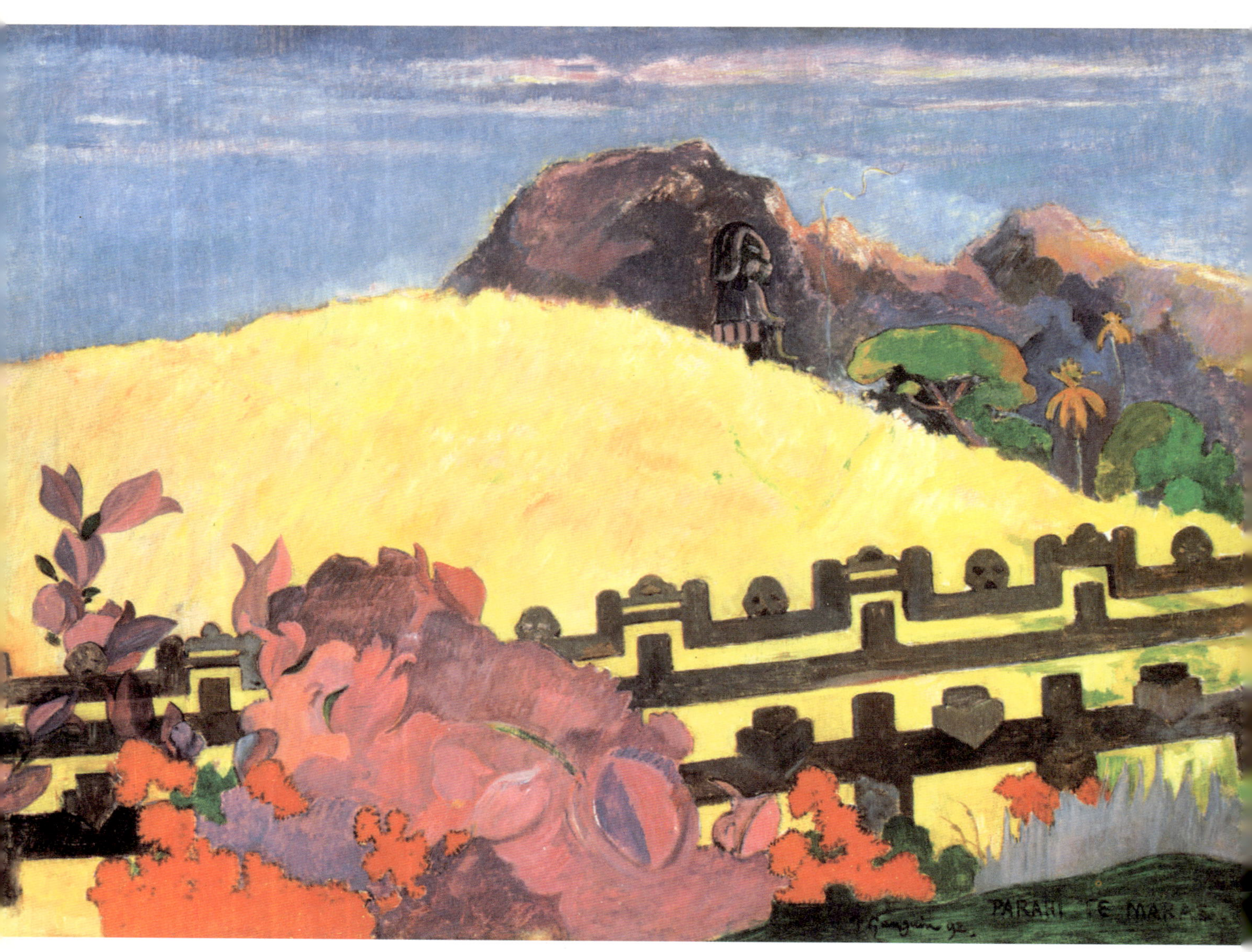

The Sacred Mountain (Parahi te Marae), 1892
Oil on canvas, 66 x 88.9 cm (26 x 35 in) • Philadelphia Museum of Art

Failing to find a primitive existence in Polynesia, Gauguin invented his own primitivism. In this work collated from diverse facts, he shows a sacred *marae* (enclosure) in the Marquesas Islands with a large statue, similar to the statues on Easter Island.

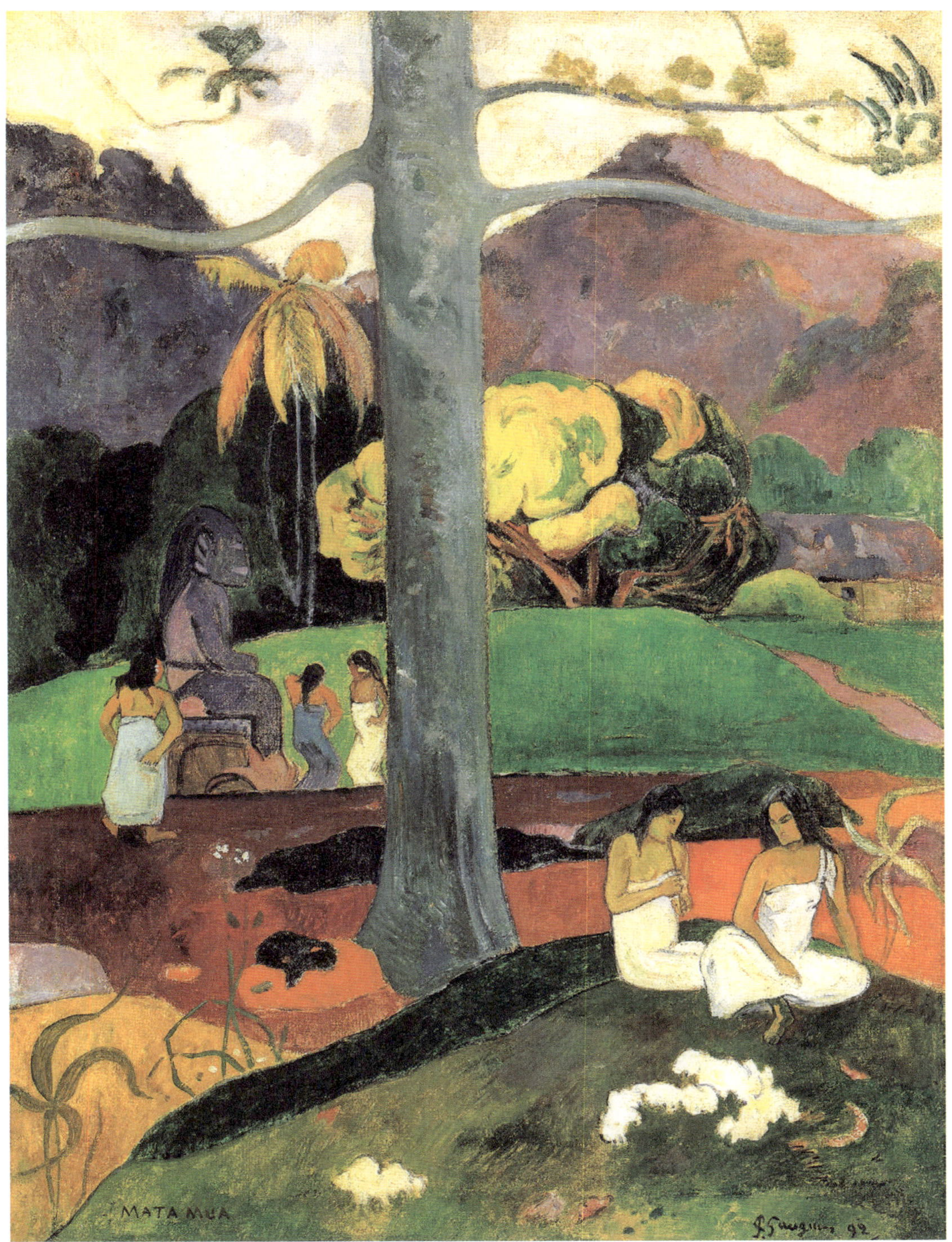

In Olden Times (Mata Mua), 1892
Oil on canvas, 91 x 69 cm (35⅞ x 27⅛ in)
• Museo Thyssen-Bornemisza, Madrid

With a mountain backdrop in a tropical paradise, women worship the deity Hina, goddess of the Moon. Gauguin hoped to find a primitive paradise; his paintings recreate his vision of olden times on the Polynesian islands.

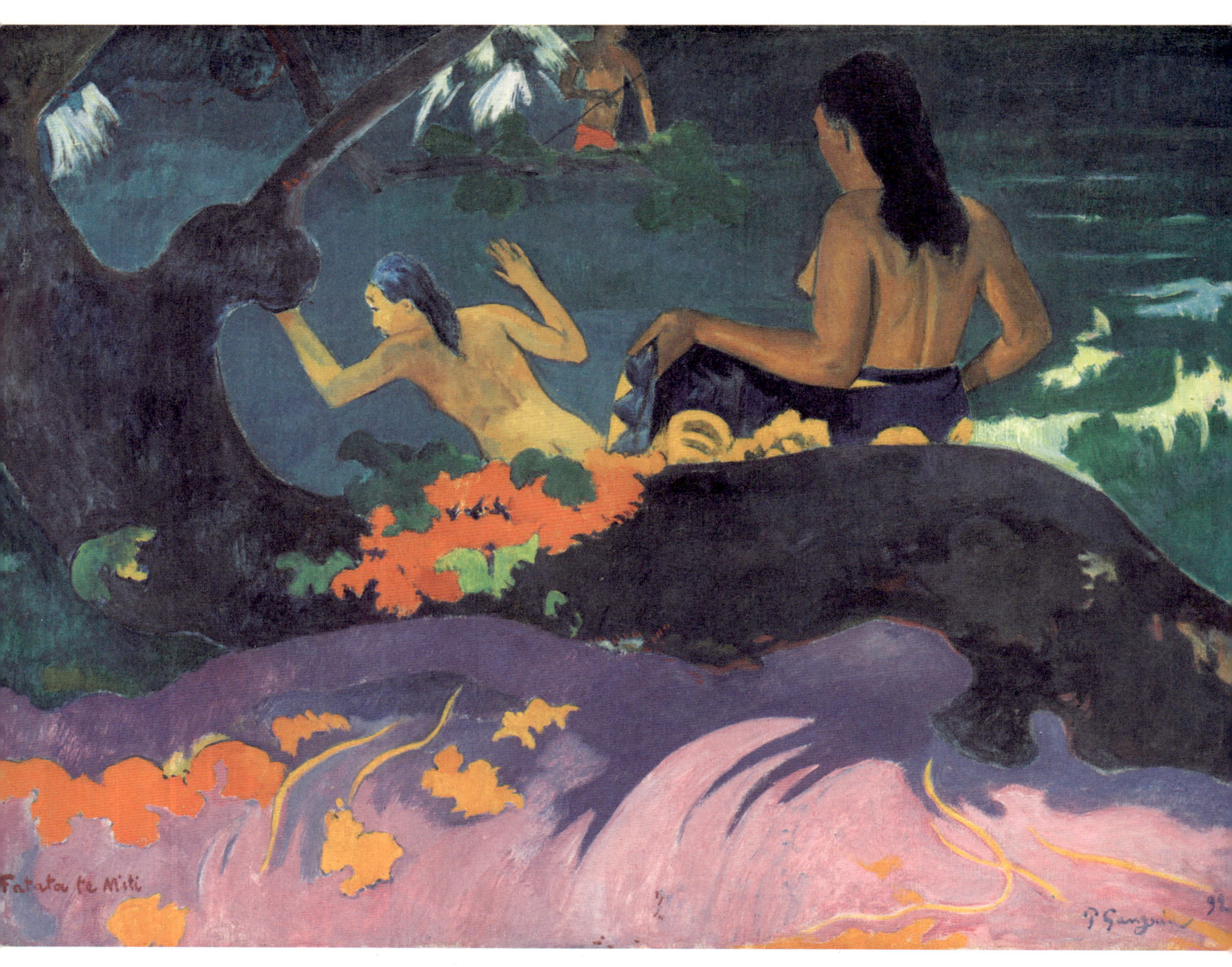

By the Sea (Fatata te Miti), 1892
Oil on canvas, 67.9 x 91.5 cm (26¾ x 36 in)
• National Gallery of Art, Washington D.C.

The brilliant pink of the island sand, scattered with phosphorescent blossoms of the hutu flower, contrast with the electric blue-green of the sea. As semi-naked women plunge into the sea for a swim, a man waits to spear a fish.

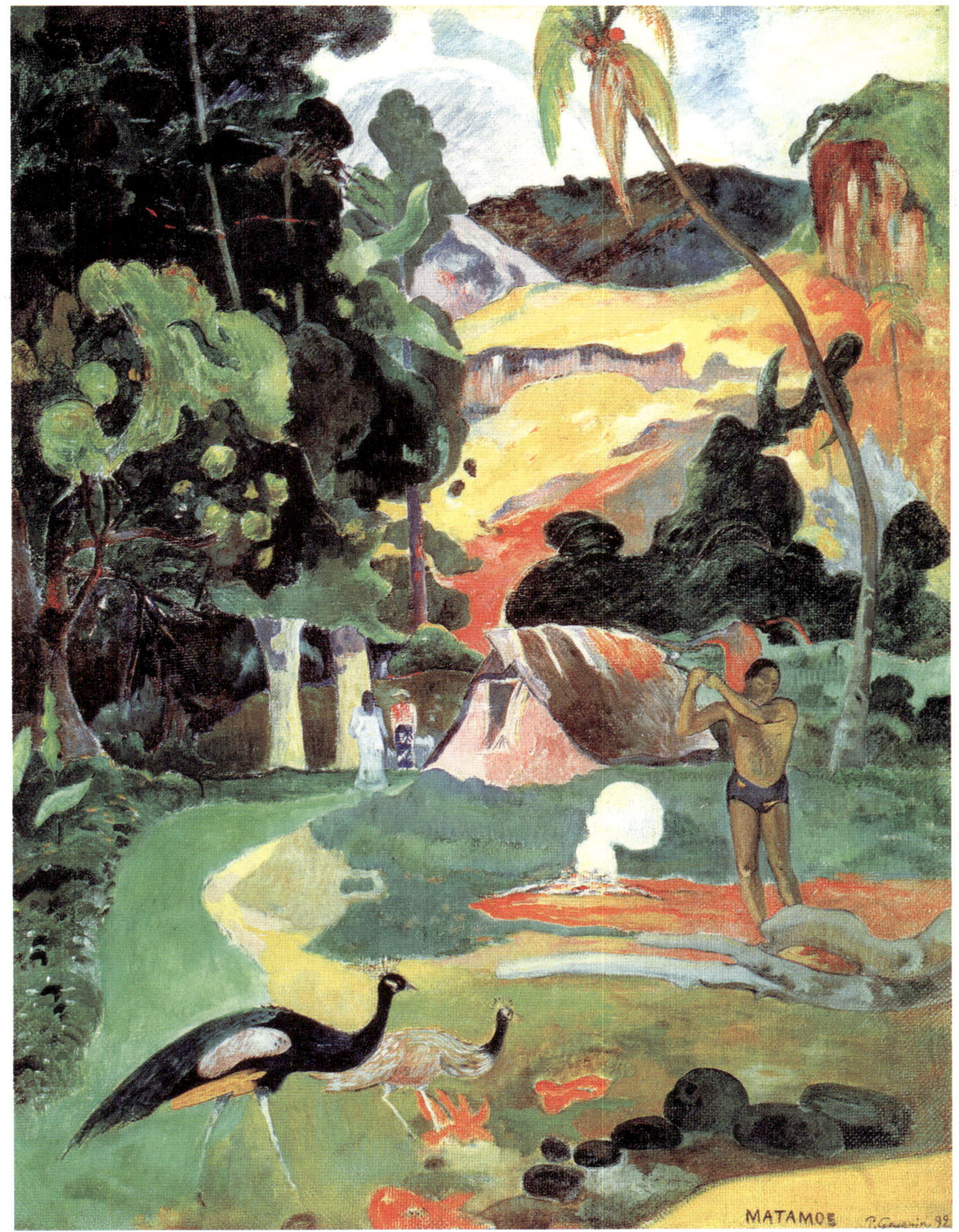

Matamoe or, Landscape with Peacocks, 1892
Oil on canvas, 115 x 86 cm (45¼ x 33⅞ in)
• Pushkin Museum, Moscow

In his manuscript *Noa Noa*, Gauguin refers to a sensation he felt when coming across this view of a man axing trees, seen as a symbolic abandonment of Gauguin's European persona to become at one with a Tahitian 'savage', primitive existence.

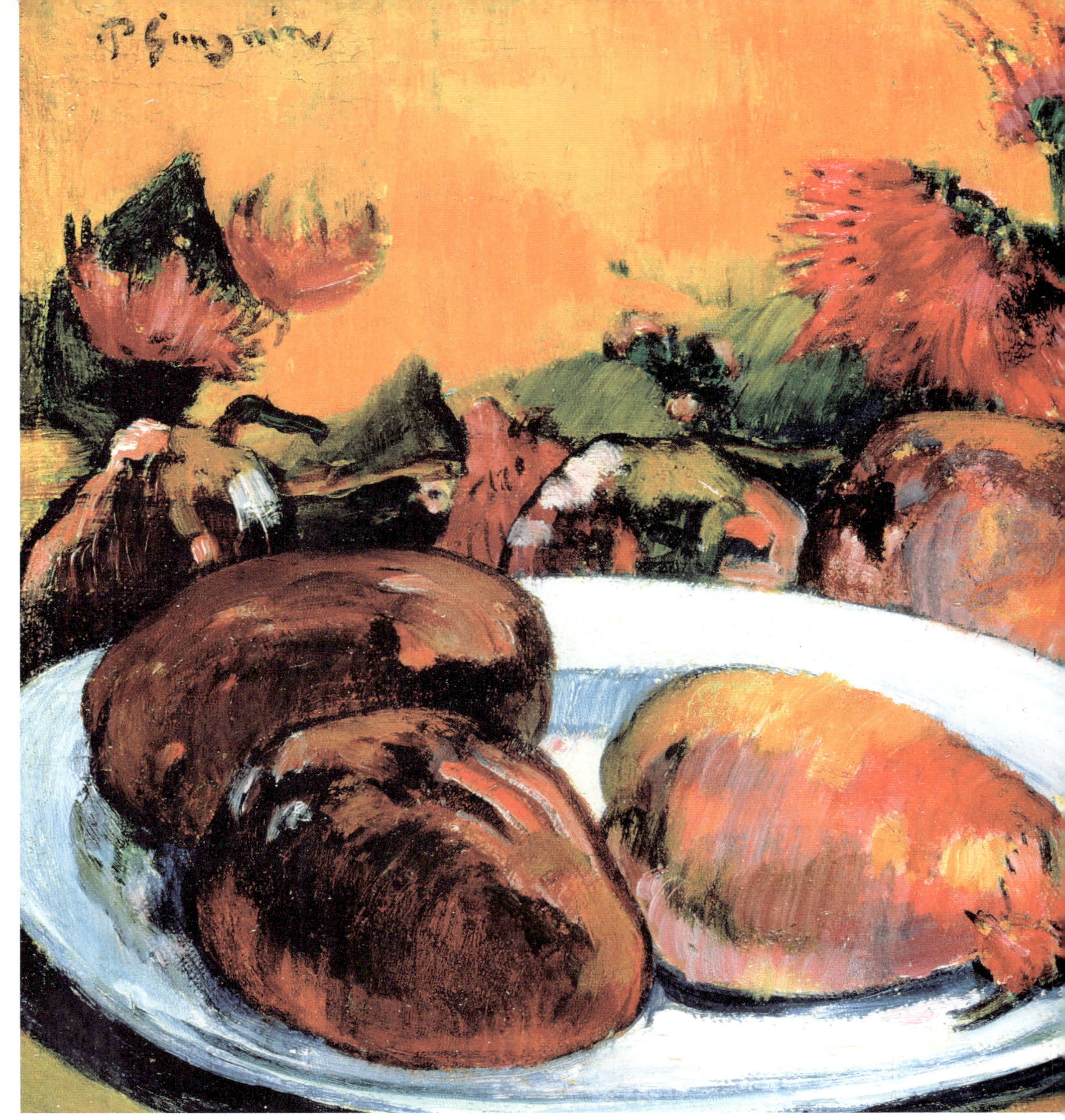

Still Life with Mangoes, 1892
Oil on canvas, 30.2 x 47.4 cm (11⅞ x 18⅔ in) • Private Collection

A painting that reveals Gauguin's skill at capturing the aura of a Polynesian island through its lush tropical produce, the ripe, juicy mango fruit. It is a perfect example of his art form Synthetism, a fusion of symbolism and sensation.

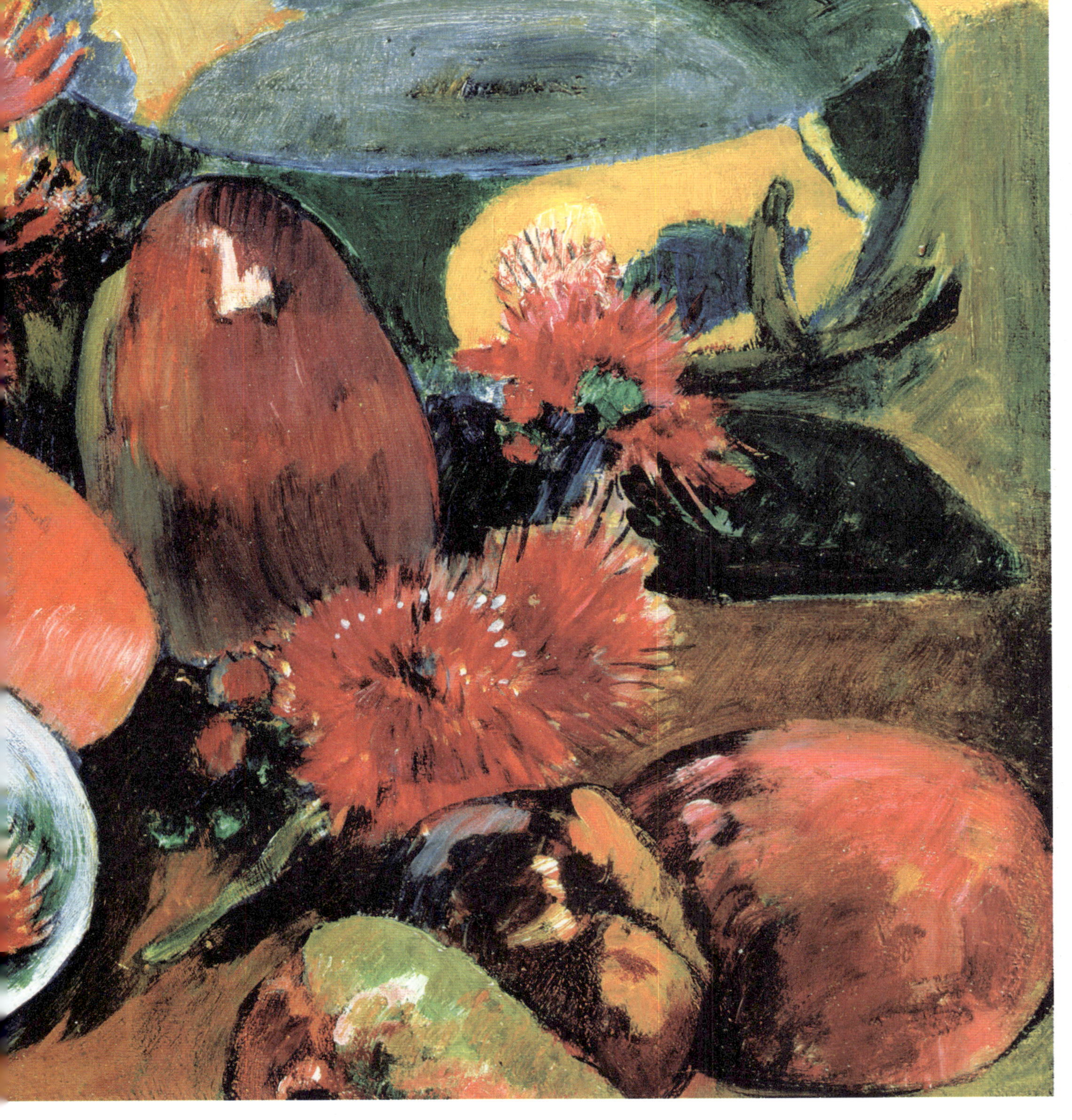

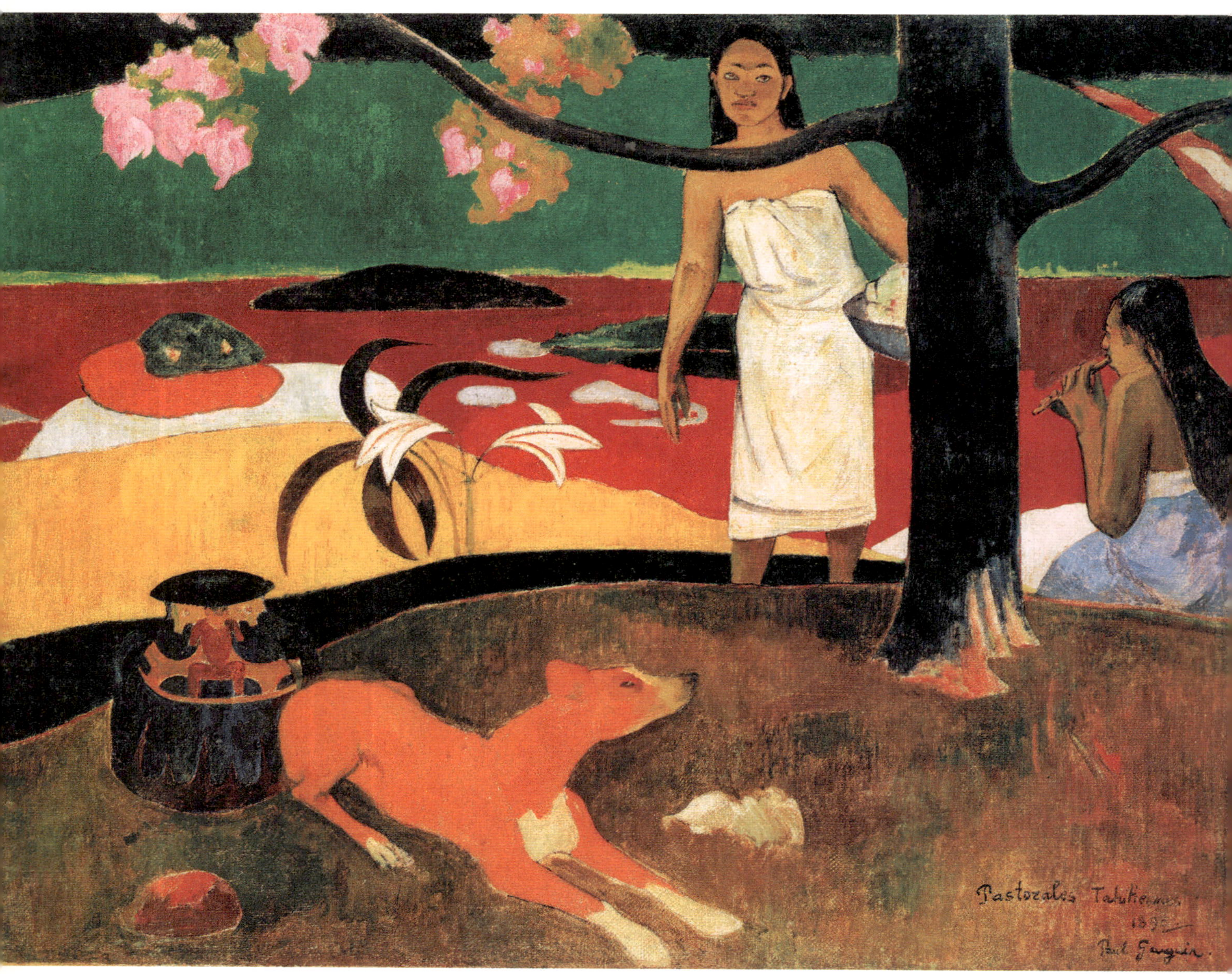

Pastorales Tahitiennes, 1893   Gauguin's interpretation of an Arcadian pastoral scene pleased him greatly. He chose a French title and
Oil on canvas, 86 x 113 cm (33⅞ x 44½ in)   described its rich complementary colour palette as 'laying on pure Veronese green and pure vermilion….'
• The State Hermitage Museum, St Petersburg

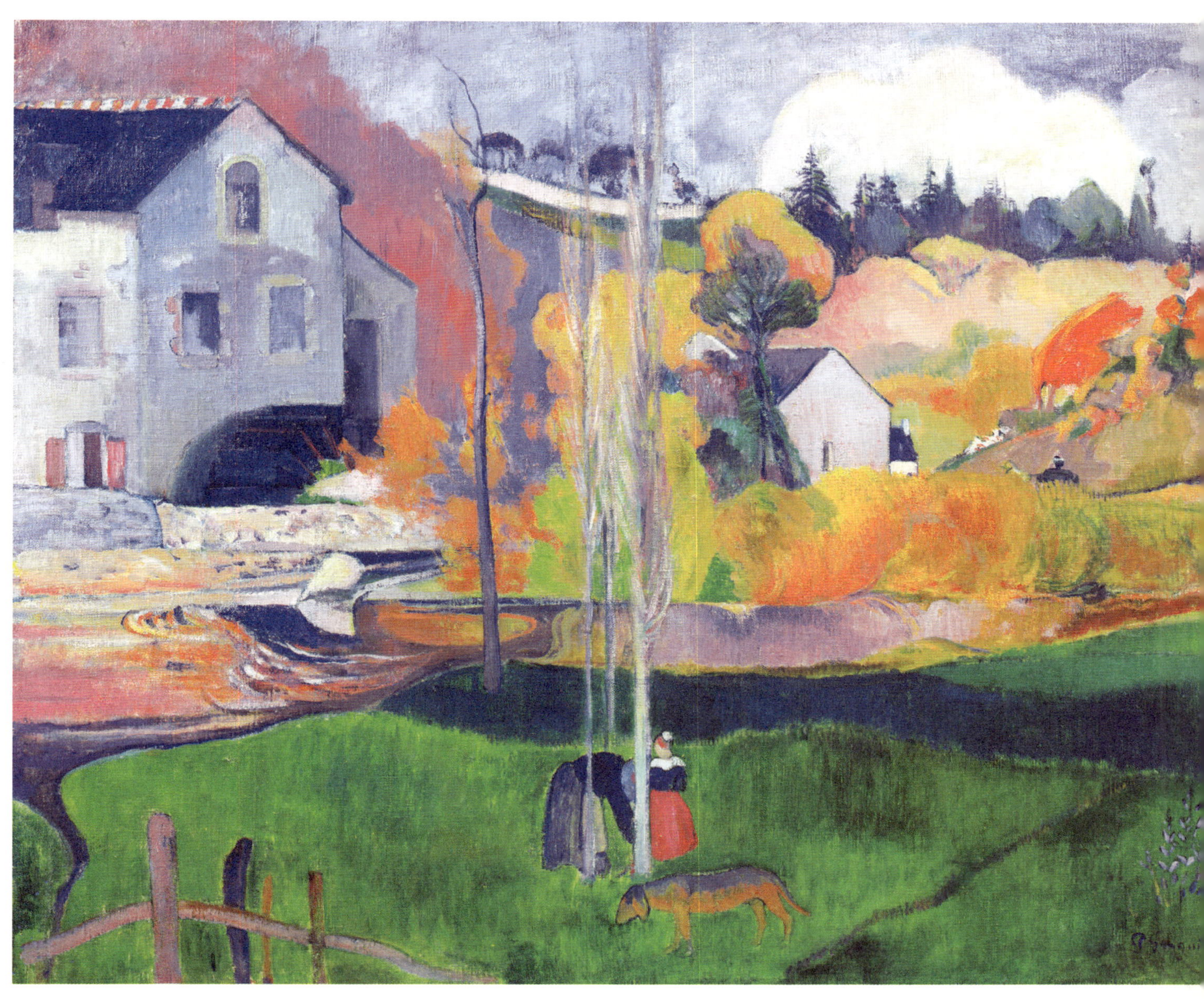

Brittany Landscape: the David Mill, 1894
Oil on canvas, 73 x 92 cm (28¾ x 36¼ in) • Musée d'Orsay, Paris

Gauguin's memories of the lush landscape of Tahiti is reflected in this painting of a local landmark in Brittany, Le Moulin David (the David Mill). The painting creates a sensual, visual response through its vibrant colour palette.

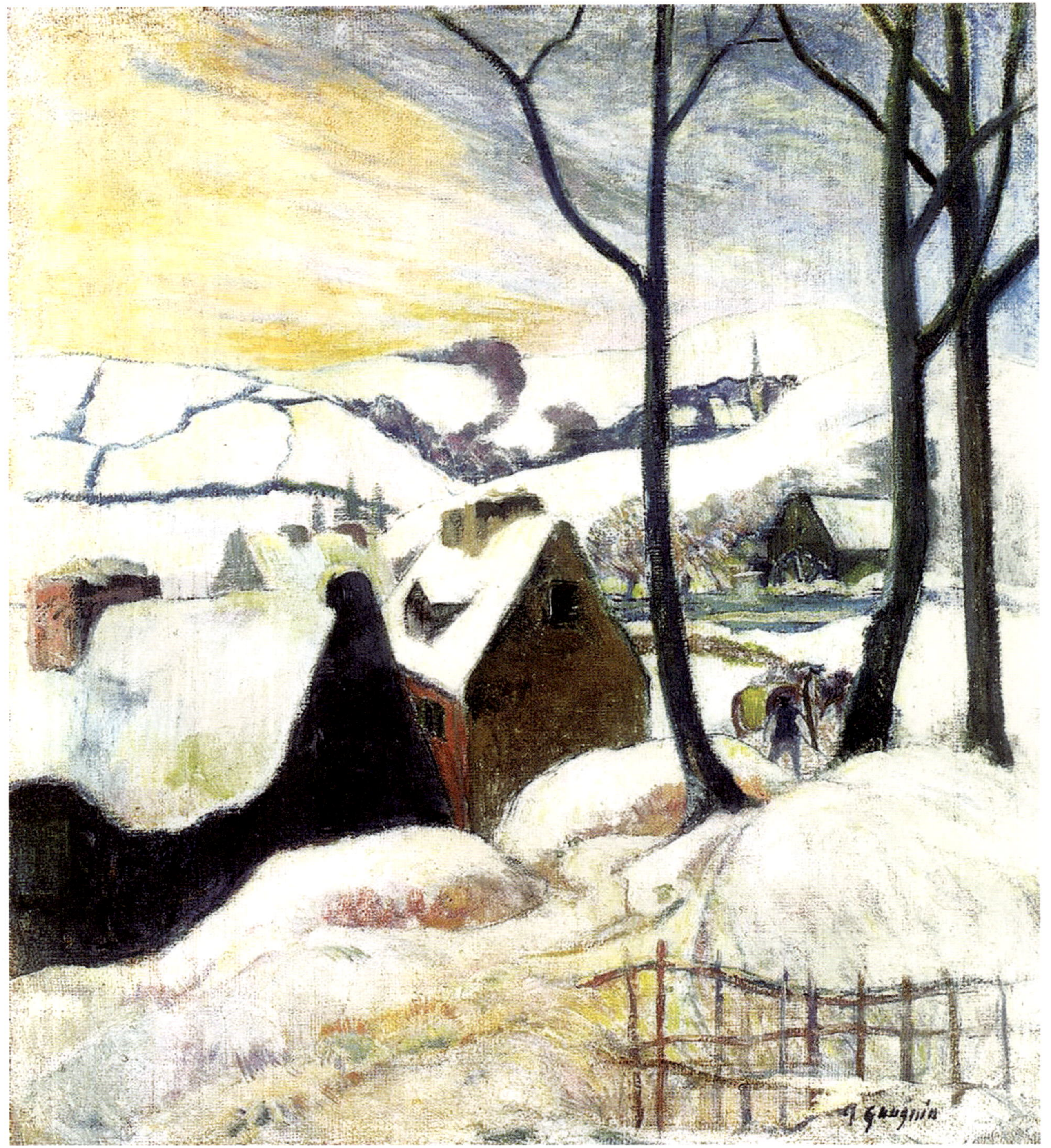

Breton Village under Snow, 1894
Oil on canvas, 76.5 x 21.5 cm (30⅛ x 8½ in) • Private Collection

On his return from Tahiti, Gauguin made his way to Pont-Aven and Le Pouldu, Brittany, spending time there between May and mid-November 1894. This is one in a series of Breton snow scenes initiated in that period.

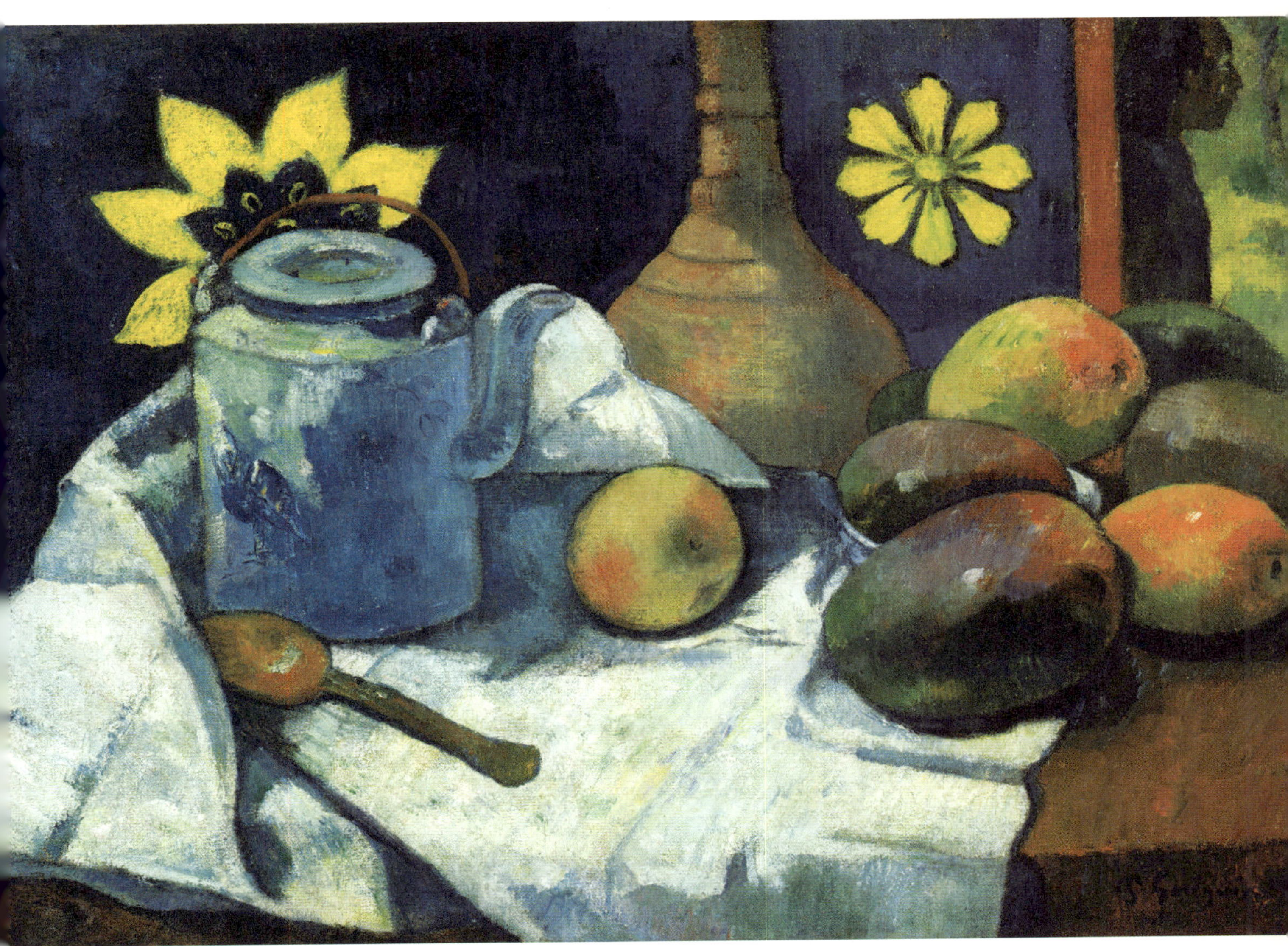

Still Life with Teapot and Fruit, 1896
Oil on canvas, 47.6 x 66 cm (18¾ x 26 in)
• Metropolitan Museum of Art, New York

Gauguin admired the art of Cézanne, collecting several works. One of his favourites was *Still Life with Fruit Dish* (1879–80). This is Gauguin's striking homage to it, a remarkable work of colour and form.

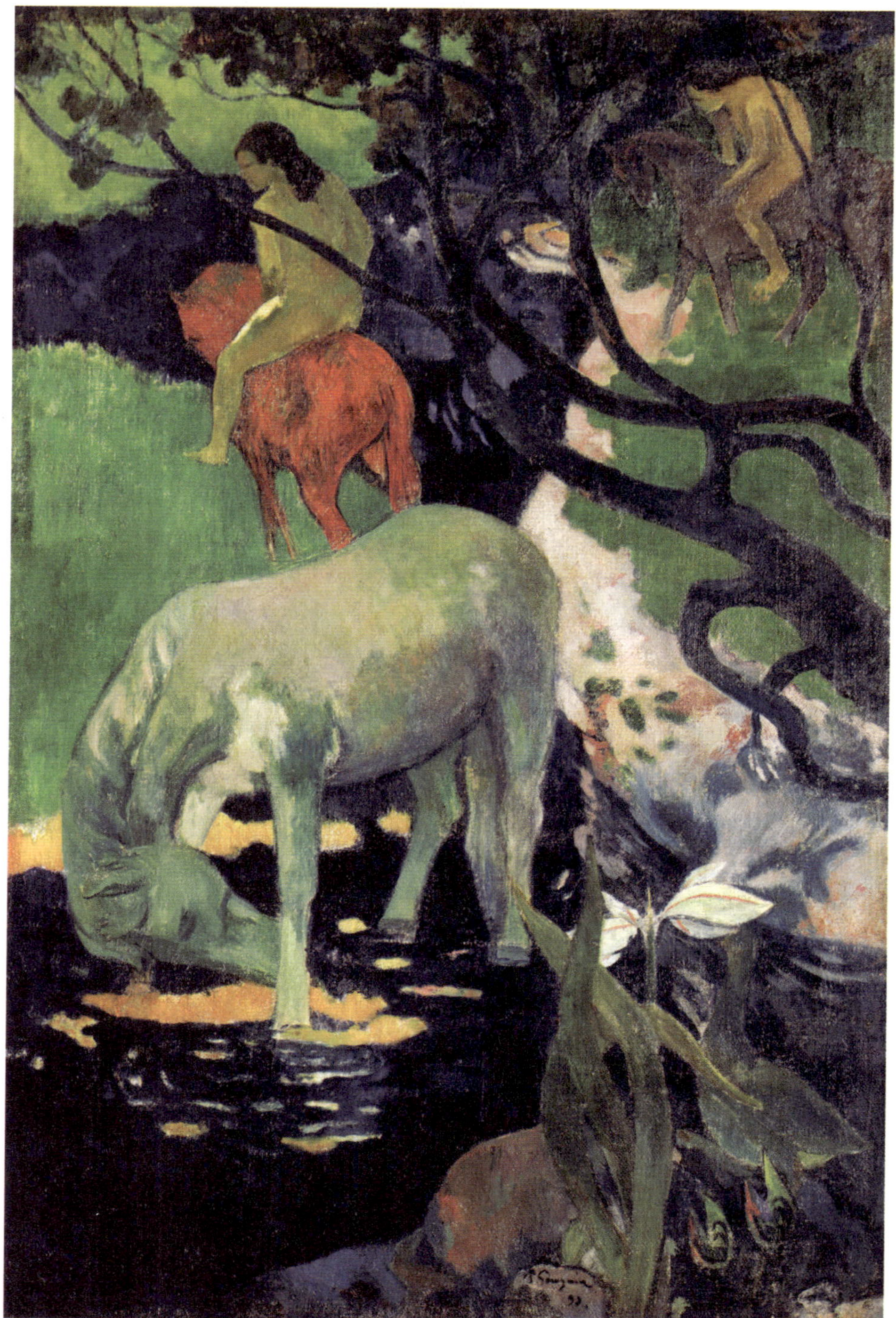

The White Horse, 1898
Oil on canvas, 140 x 91.5 cm (55⅛ x 36 in) • Musée d'Orsay, Paris

Gauguin creates a stunning scene with naked Tahitian bareback riders glimpsed through a verdant forest of trees and bushes. A riderless white horse, dappled green under the leafy canopy, stops by a stream to drink.

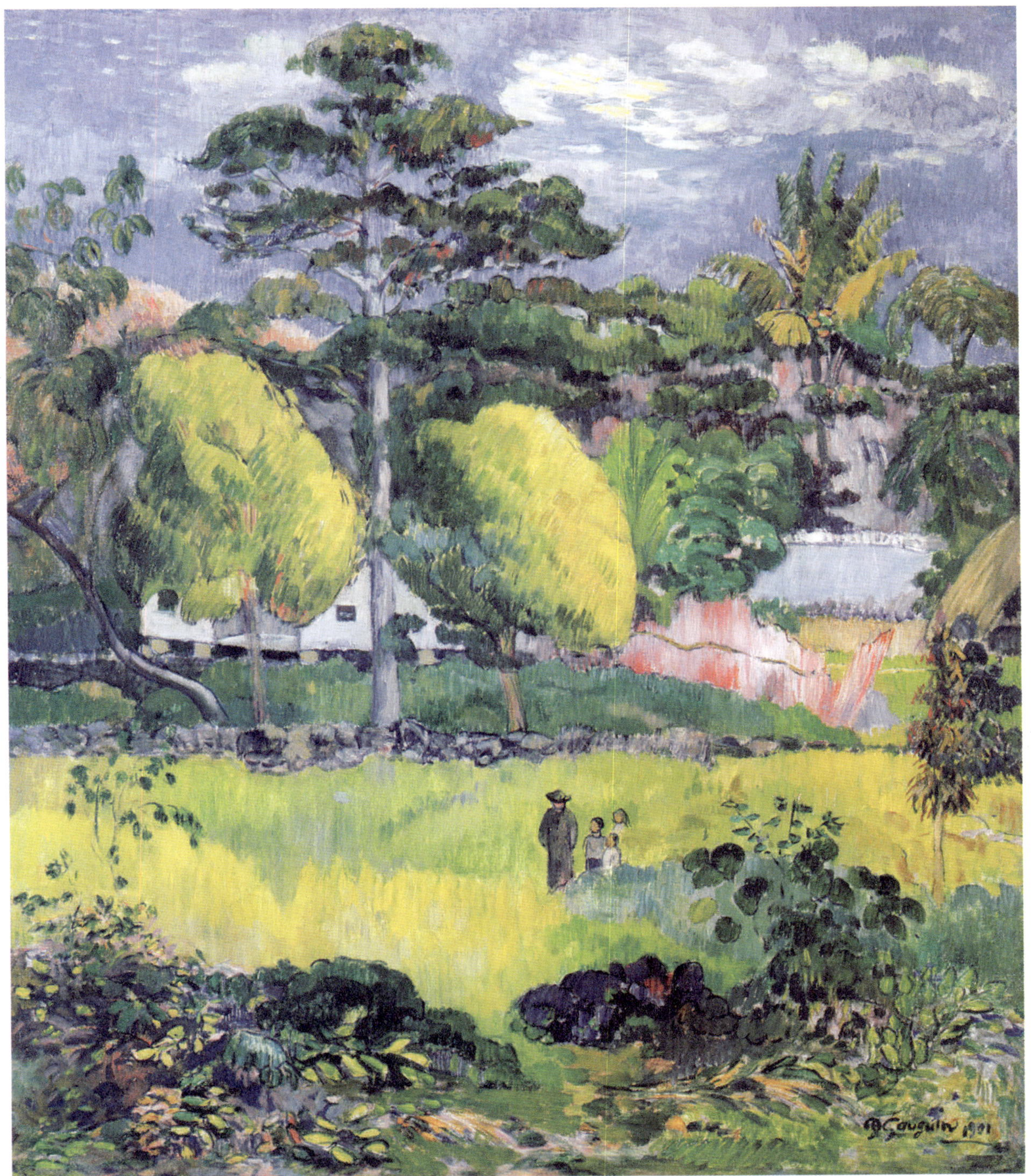

Landscape, 1901
Oil on canvas, 76 x 65 cm (29⅞ x 25⅝ in) • Musée de l'Orangerie, Paris

Possibly set in Hiva Oa. The title was changed from *The Priest and the Children* (*Le Curé et les enfants*). In the work one can see small figures, a man – possibly a missionary – walking with children near local dwellings.

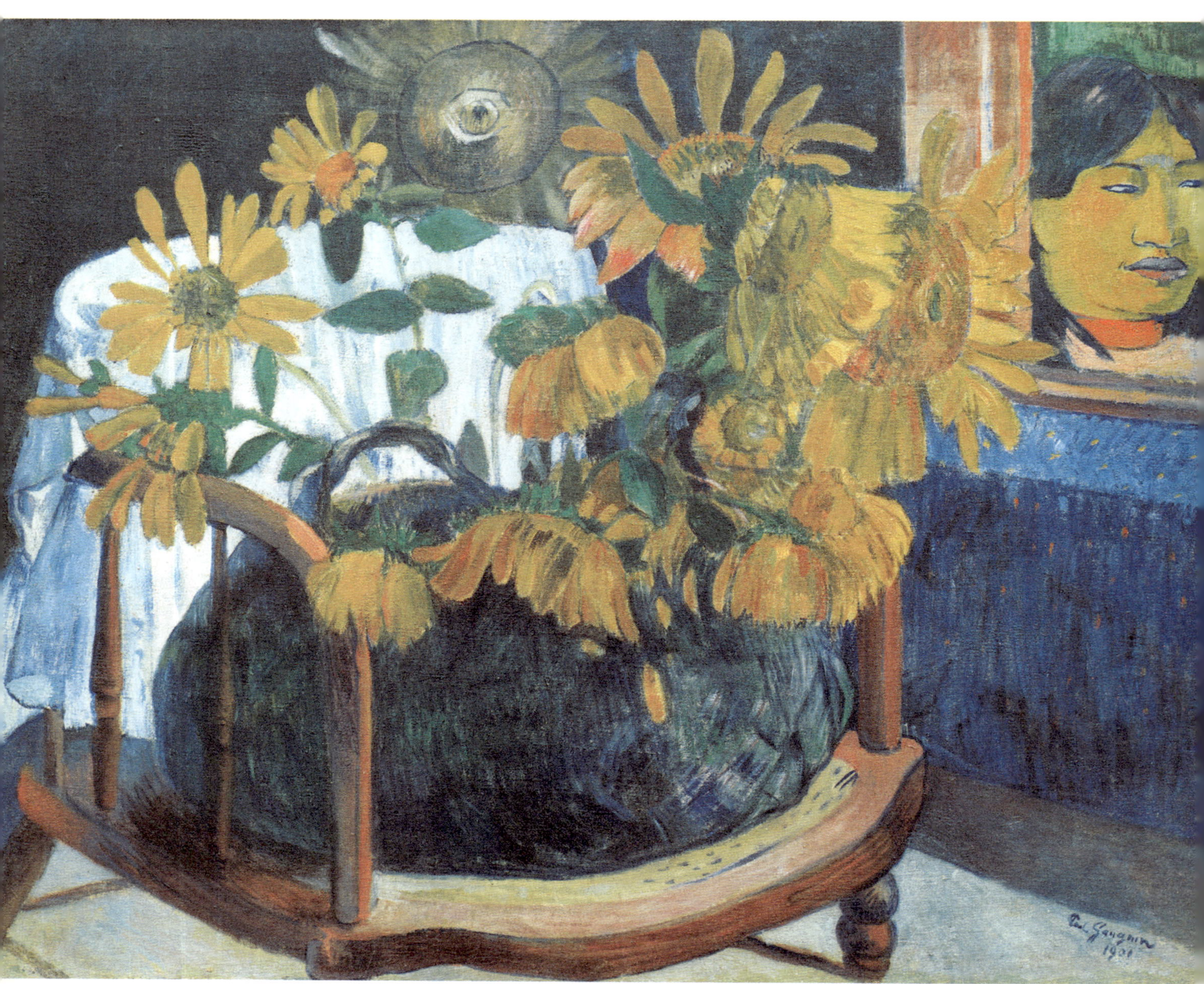

Sunflowers, 1901
Oil on canvas, 72 x 91 cm (28⅓ x 35⅞ in)
• The State Hermitage Museum, St Petersburg

Gauguin made a request to his friend George-Daniel de Monfreid to send him some sunflower seeds, which he grew in his garden in Atuona. In this mystical still life, an all-seeing eye replaces a sunflower head.

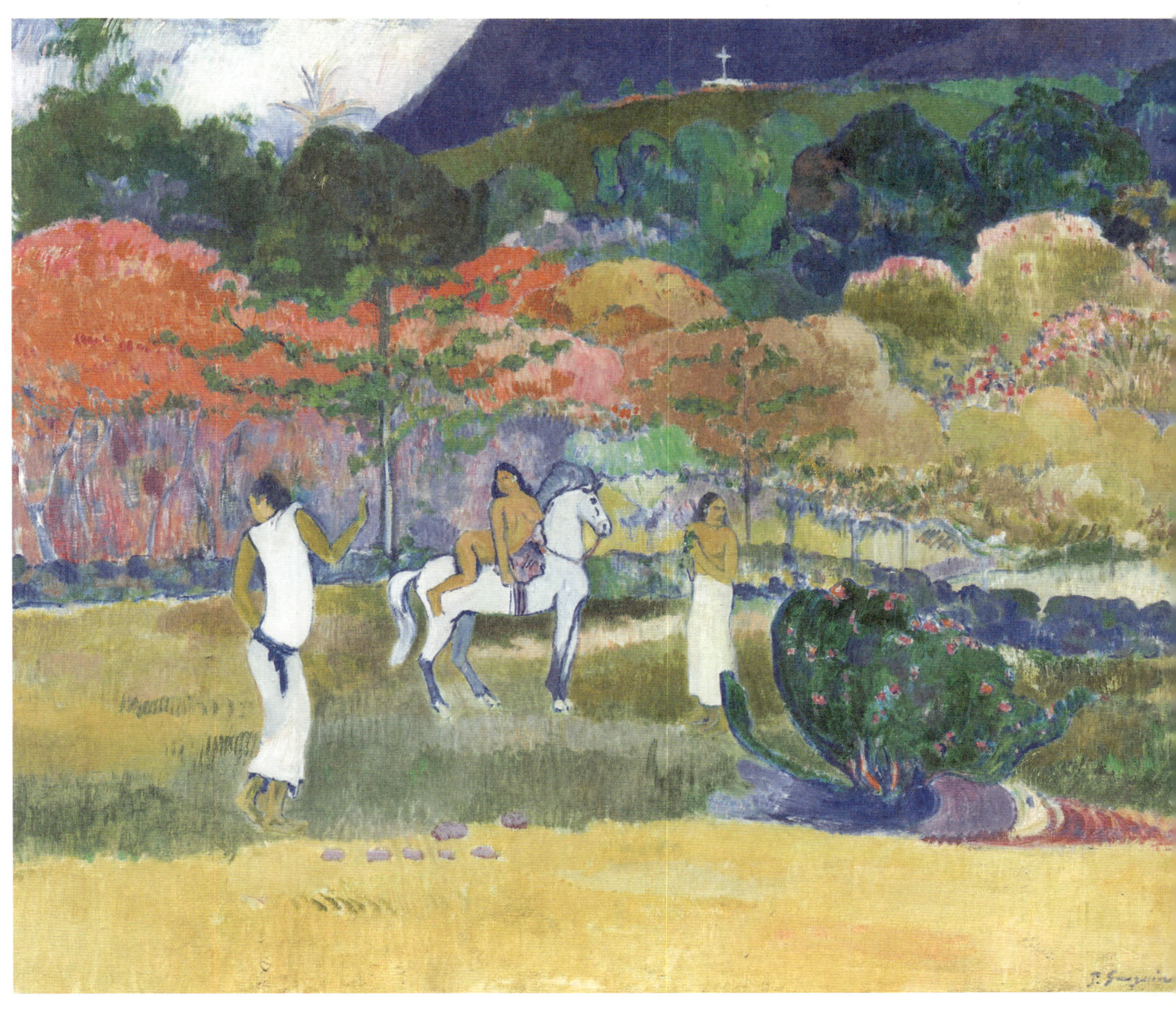

Women and a White Horse, 1903
Oil on canvas, 73.3 x 91.7 cm (28⅞ x 36⅛ in)
• Museum of Fine Arts, Boston

In a tropical paradise women converse with a naked woman on a white horse. Above the verdant backdrop the Christian cross of the local Mission appears. In Polynesia the colour white was associated with the worship of gods and with death.

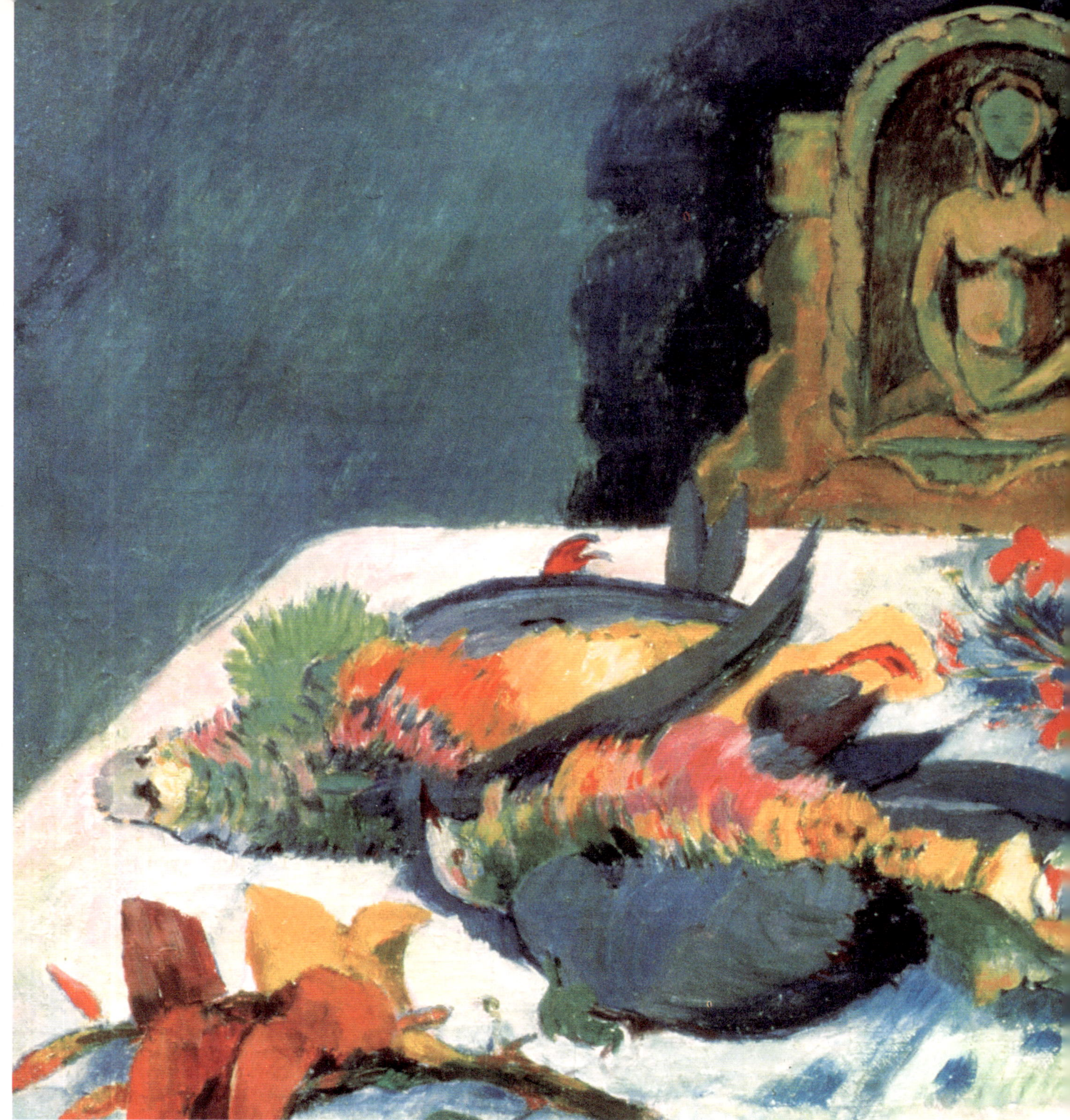

Still Life with Parrots, 1902
Oil on canvas, 62 x 76 cm (24⅜ x 29⅞ in) • Pushkin Museum, Moscow

Gauguin created the ceramic sculpture of the Tahitian goddess Hina, portrayed in the work. It sits on a tablecloth covering a traveller's trunk. Brightly coloured dead offerings include flowers and parrots, possibly symbolic of the short-lived life on Earth.

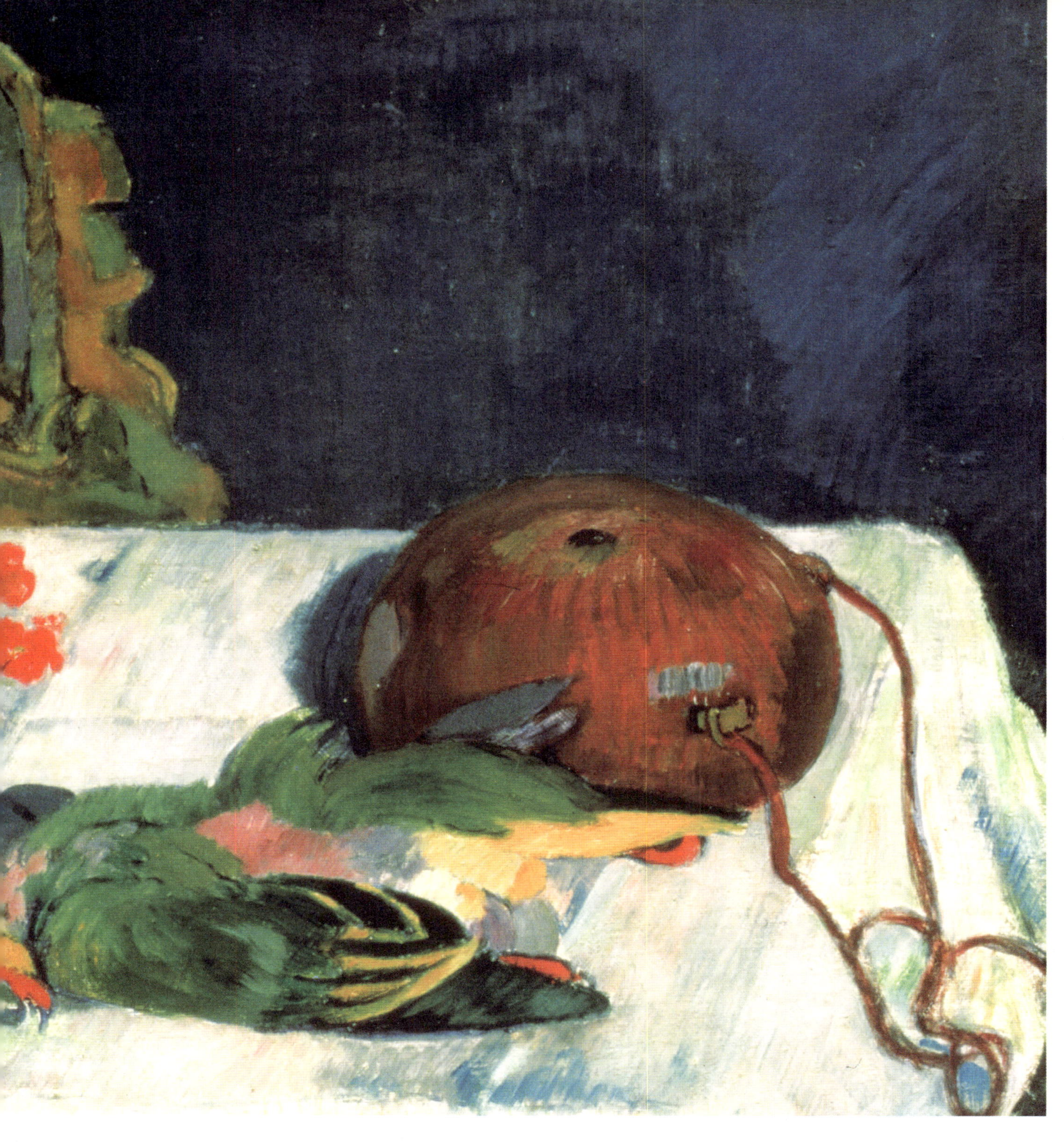

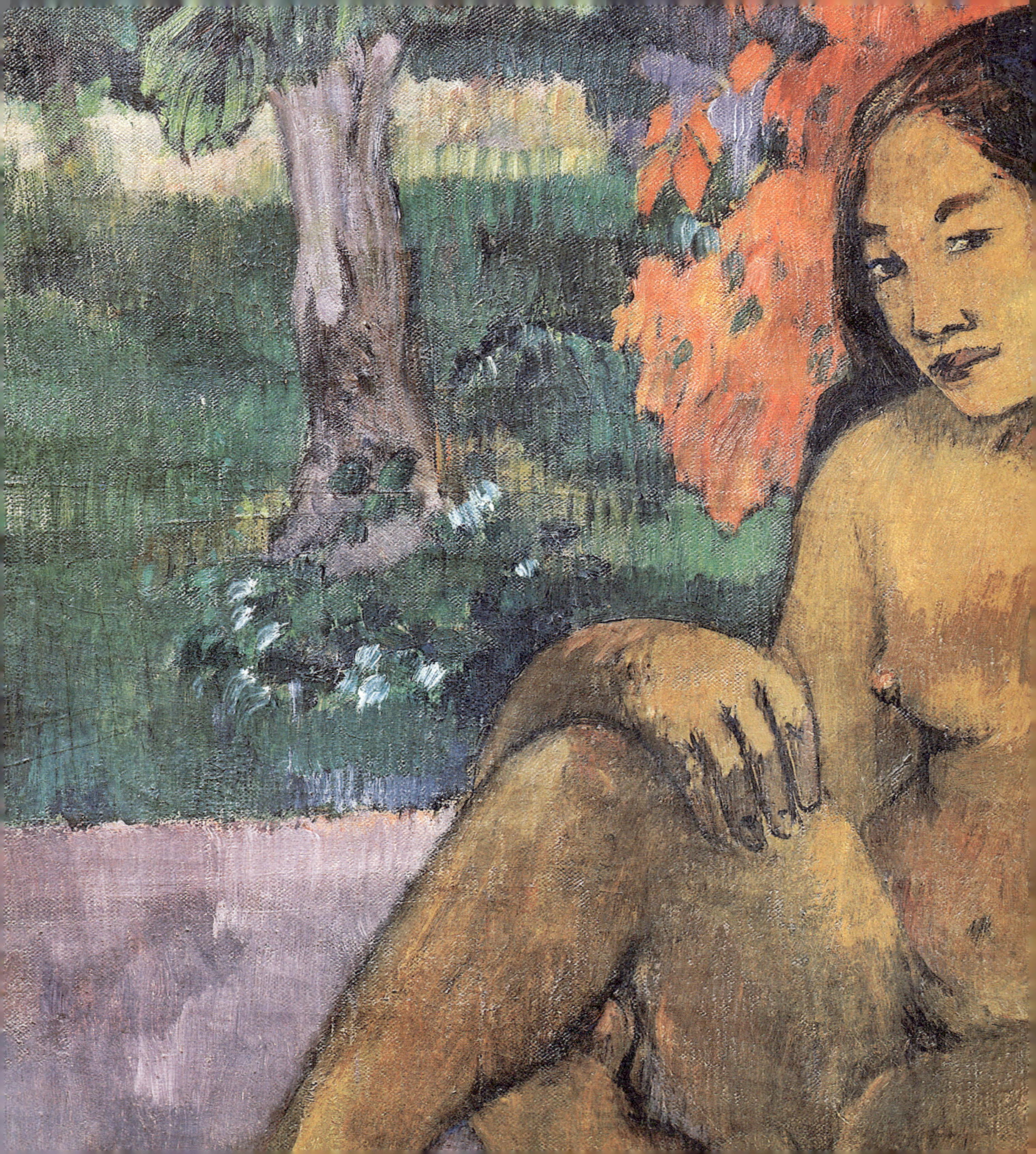

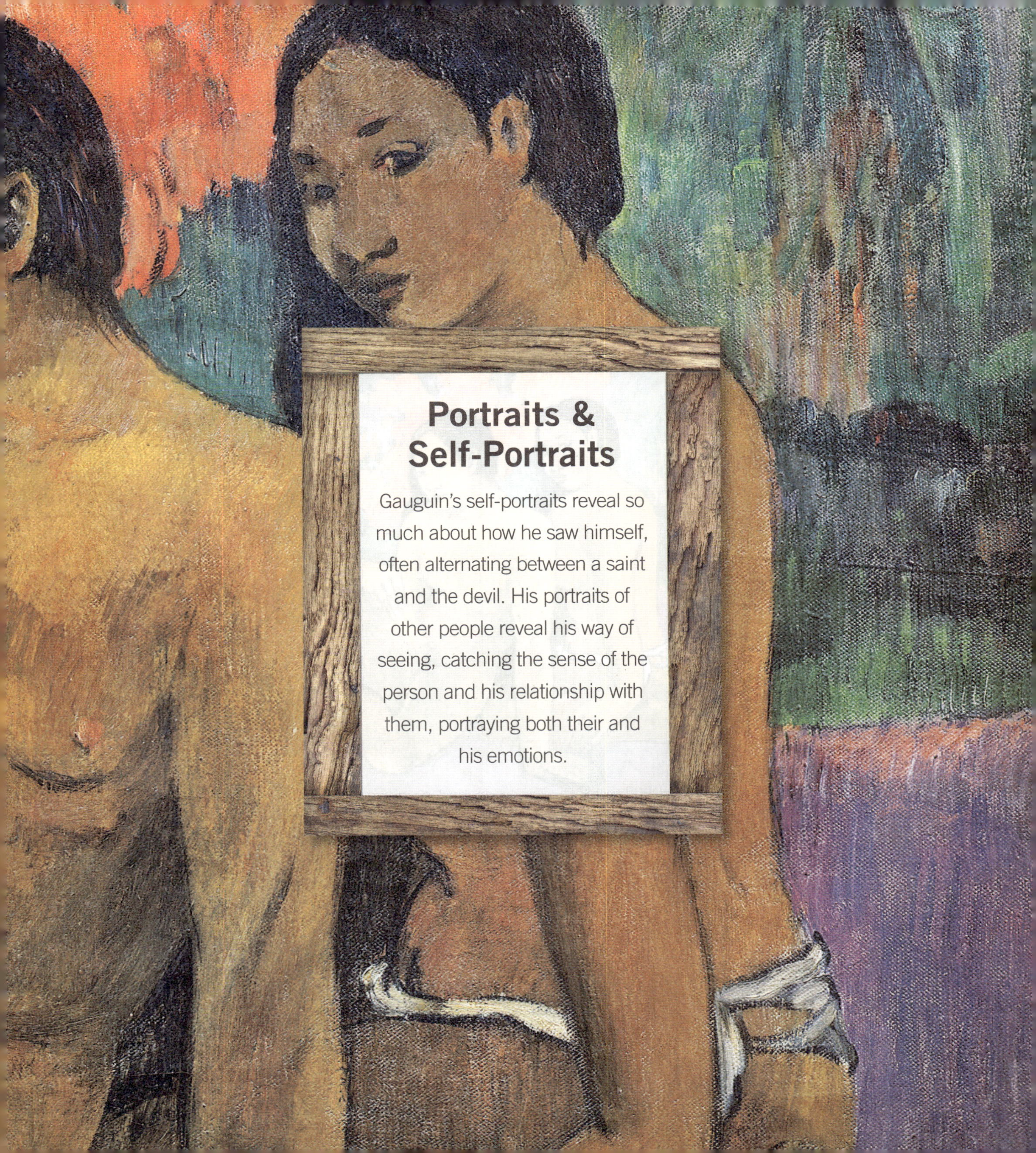

Portraits & Self-Portraits

Gauguin's self-portraits reveal so much about how he saw himself, often alternating between a saint and the devil. His portraits of other people reveal his way of seeing, catching the sense of the person and his relationship with them, portraying both their and his emotions.

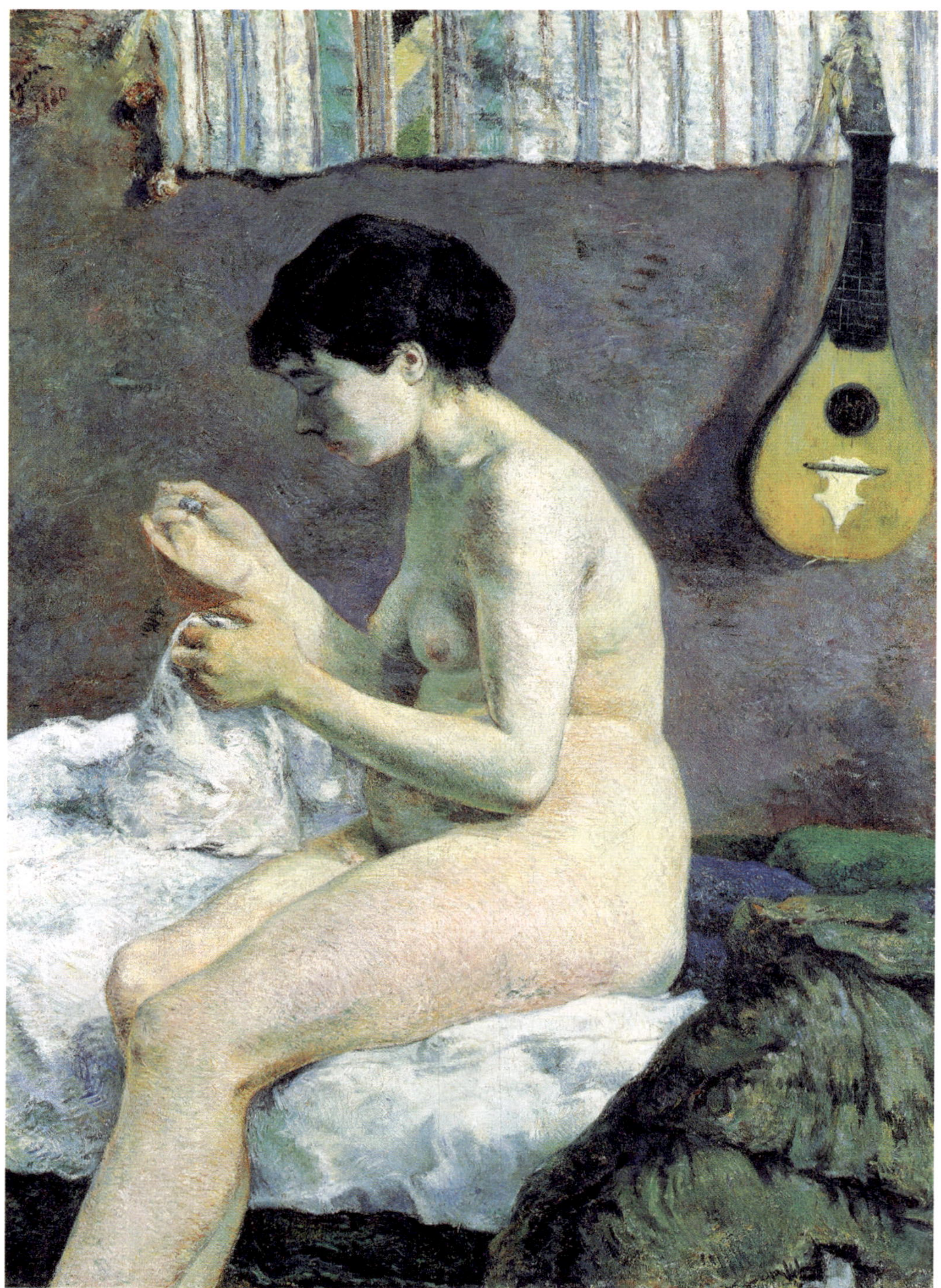

Study of Nude, Suzanne Sewing, 1880
Oil on canvas, 114.5 x 79.5 cm (45⅛ x 31⅓ in)
• Ny Carlsberg Glyptotek, Copenhagen

The pose is similar to the earlier *Mette Sewing* (1878). Gauguin creates a subtle, naturalistic portrait of his servant girl seated nude, sewing. Exhibited at the Sixth Impressionist Exhibition, it was greatly praised by art critics.

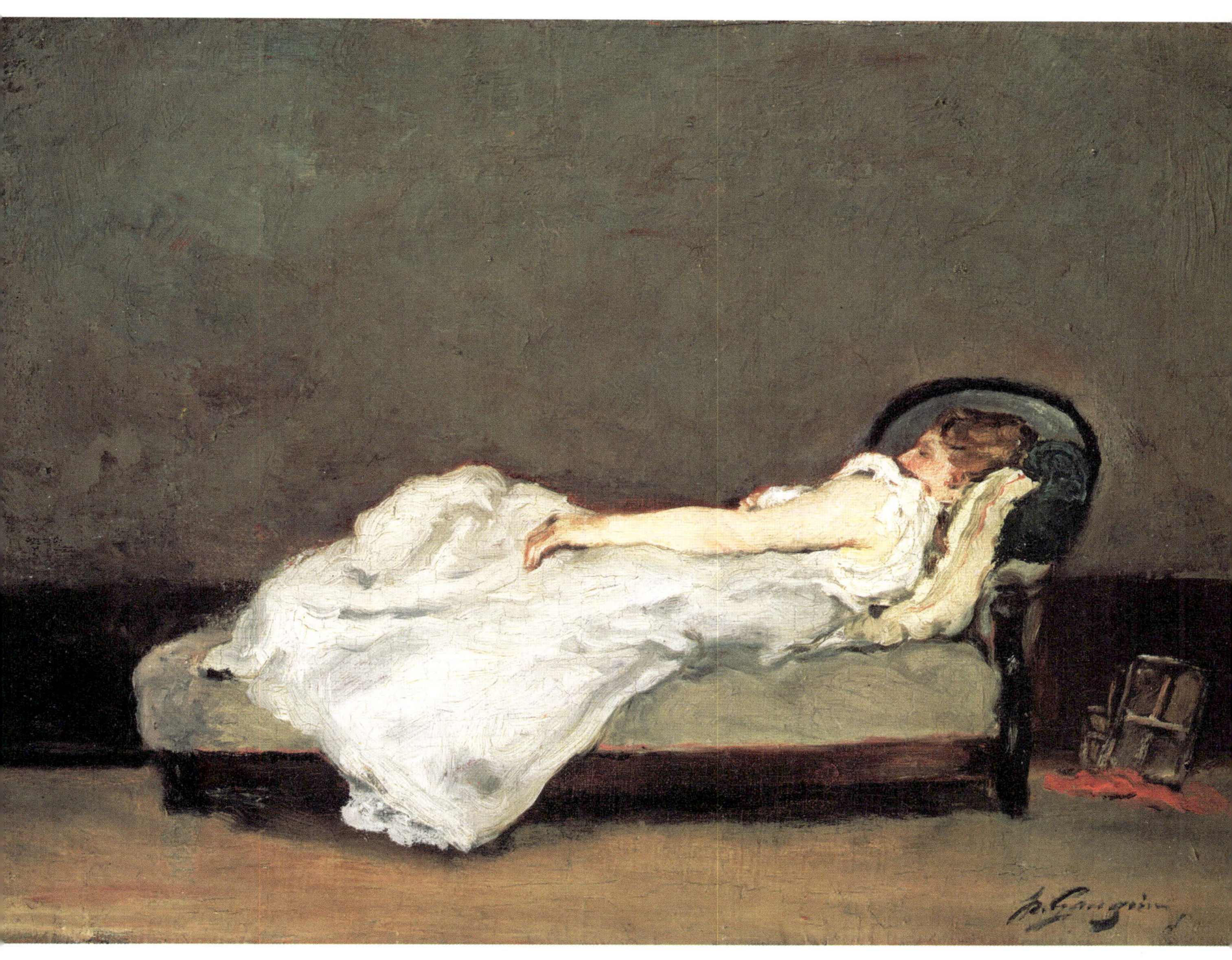

**Fair-haired Woman Asleep on a Sofa
(aka Mette Sleeping),** *c.* **1875**

Oil on canvas, 24 x 33 cm (9½ x 13 in) • Private Collection

It is thought that this small, exquisite painting is of Gauguin's wife Mette, asleep on a family sofa. It would date to *c.* 1875, when Gauguin was heavily influenced by the work of portrait painter Corot.

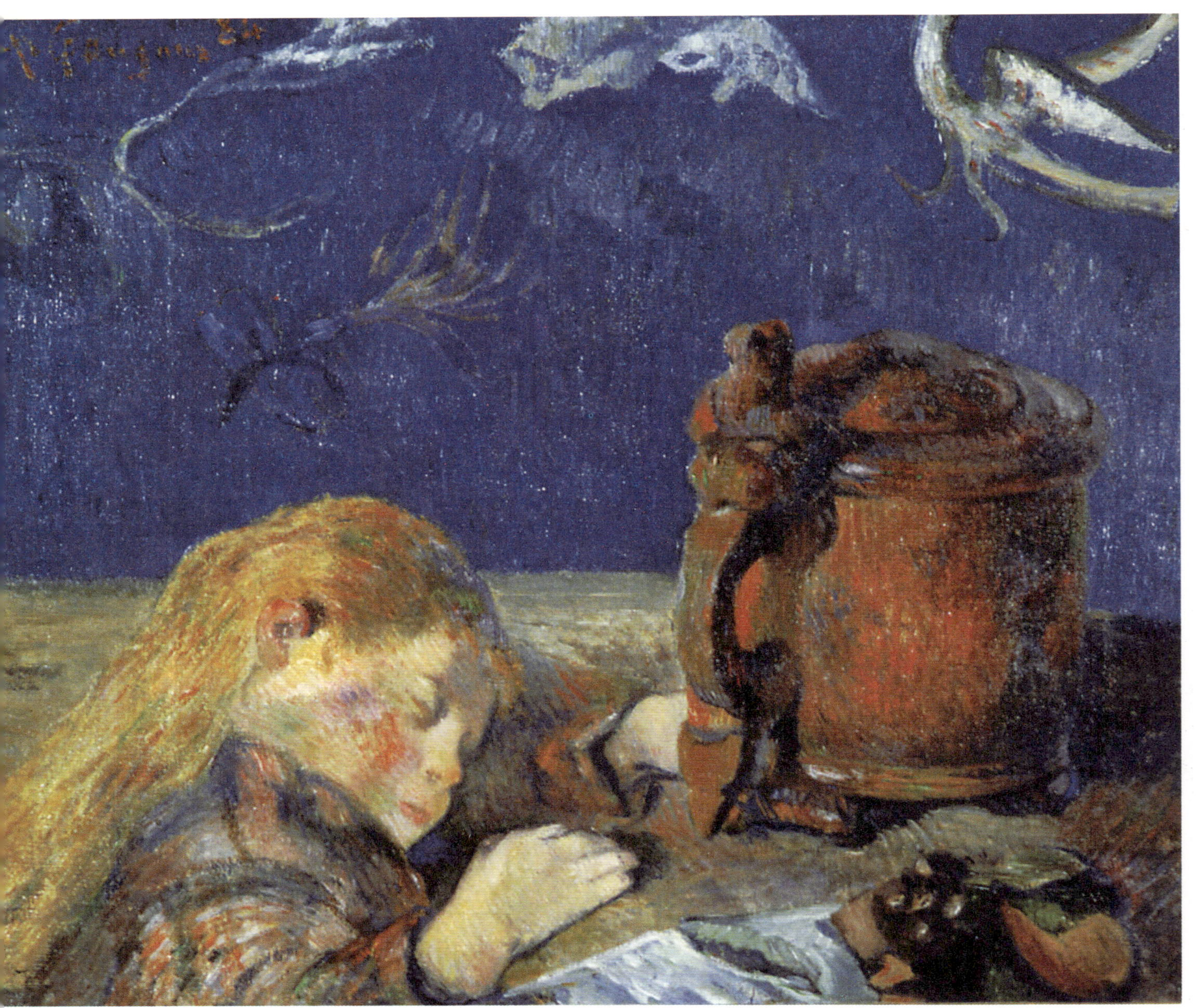

Clovis Gauguin (Sleeping Child), 1884
Oil on canvas, 46 x 55.5 cm (18⅛ x 21⅞ in) • Private Collection

Prior to the 1886 portrait of Clovis, Gauguin's young son had long golden hair worn in ringlets, and wore dresses, as was the custom for young boys until the early twentieth century. The child slumbers at the table.

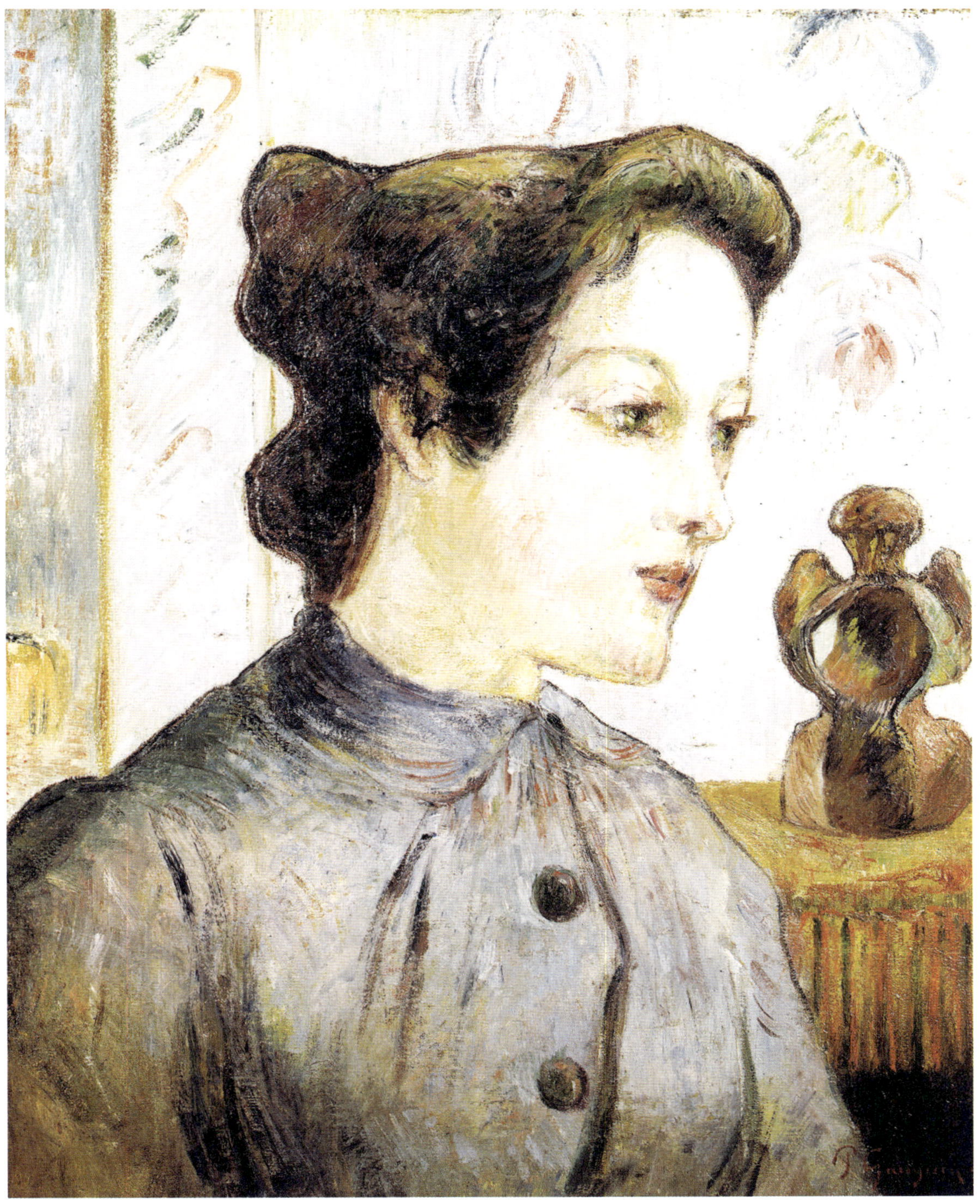

Portrait of a Young Woman, 1886
Oil on canvas, 46 x 38 cm (18 x 15 in)
• Bridgestone Museum of Art, Tokyo

By 1886 Gauguin, like other artists, had moved beyond Impressionism, experimenting with his own creation: Synthetist art. One can see the artist's ceramic sculpture – visible in *Still Life with a Profile of Laval* (1886) – in the background.

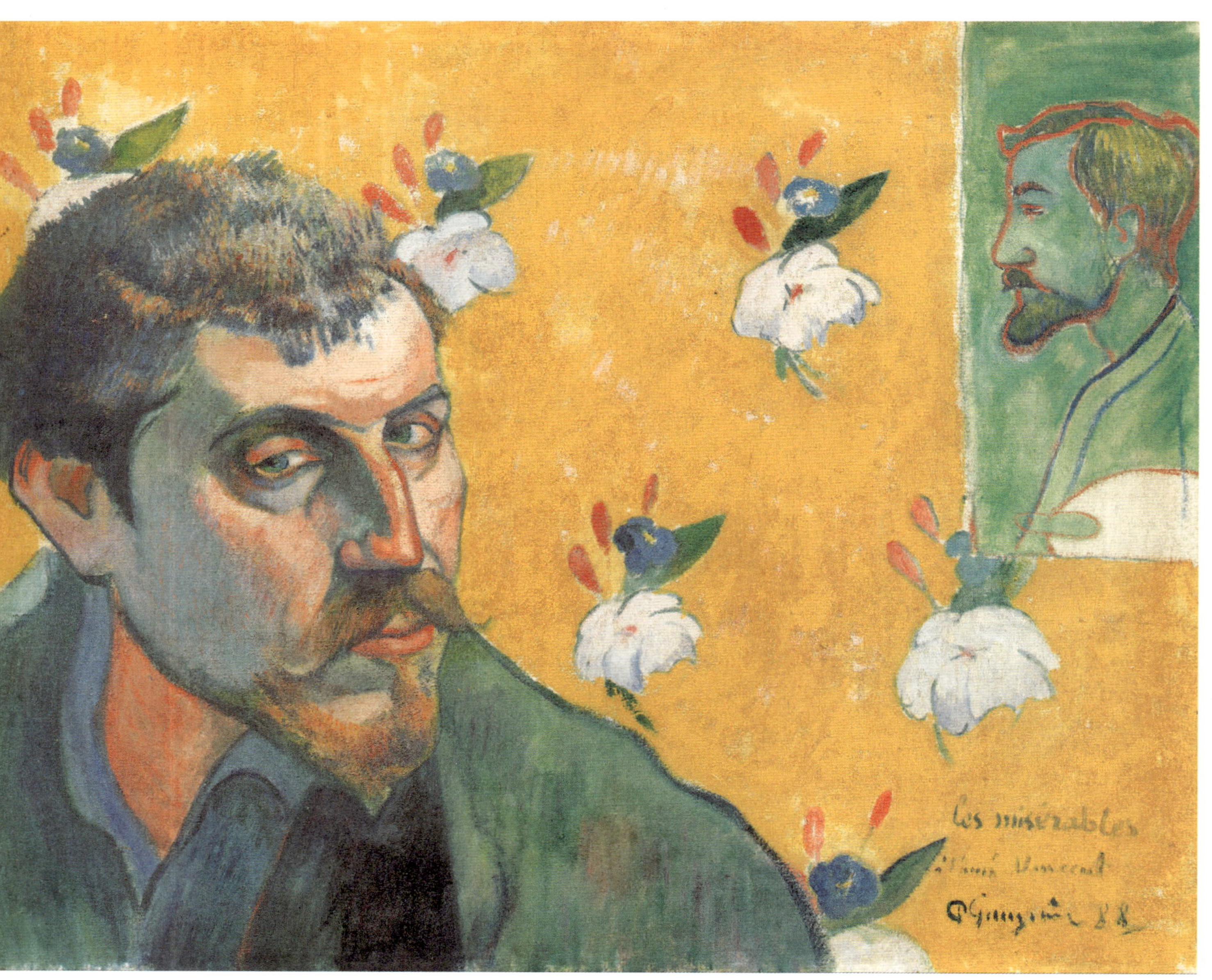

Self-Portrait, Les Misérables, 1888
Oil on canvas, 45 x 55 cm (17¾ x 21⅓ in)
• Van Gogh Museum, Amsterdam

Van Gogh and Gauguin wanted character portraits of each other before their Arles venture. Gauguin painted himself as Victor Hugo's *Les Misérables* character Jean Valjean. 'It is the face of an outlaw....', and Van Gogh painted himself as a Buddhist monk.

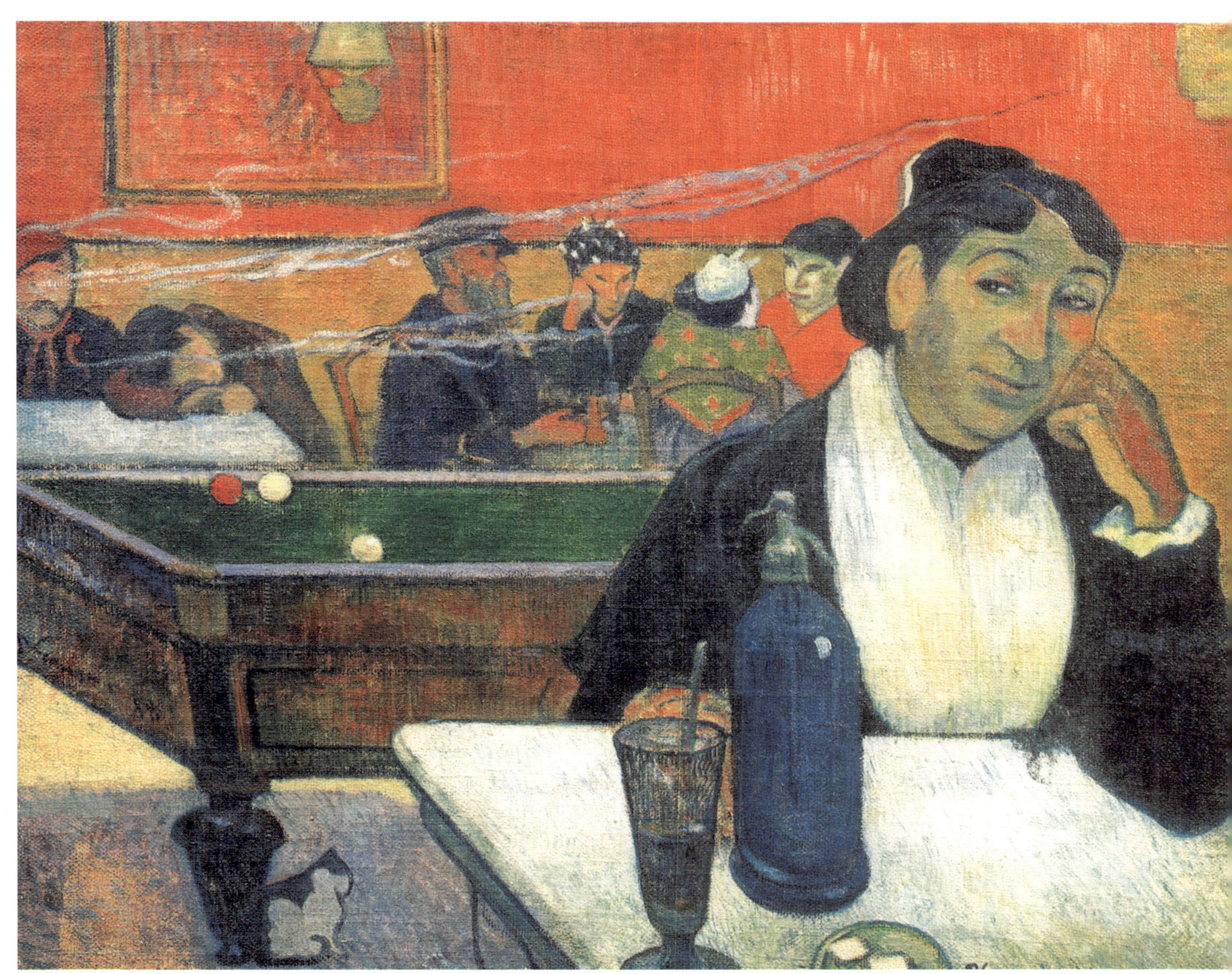

Café at Arles (Café de Nuit), 1888
Oil on canvas, 72 x 92 cm (28⅓ x 36¼ in) • Pushkin Museum, Moscow

Soon after arriving in Arles, Gauguin painted a portrait of Madame Marie Ginoux, proprietor of the local *café de nuit*, the Café de la Gare. Madame Ginoux, wearing traditional black and white Arlésienne costume, is portrayed in the café interior.

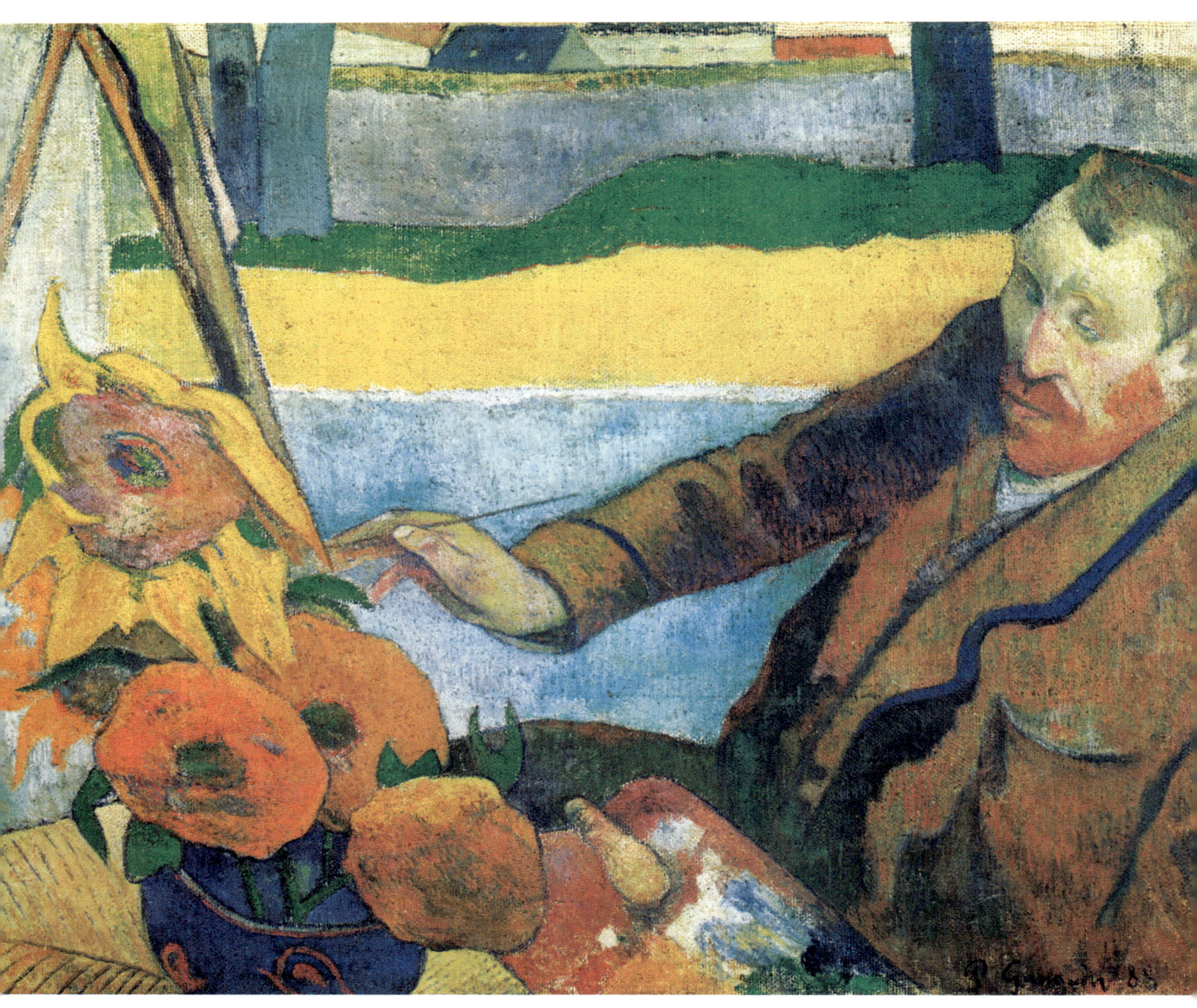

Van Gogh Painting Sunflowers, 1888
Oil on canvas, 73 x 91 cm (28¾ x 35⅞ in)
• Van Gogh Museum, Amsterdam

Gauguin portrays Van Gogh deep in concentration at his easel, painting sunflowers. In the intimacy of the Yellow House studio we are brought face to face with the Dutch painter at work, absorbed in his subject.

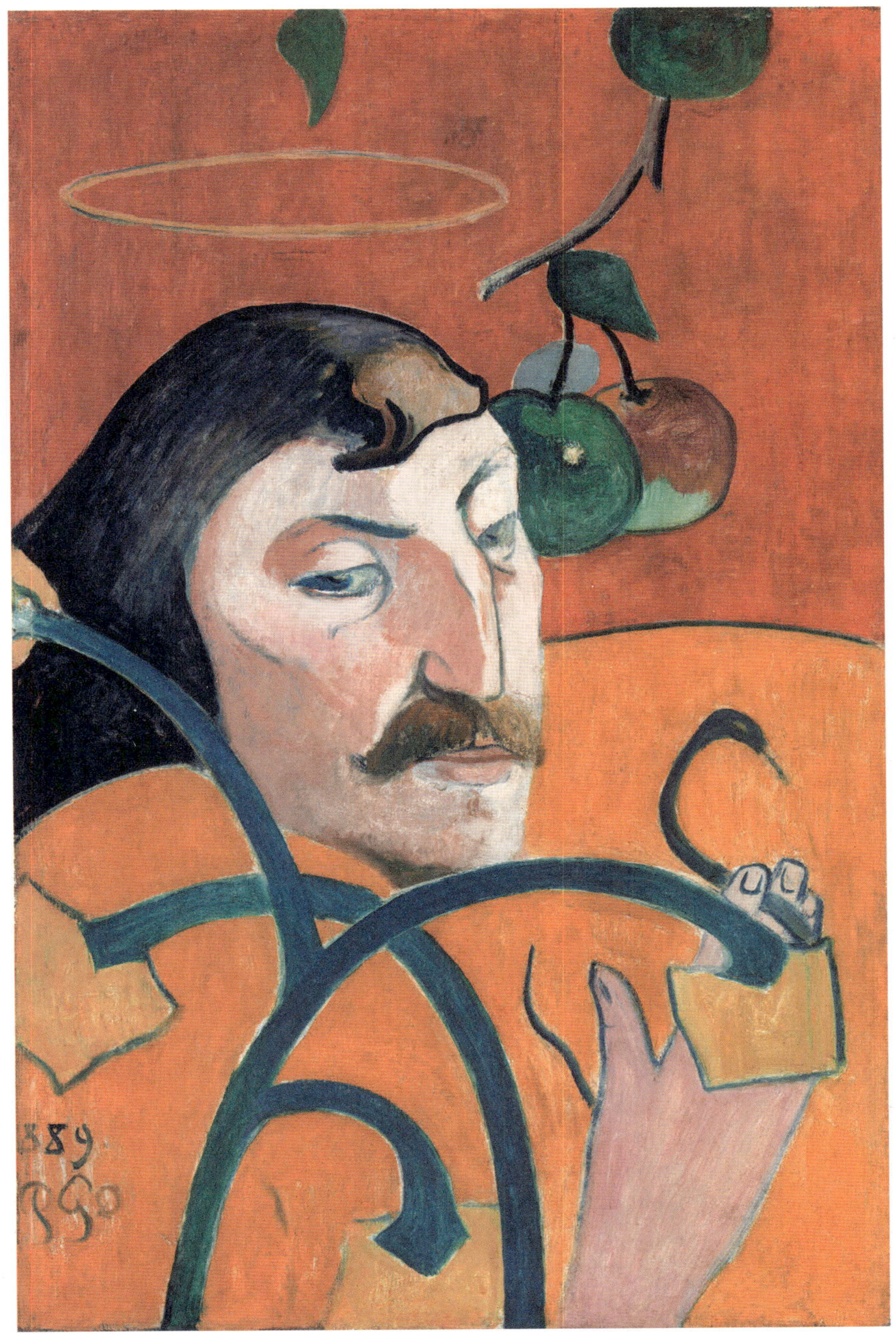

Self-Portrait, 1889

Oil on wood, 79.2 x 51.3 cm (31⅛ x 20⅓ in)

• National Gallery of Art, Washington D.C.

An unusual self-portrait of Gauguin portrayed as a haloed saint with devilish demeanour, holding a snake. The rich colour palette serves to heighten the Synthetism generated by his gaze towards the spectator.

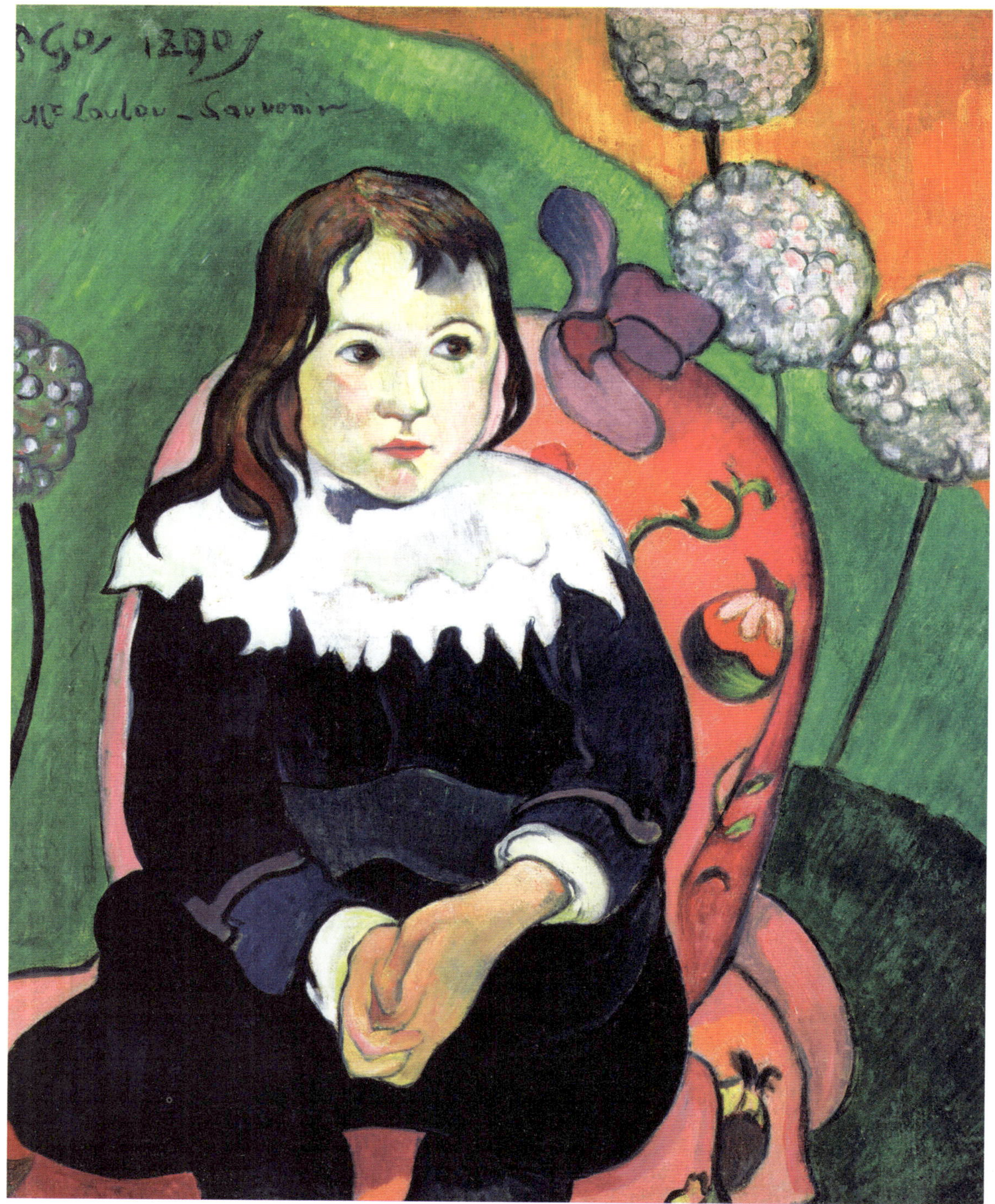

M. Loulou (Louis Le Ray), 1890
Oil on canvas, 55 x 46.2 cm (21⅔ x 18⅓ in)
• The Barnes Foundation, Philadelphia

Gauguin had a gentle touch in the art of depicting a child's character. Here, he captures the quiet personality of a young boy, the son of Gauguin's associate, who sits on a rose-blush chair, surrounded by floral blooms.

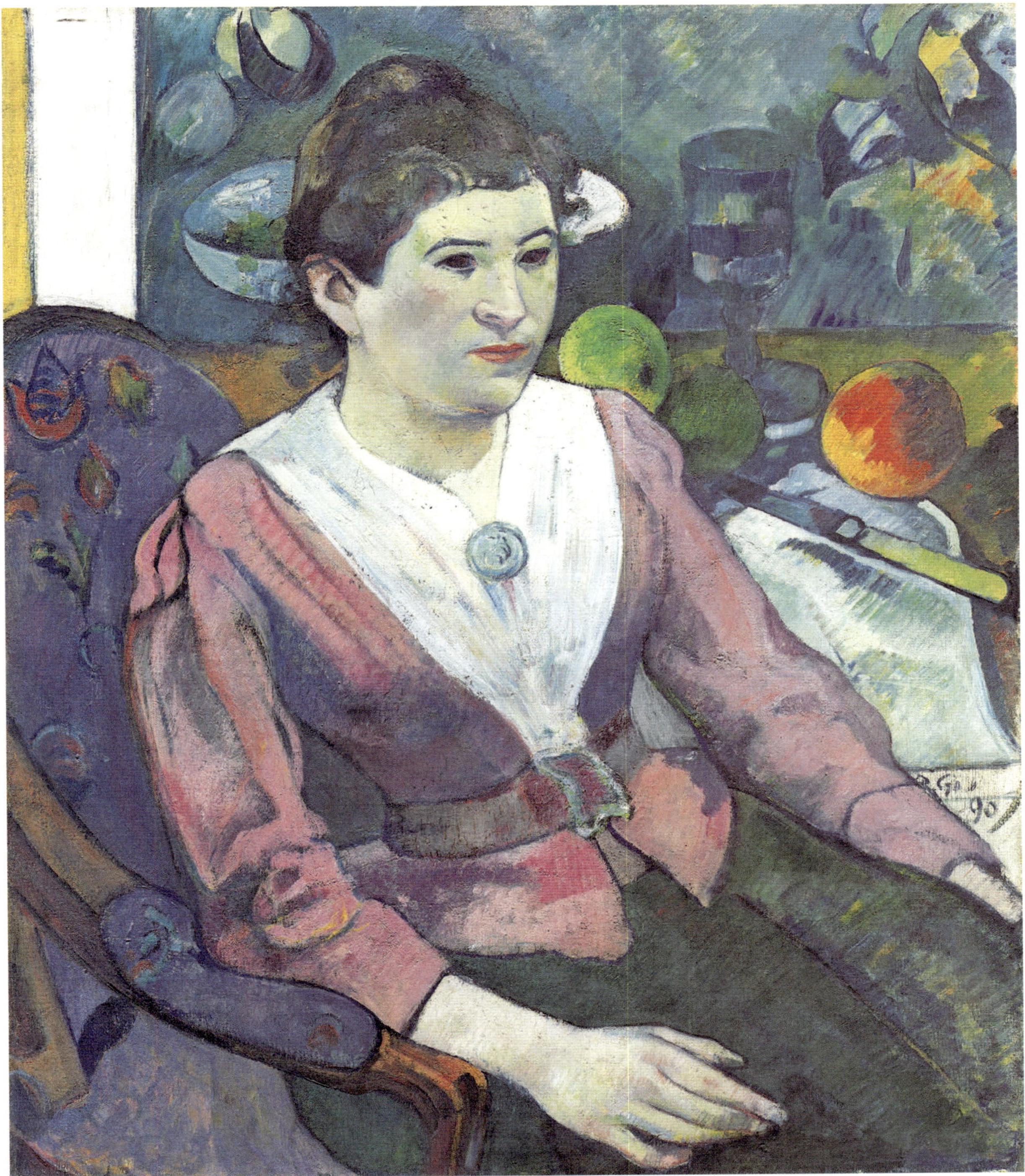

Woman in Front of a Still Life by Cézanne, 1890
Oil on linen canvas, 65.3 x 54.9 cm (25¾ x 21⅜ in)
• The Art Institute of Chicago

During his career as a successful stockbroker, Gauguin collected many paintings by Cézanne, an artist he admired. In this portrait of an unknown sitter, Gauguin includes Cézanne's *Still Life with Fruit Dish* (1879–80), which he owned.

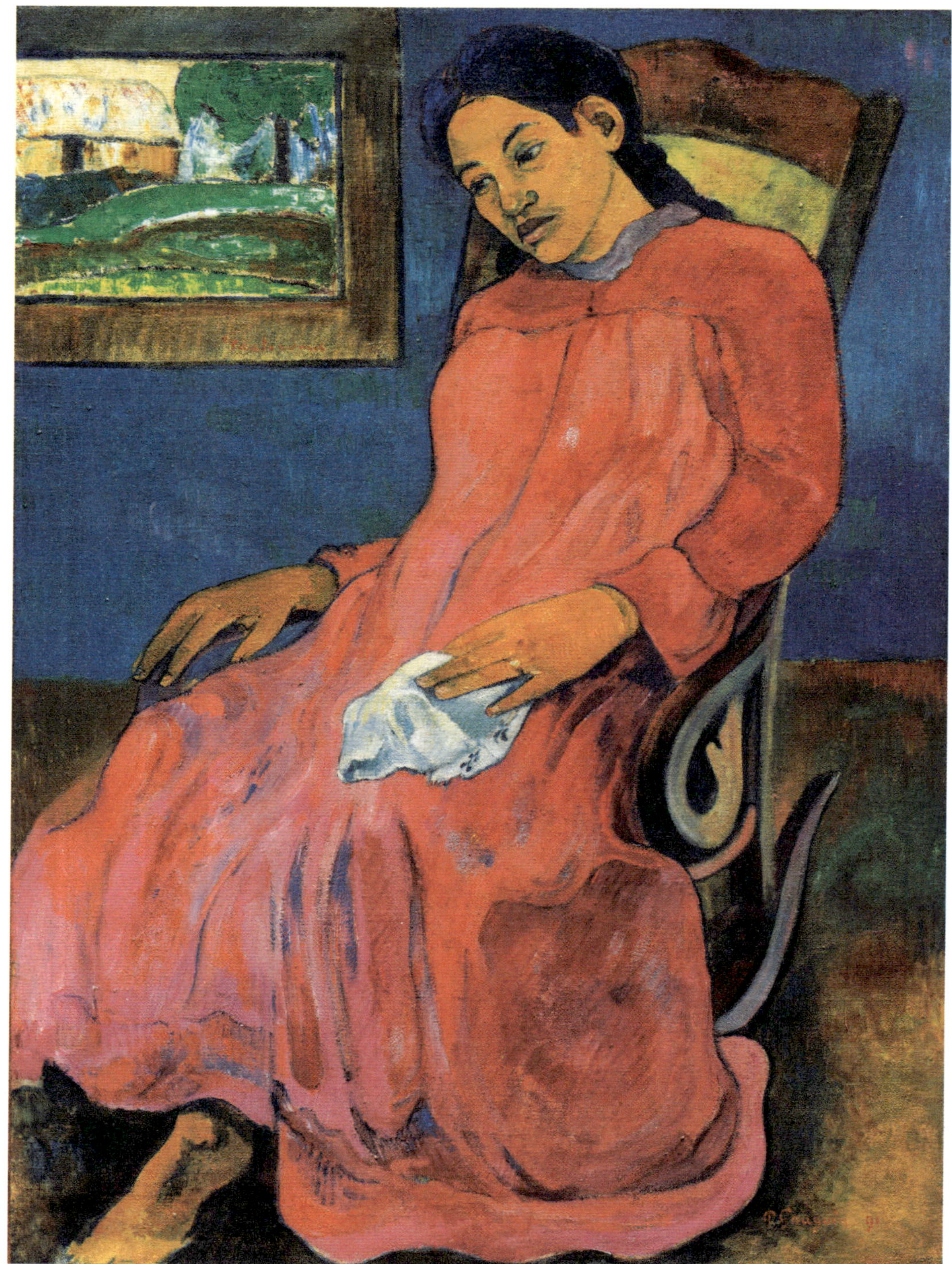

Melancholic (Faaturuma), 1891
Oil on canvas, 93 x 68.3 cm (36⅜ x 26⅞ in)
• Nelson-Atkins Museum of Art, Kansas City

Faaturuma is a Tahitian word for an overcast sky. Gauguin implies melancholy in the demeanour of the young woman seated in a rocking chair. She is downcast. The brightness of her red dress contrasts with her sad expression.

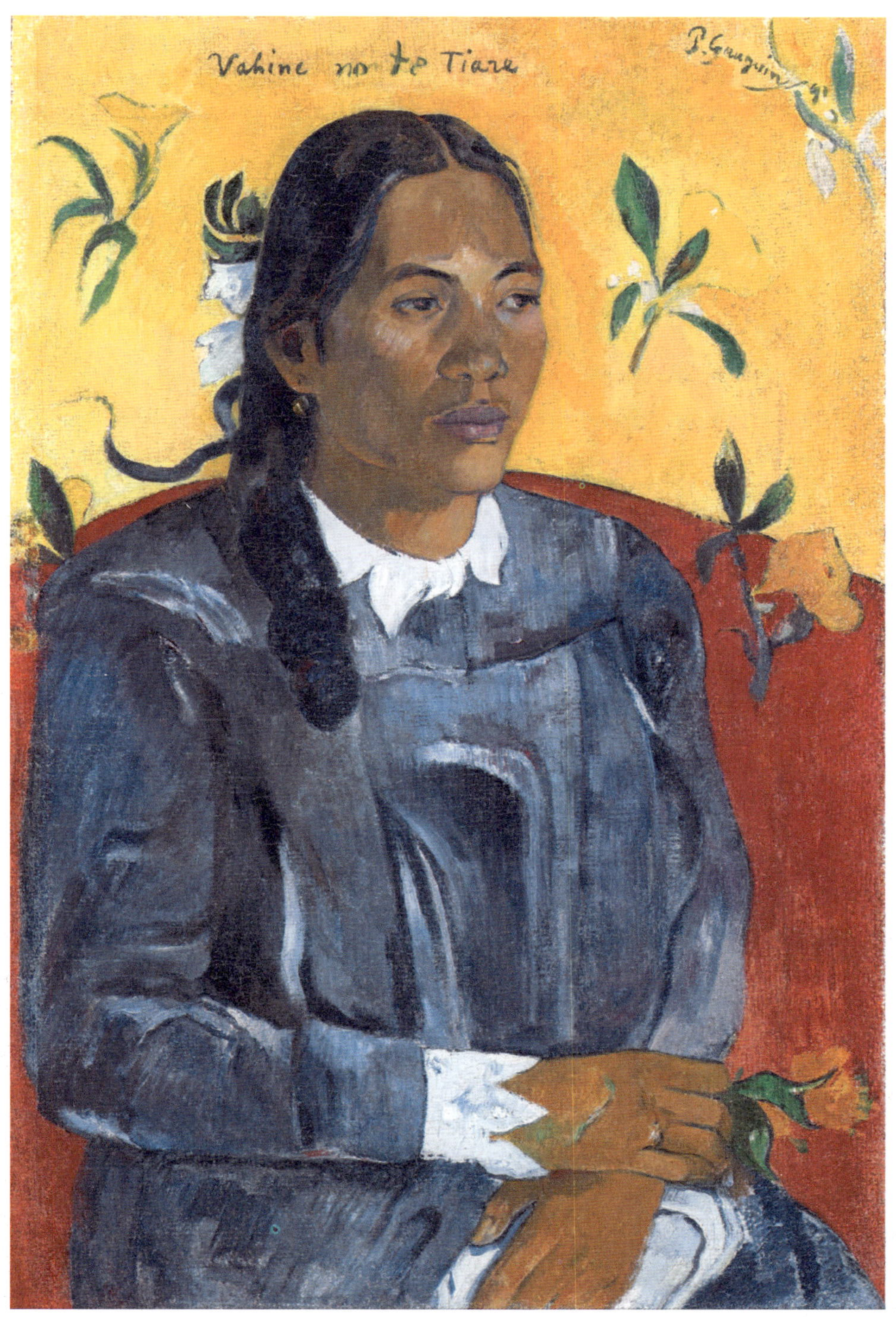

Woman with a Flower (Vahine no te Tiare), 1891
Oil on canvas, 70 x 46 cm (27⅔ x 18 in)
• Ny Carlsberg Glyptotek, Copenhagen

Gauguin's colour-saturated portrait captures innocence in the youthful beauty of a Polynesian *vahine* (woman). She holds a fragrant flower, *tiare*, traditionally used to make welcoming garlands for island visitors.

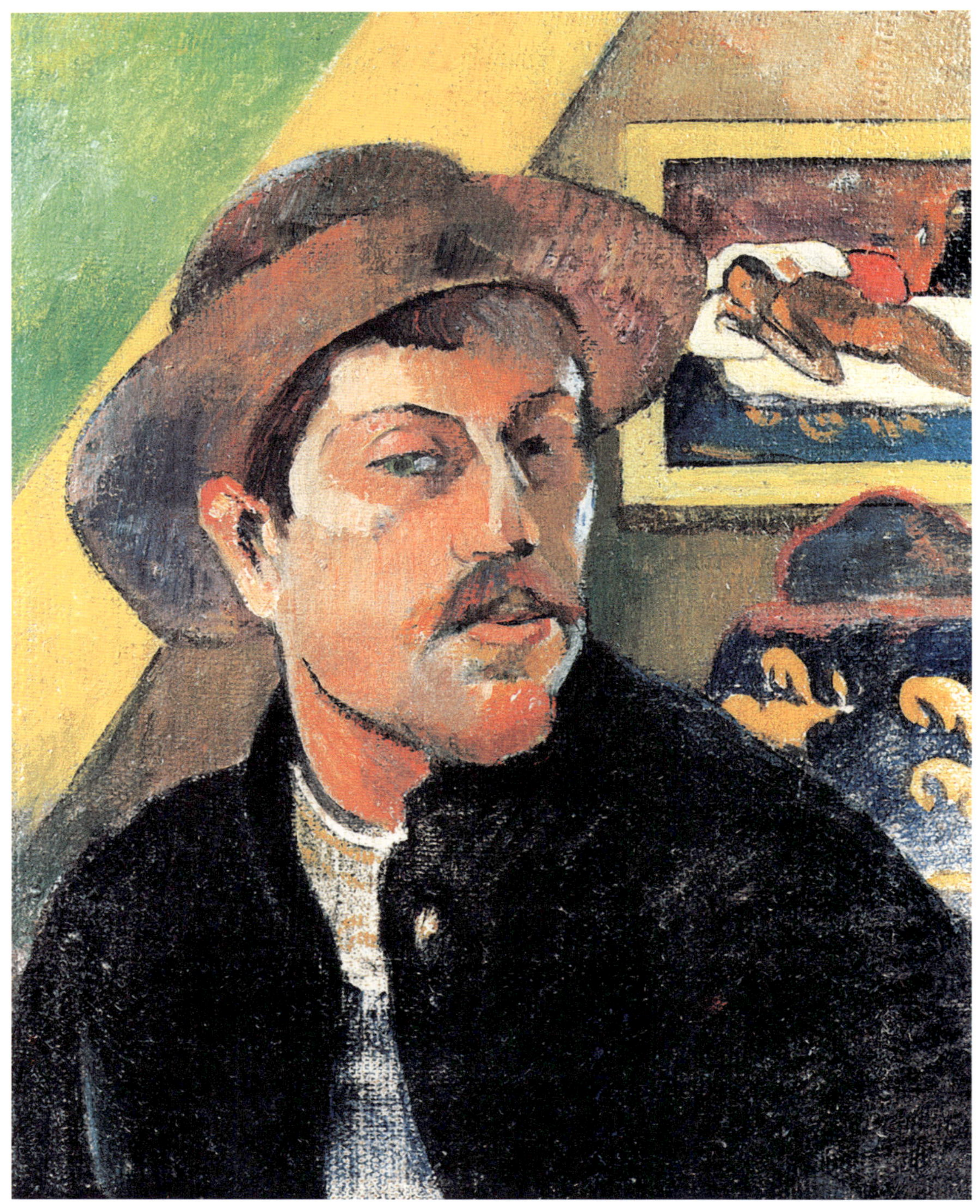

Self-Portrait in a Hat, 1893–94
Oil on canvas, 46 x 38 cm (18⅛ x 15 in) • Musée d'Orsay, Paris

After mixed reviews of his Paris exhibition of Tahitian paintings, Gauguin, in his 'Tahitianized' Paris studio, portrayed himself with defiant expression, wearing a fedora and black jacket, surrounded by paintings and memorabilia from his first sojourn in Polynesia.

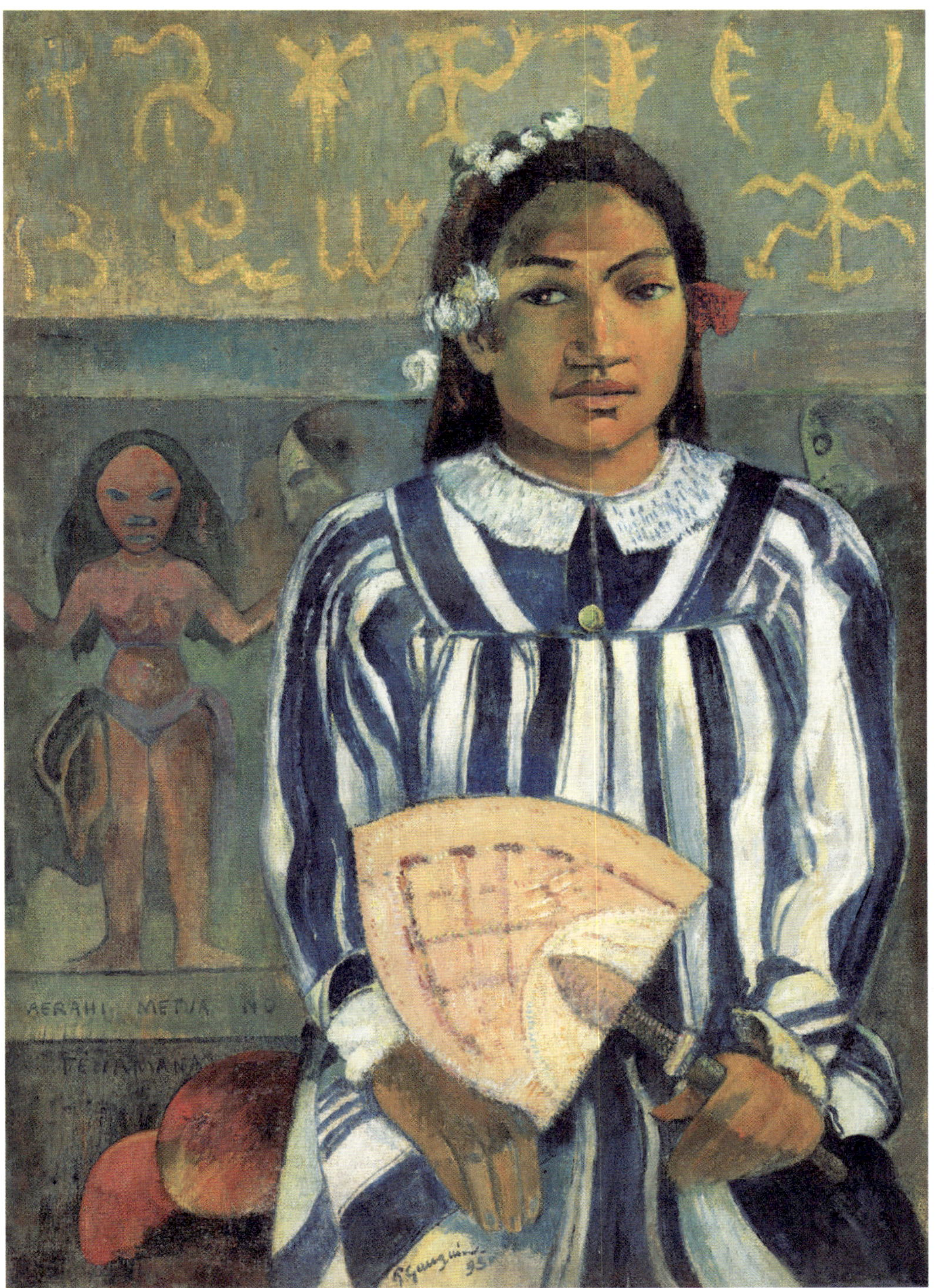

The Ancestors of Tehamana, or Tehamana Has Many Parents (Merahi Metua no Tehamana), 1893
Oil on canvas, 76.3 x 54.3 cm (30 x 21⅗ in)
• The Art Institute of Chicago

In a European-style dress given out by Christian missionaries, Tehamana, red flower in hair, sits in front of a frieze of undecipherable Polynesian script and Gauguin's depiction of the ancient deity Hina, to whom all Tahitians believed they were related.

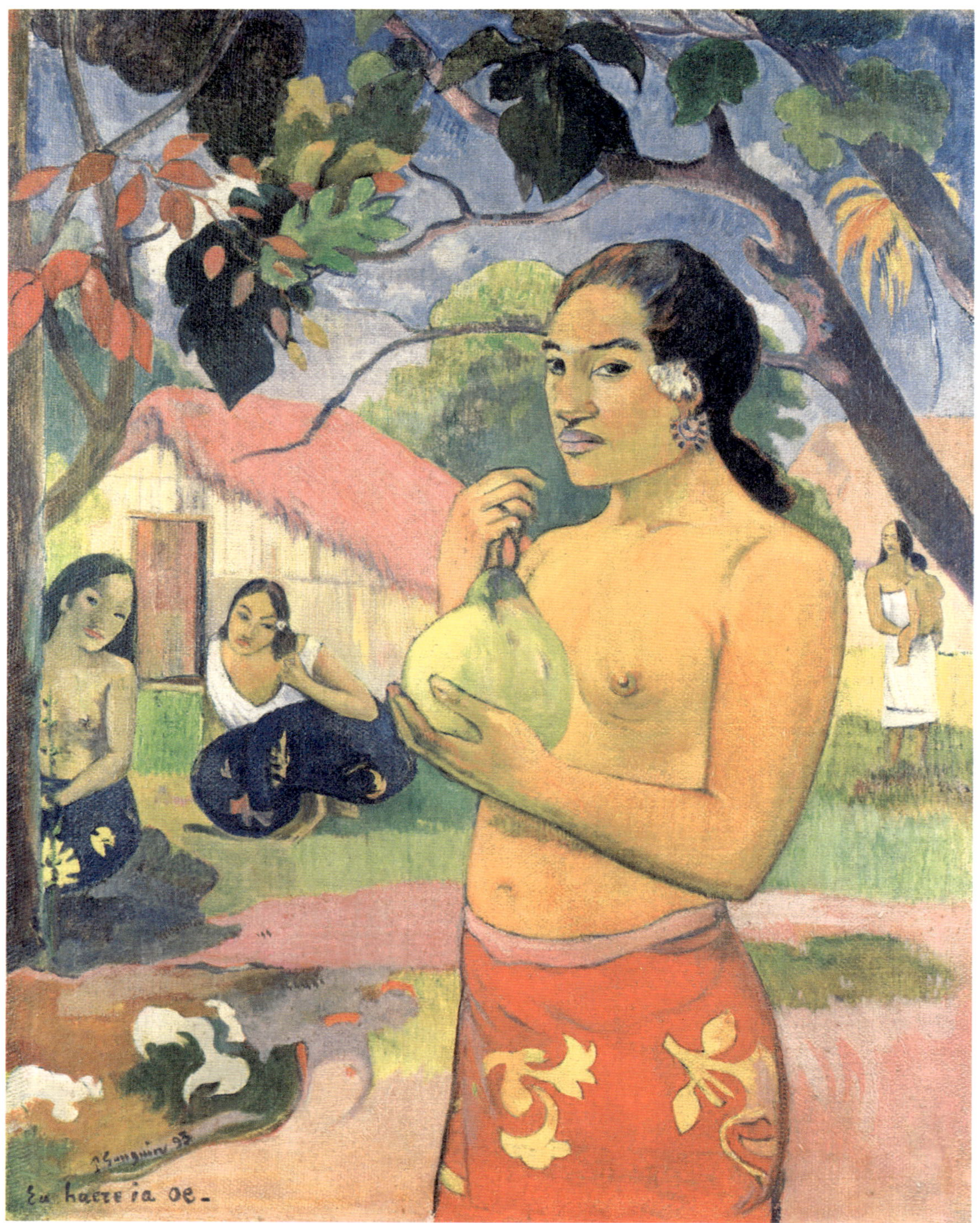

Woman with Mango, 1893
Oil on canvas, 92 x 73 cm (36¼ x 28¾ in)
• The State Hermitage Museum, St Petersburg

Purchased by Edgar Degas, a staunch supporter of Gauguin's art, *Woman with Mango* depicts Tehamana, a 13-year-old girl who lived with Gauguin as his *vahine*. She appears in many of his finest works, created in 1892–93.

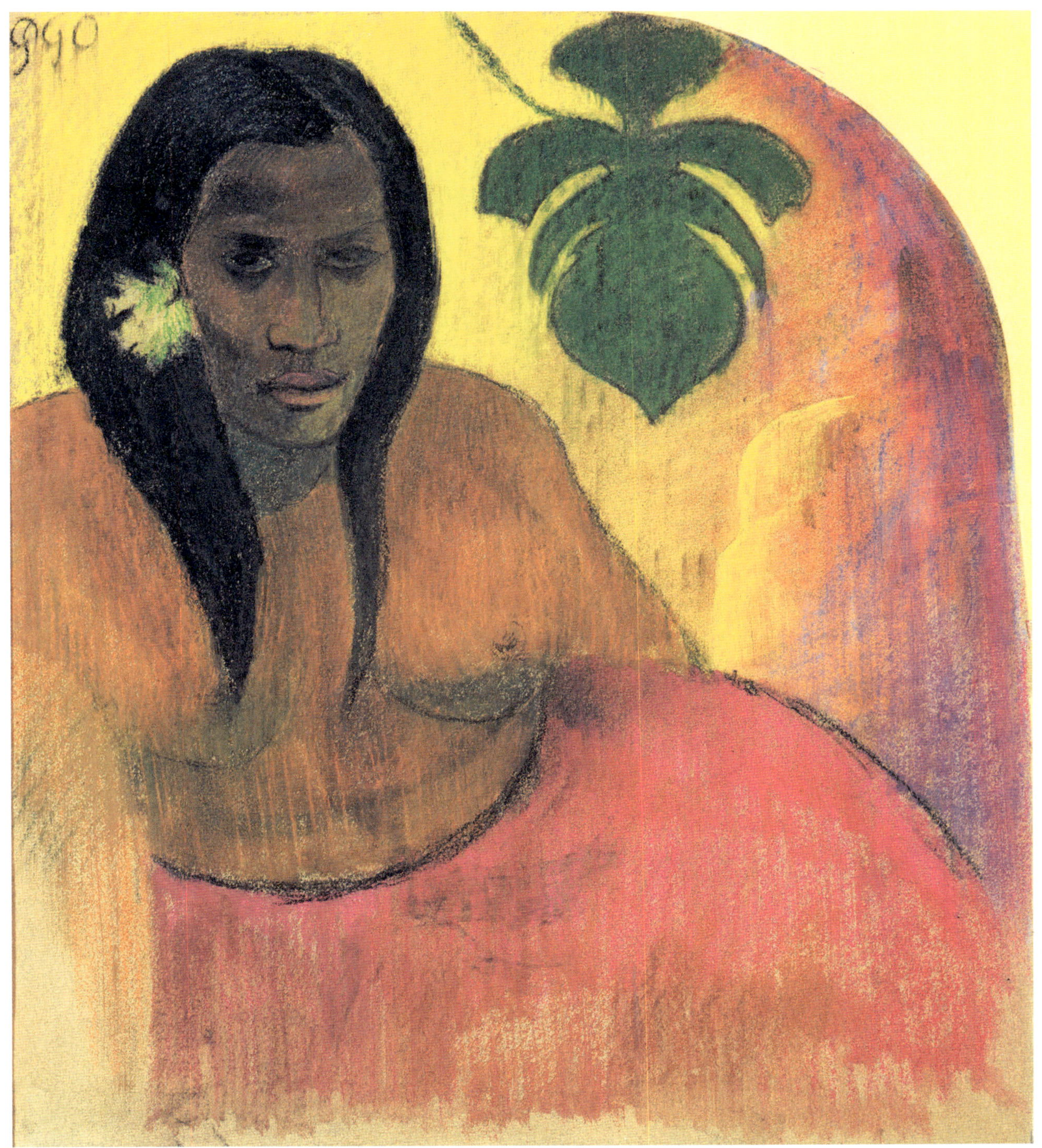

Tahitian Woman, *c.* 1894
Charcoal and pastel on paper laid down on board,
54.9 x 49.5 cm (21⅜ x 19½ in)
• Brooklyn Museum, New York

Gauguin was a prolific sketcher, working in many mediums. Here, in charcoal and pastel on paper, glued to yellow wove paper, he creates a warm harmony of colour in this intimate, sultry portrait of a Tahitian woman.

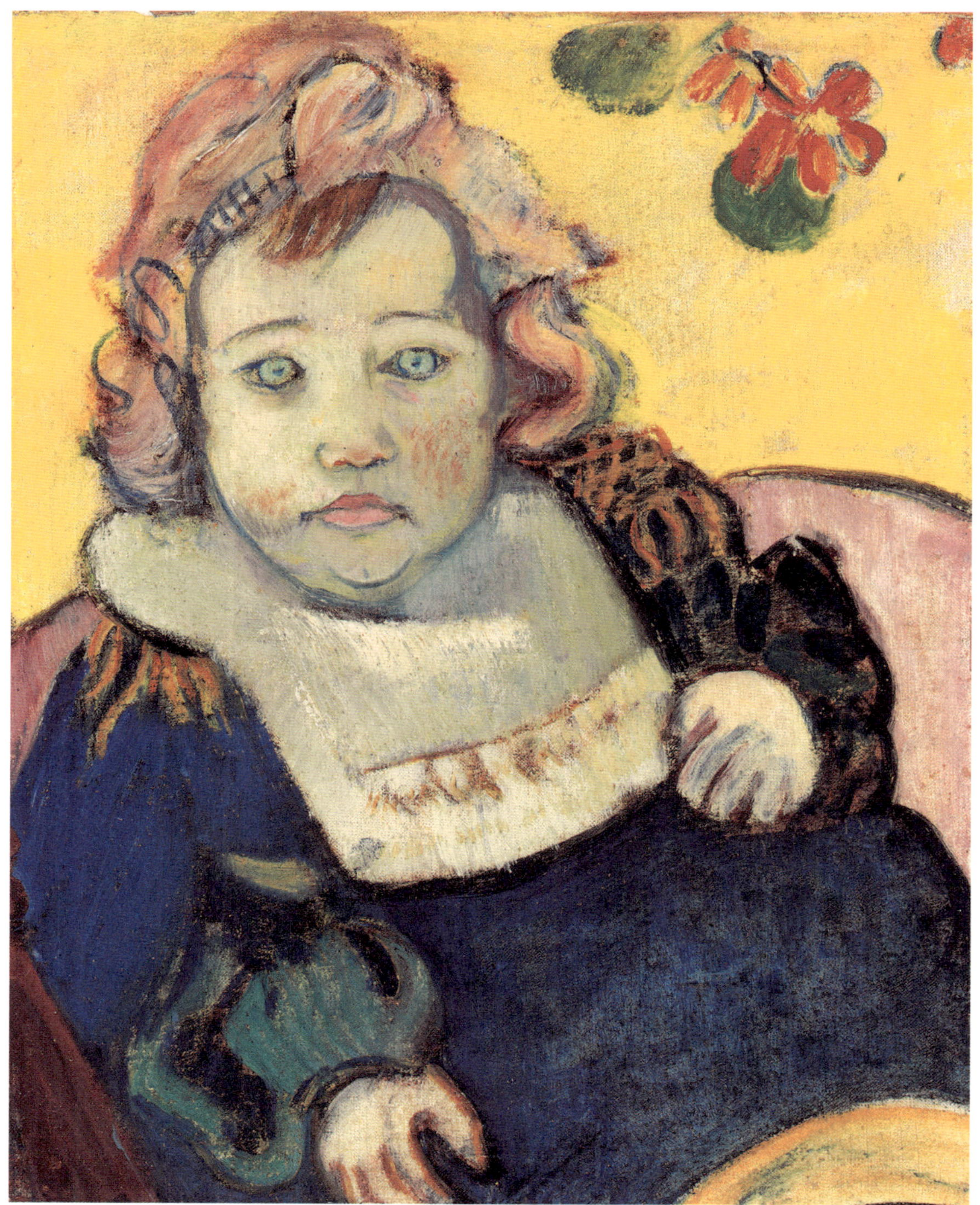

Child with Bib, 1895
Oil on canvas, 32.1 x 25.4 cm (12⅔ x 10 in) • Private Collection

In this portrait commissioned and painted in Paris, prior to Gauguin journeying to Tahiti, the artist illustrates the baby's individual character, primarily through limpid, pale green eyes that are transfixed on the viewer.

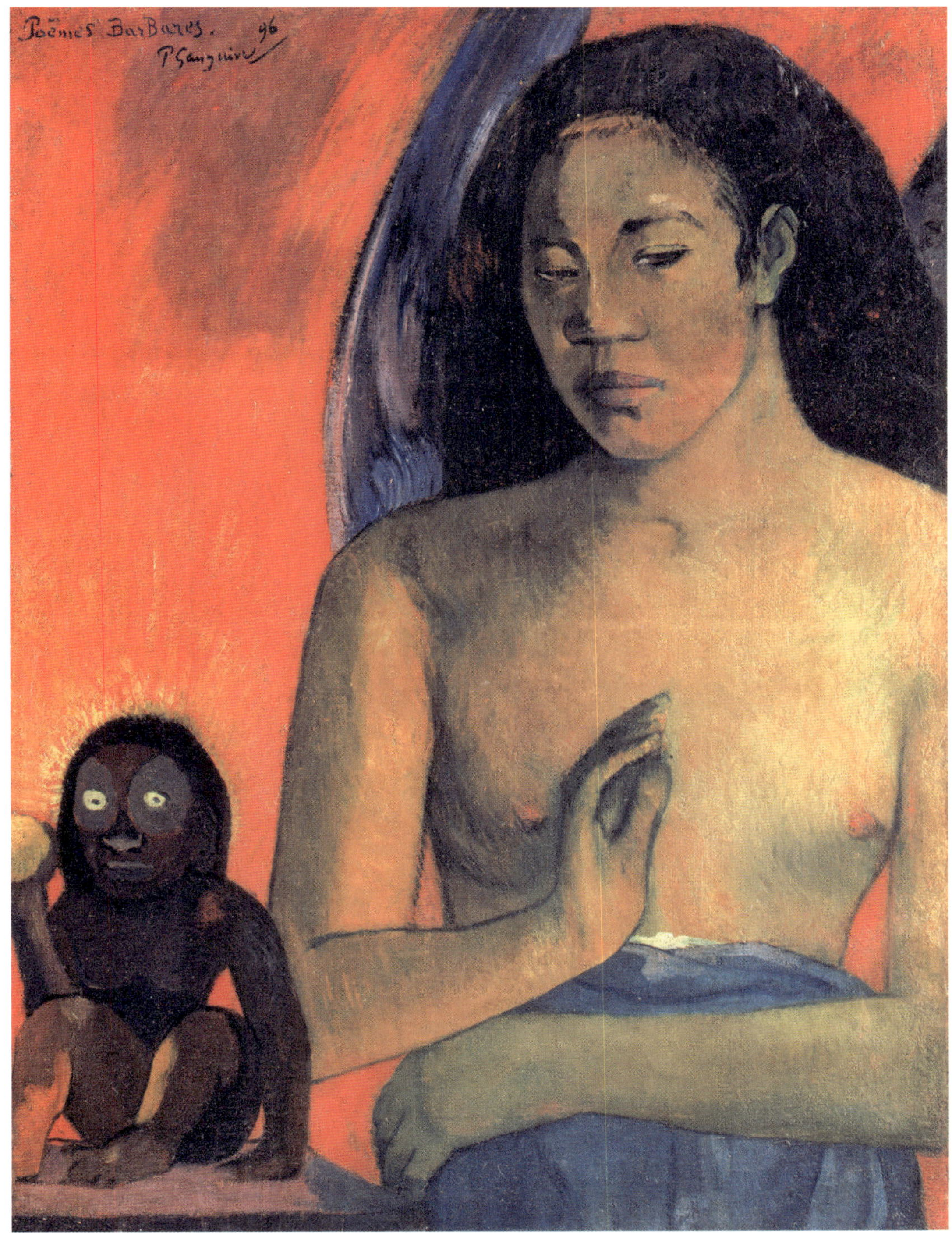

Savage Poems, 1896
Oil on canvas, 62.9 x 47 cm (24¾ x 18½ in)
• Fogg Museum, Harvard Art Museums, Cambridge, Massachusetts

The title is taken from *Poèmes barbares* (Barbaric Poems, 1862), by French poet Charles Leconte de Lisle (1818–94), featuring magical creatures on the island of Tahiti. From the poems Gauguin visualizes a winged female, and Ta'aroa, a Tahitian deity.

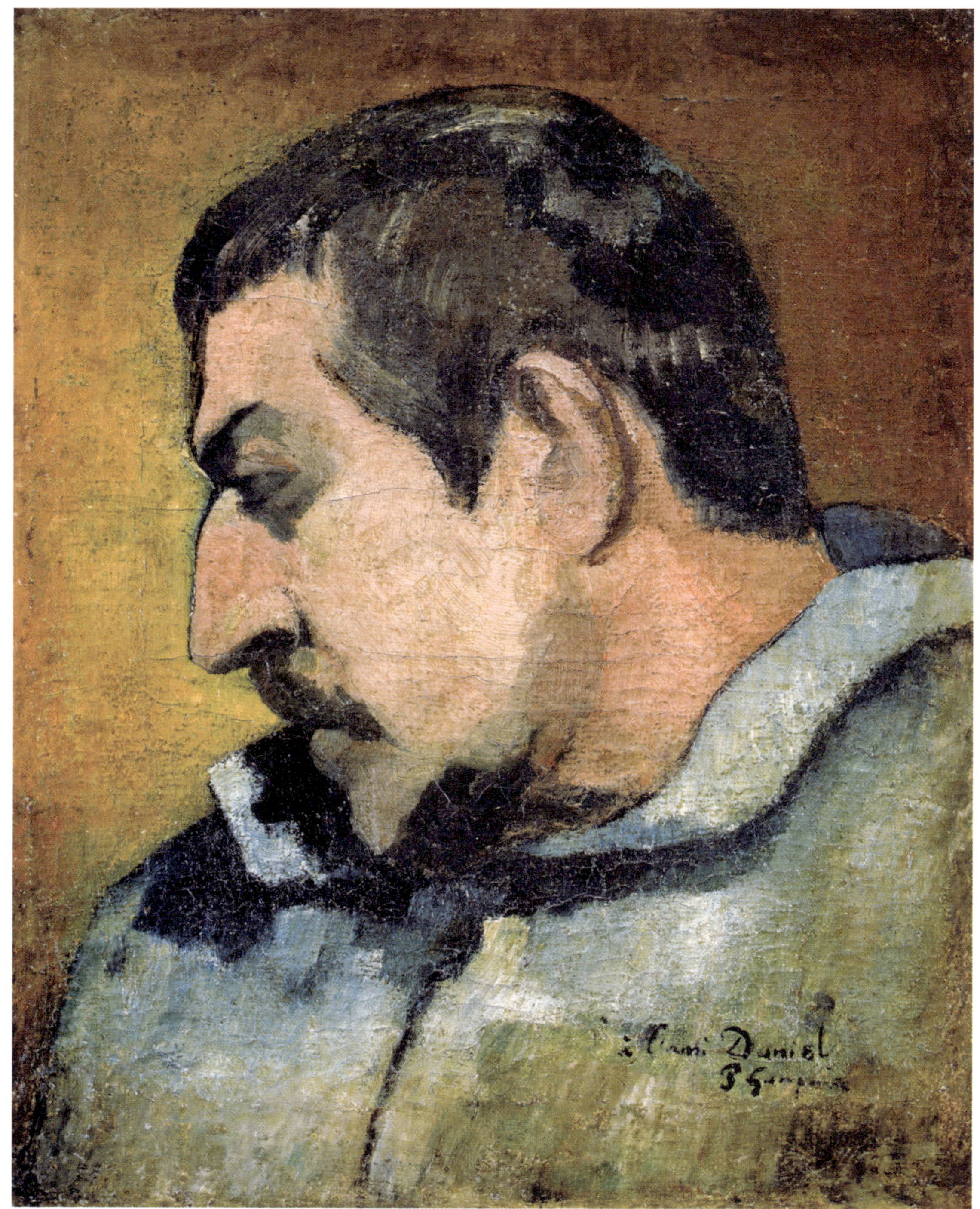

Self-Portrait, 1896

Oil on canvas, 40 x 32 cm (15¾ x 12⅓ in) • Musée d'Orsay, Paris

A self-portrait, depicting Gauguin in profile, dedicated to his friend and biographer the Symbolist poet George-Daniel de Monfreid. Hues of green and golden ochre create an evocative, intimate portrayal.

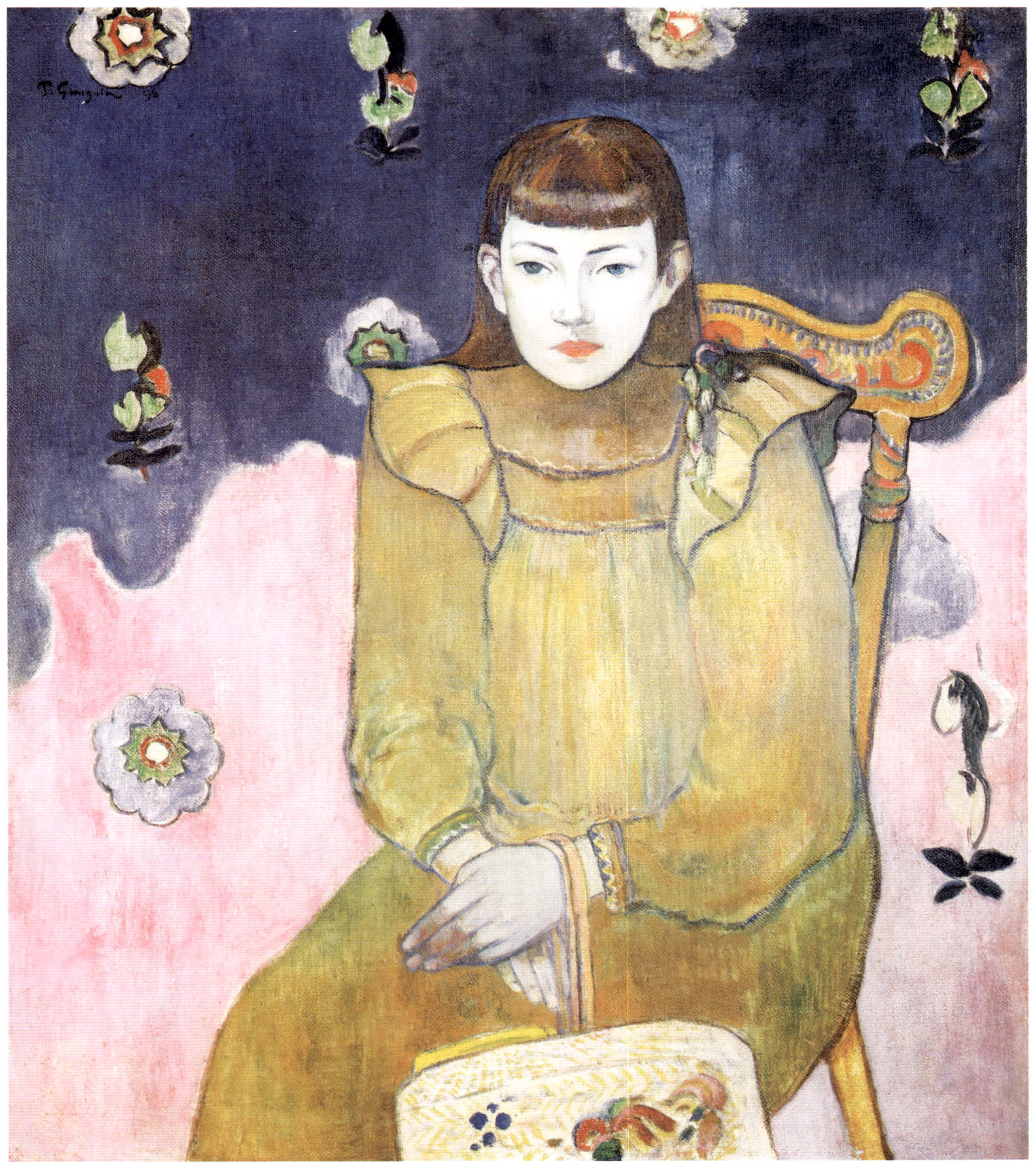

Portrait of Vaite Goupil, 1896
Oil on canvas, 75 x 65 cm (29½ x 25⅗ in) • Ordrupgaard, Copenhagen

At Gauguin's request, Auguste Goupil, a wealthy French lawyer in residence on his plantation near Papeete, commissioned a portrait of his daughter, Jeanne, whose Tahitian name was Vaite. The portrait's Symbolist quality is accentuated in its background decoration and colour contrasts.

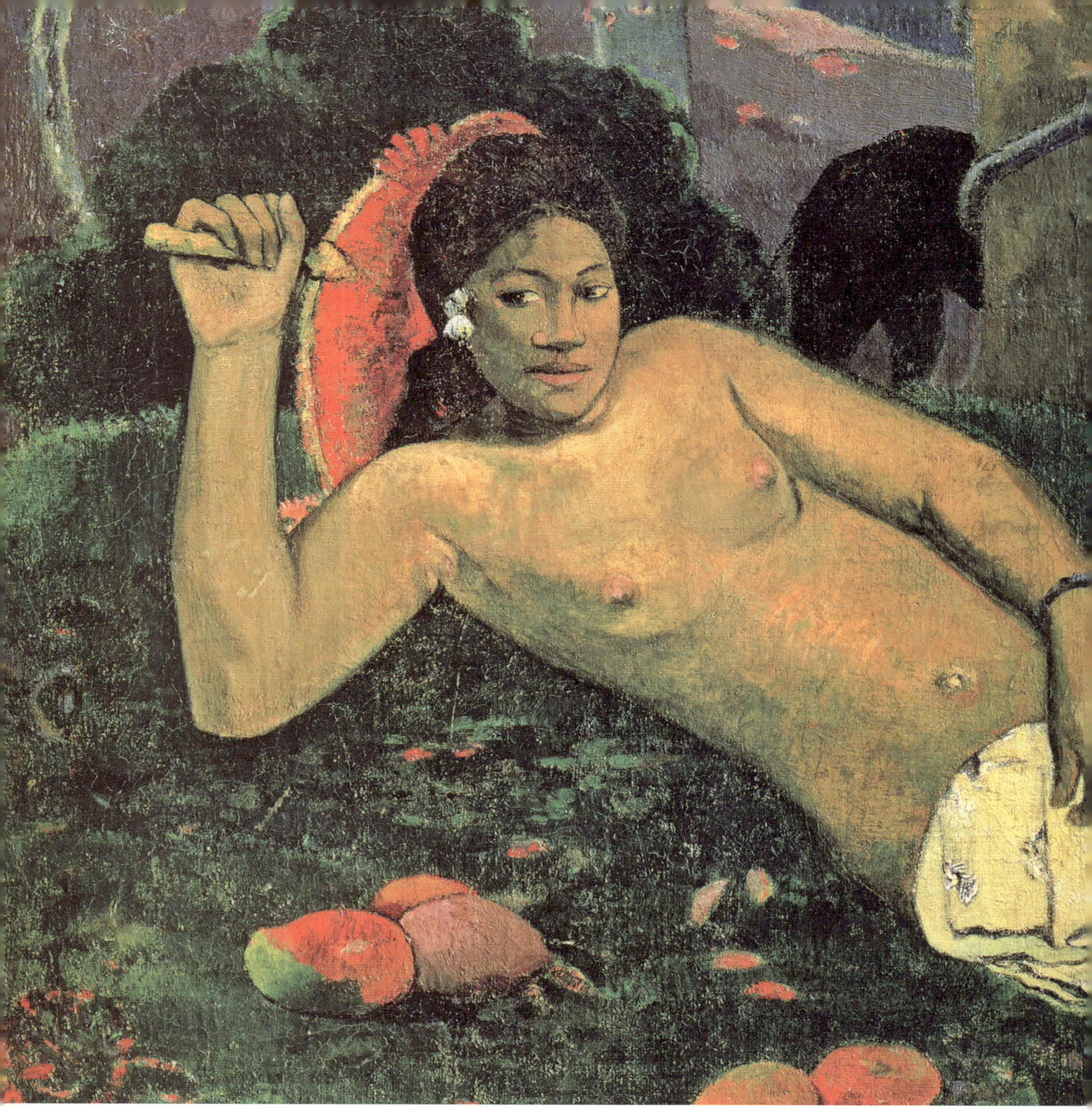

The King's Wife (Te Arii Vahine), 1896
Oil on canvas, 97 x 130 cm (38⅓ x 51⅓ in)
• Pushkin Museum, Moscow

In April 1896, Gauguin wrote to the Symbolist poet and art collector de Monfreid, 'I've just done a big painting … a naked queen reclining on a green rug…. I don't think I have ever done anything with such deep resonant colours.'

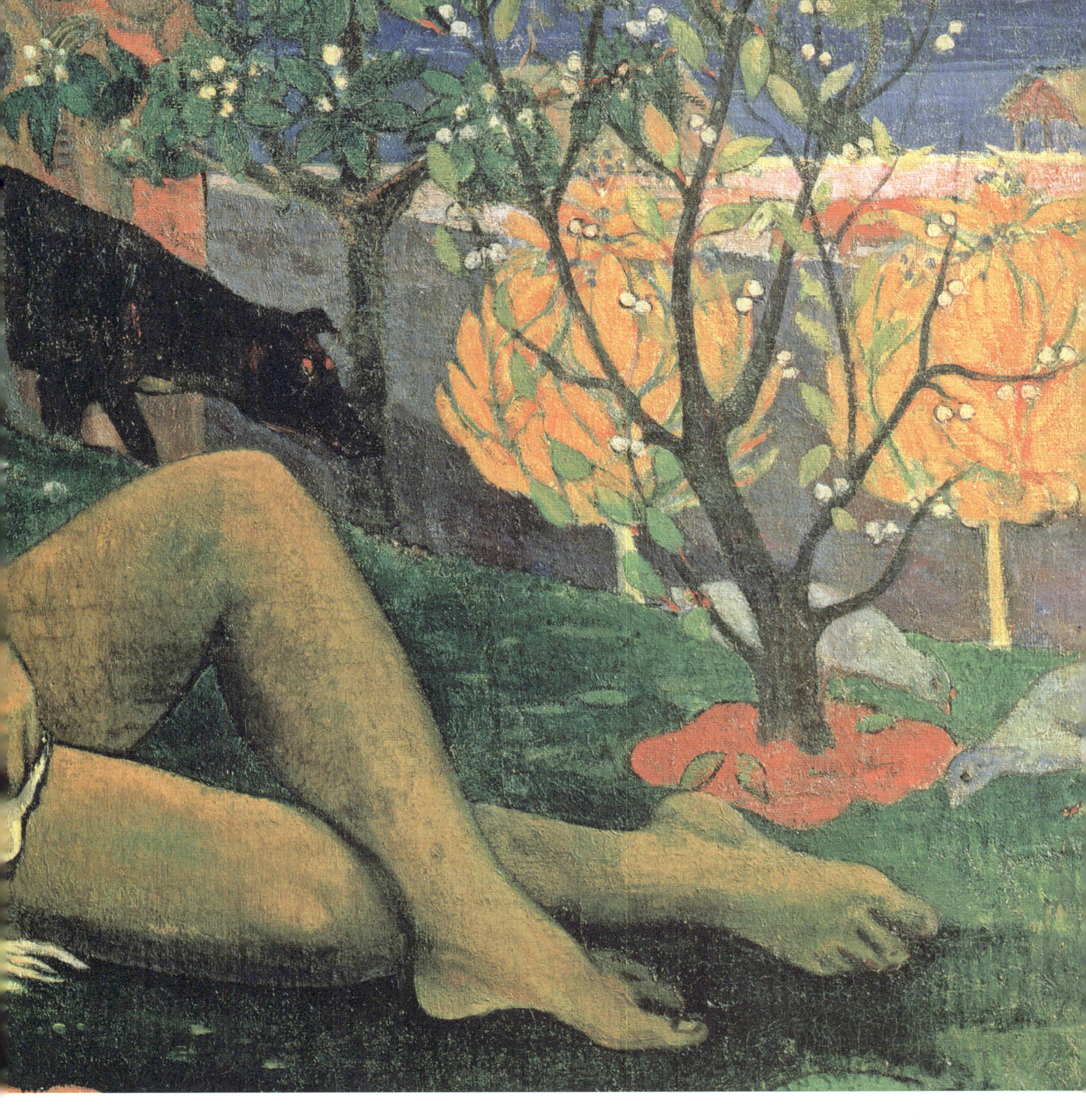

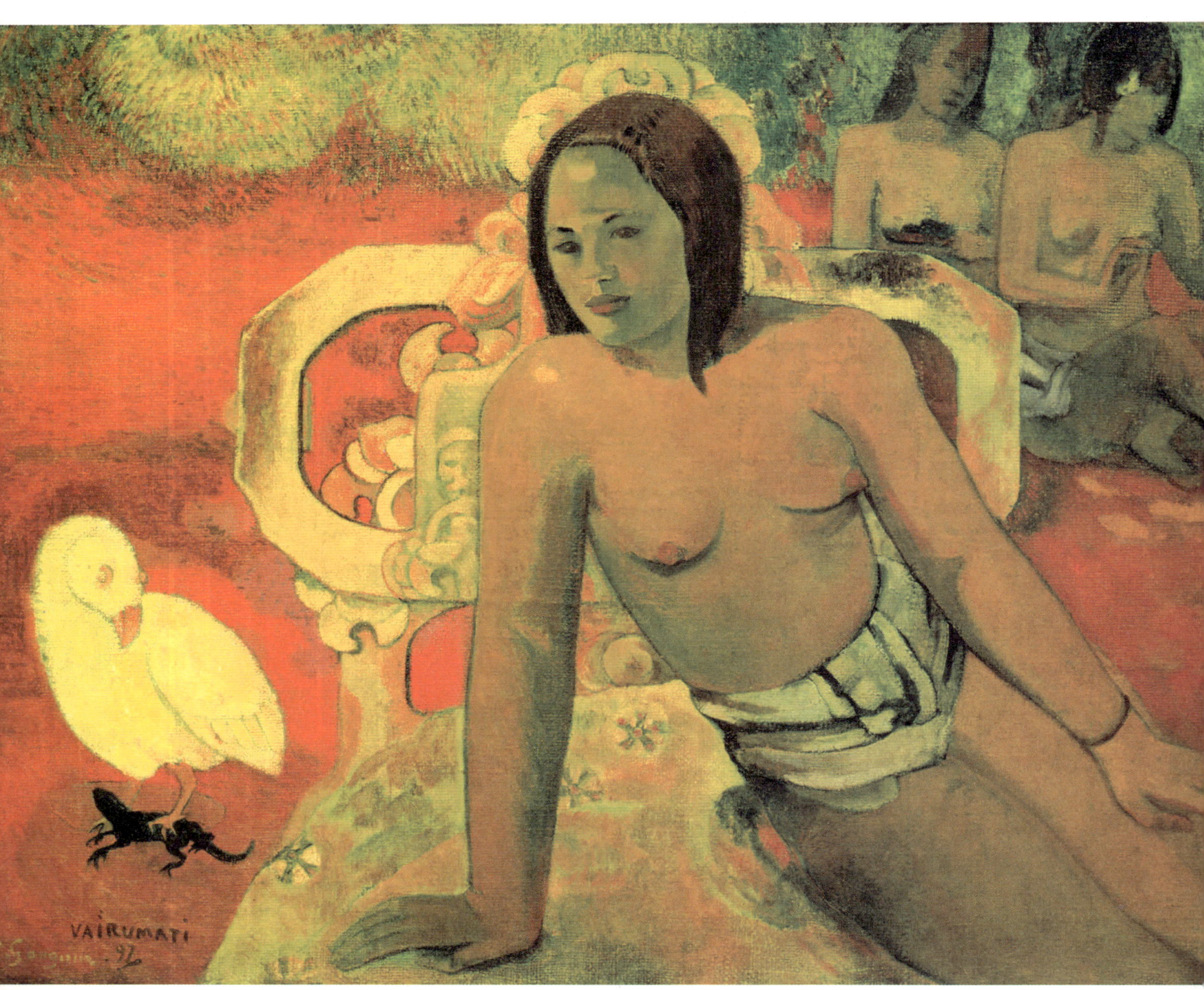

Vairumati, 1897
Oil on canvas, 73 x 94 cm (28¾ x 37 in) • Musée d'Orsay, Paris

Painted in Martinique, this masterpiece by Gauguin depicts a young girl posing as the immortal goddess Vairumati, a Maori 'Eve'. Close to her a white bird holds a lizard in its claws, a Tahitian symbol of life's recurring cycle.

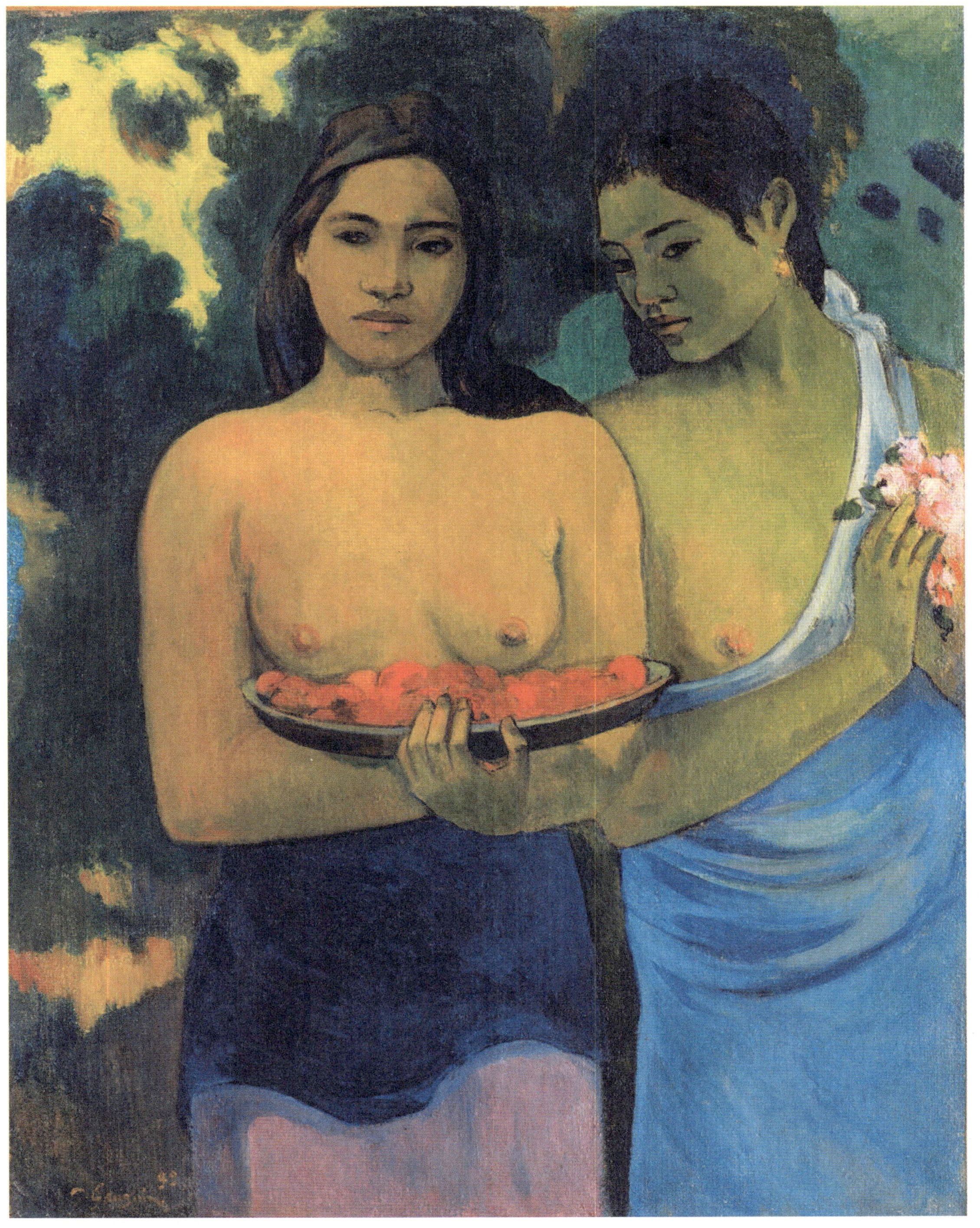

Two Tahitian Women, 1899
Oil on canvas, 94 x 72.4 cm (37 x 28½ in)
• Metropolitan Museum of Art, New York

Gauguin portrays 'Tahitian Eve' whom he described as 'very subtle, very knowing in her naïveté …
capable of walking around naked without shame'. The young Tahitians appear also in *Tahitian Pastoral
(Faa Iheihe)* (1898 frieze) and *Fruit Gathering (Rupe Rupe)* of 1899.

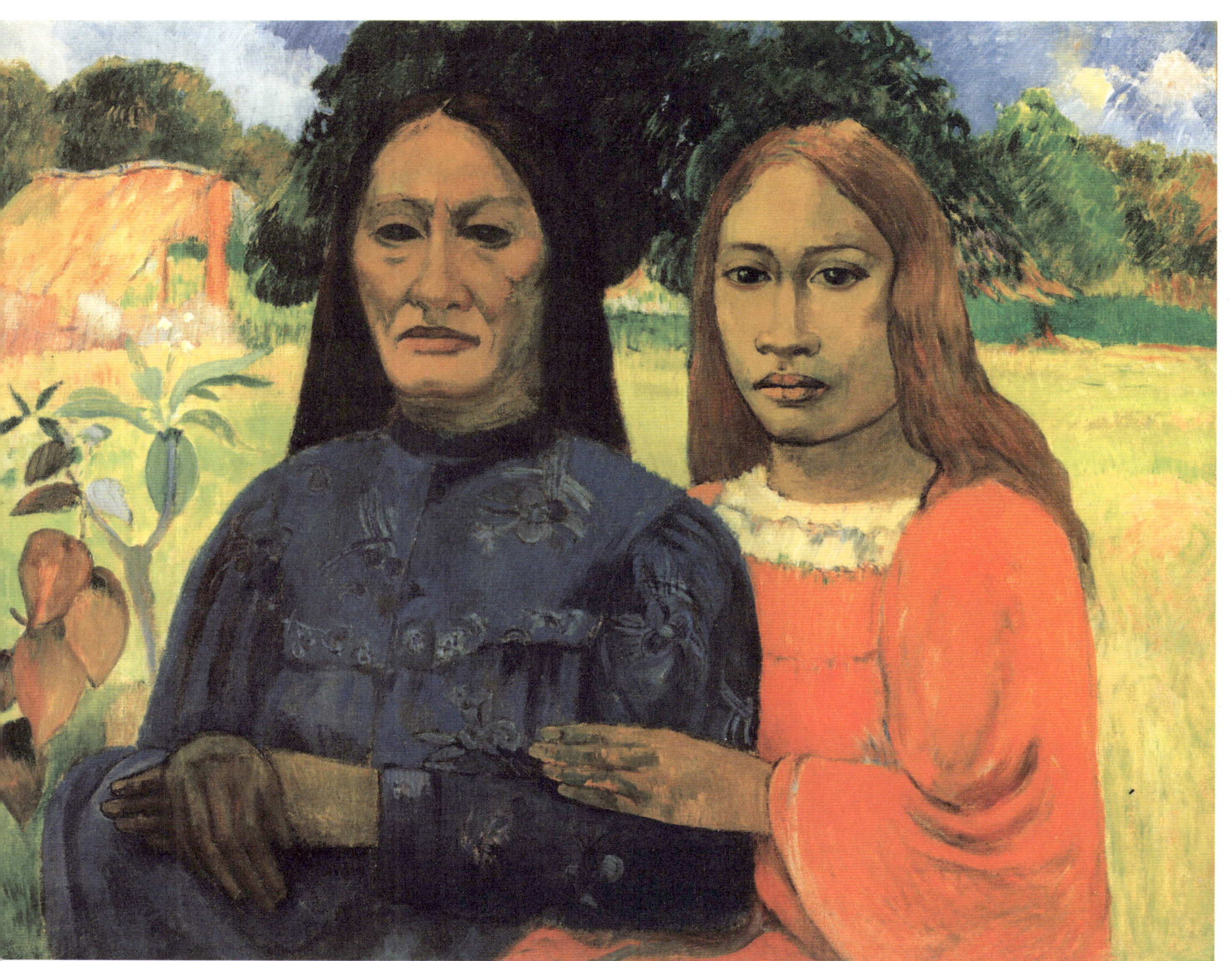

Two Women, 1901–02
Oil on canvas, 73.7 x 92.1 cm (29 x 36¼ in)
• Metropolitan Museum of Art, New York

Copied from a photograph of an older and younger woman, seated side by side on steps, Gauguin recreates their likenesses, transferred to a background set in a Polynesian landscape with vernacular dwelling house and beautiful landscape.

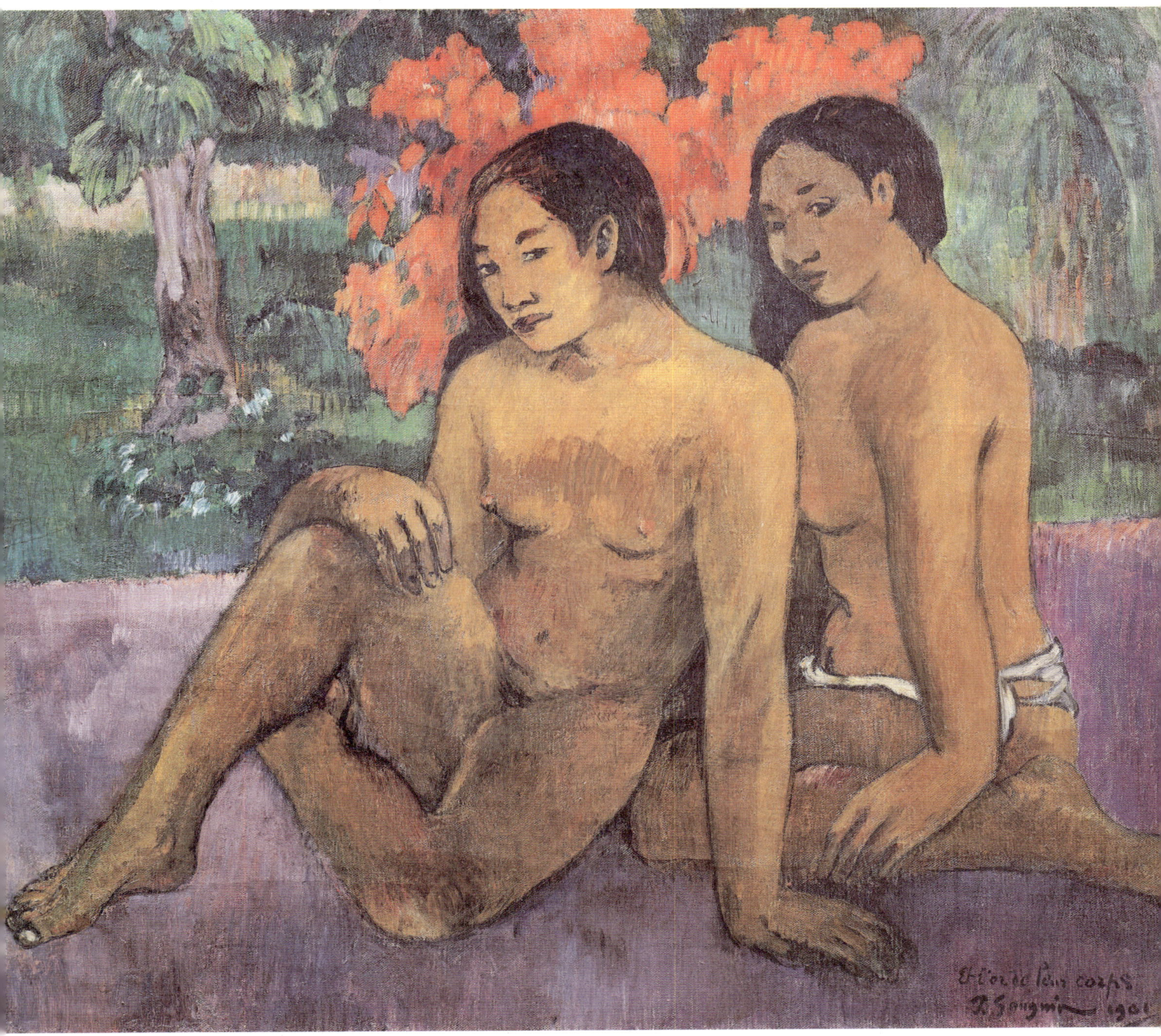

And the Gold of their Bodies, 1901
Oil on canvas, 67 x 76 cm (26⅔ x 29⅞ in) • Musée d'Orsay, Paris

A stunningly beautiful depiction of two young Polynesian women, Gauguin stresses their youthful bodies, golden skin and gentle natures as they gaze out to the spectator from a tropical island 'paradise' of Gauguin's creation.

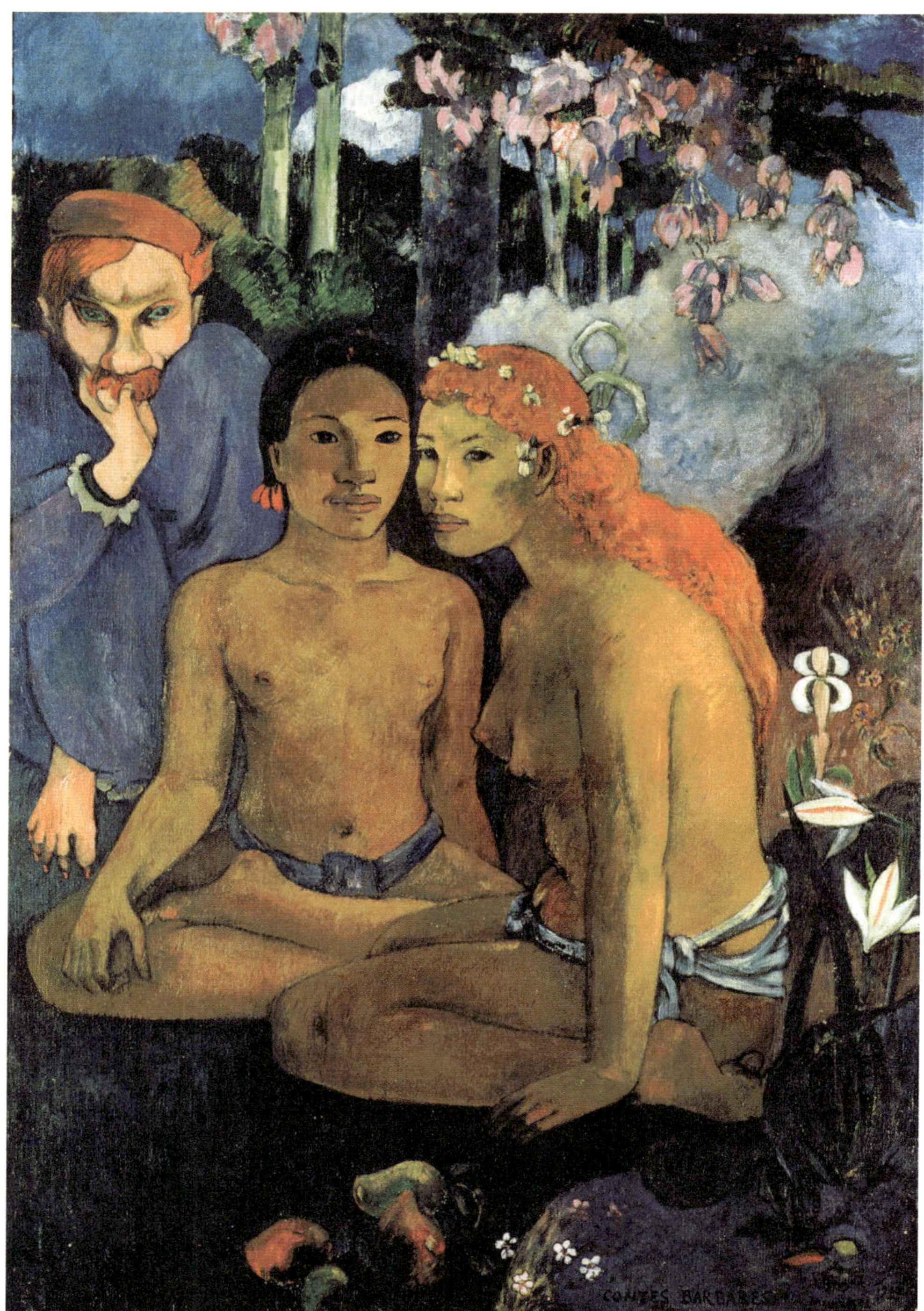

Barbarian Tales (Contes barbares), 1902
Oil on canvas, 130 x 91.5 cm (51⅛ x 36 in)
• Museum Folkwang, Essen, Germany

Gauguin's past and present life came together in this portrait. Two native Polynesian women represent his 'primitive' life, and like a ghoul at a feast, Gauguin's deceased friend, Dutch painter Meijer de Haan (1852–95), may represent the 'civilized' life Gauguin left in France.

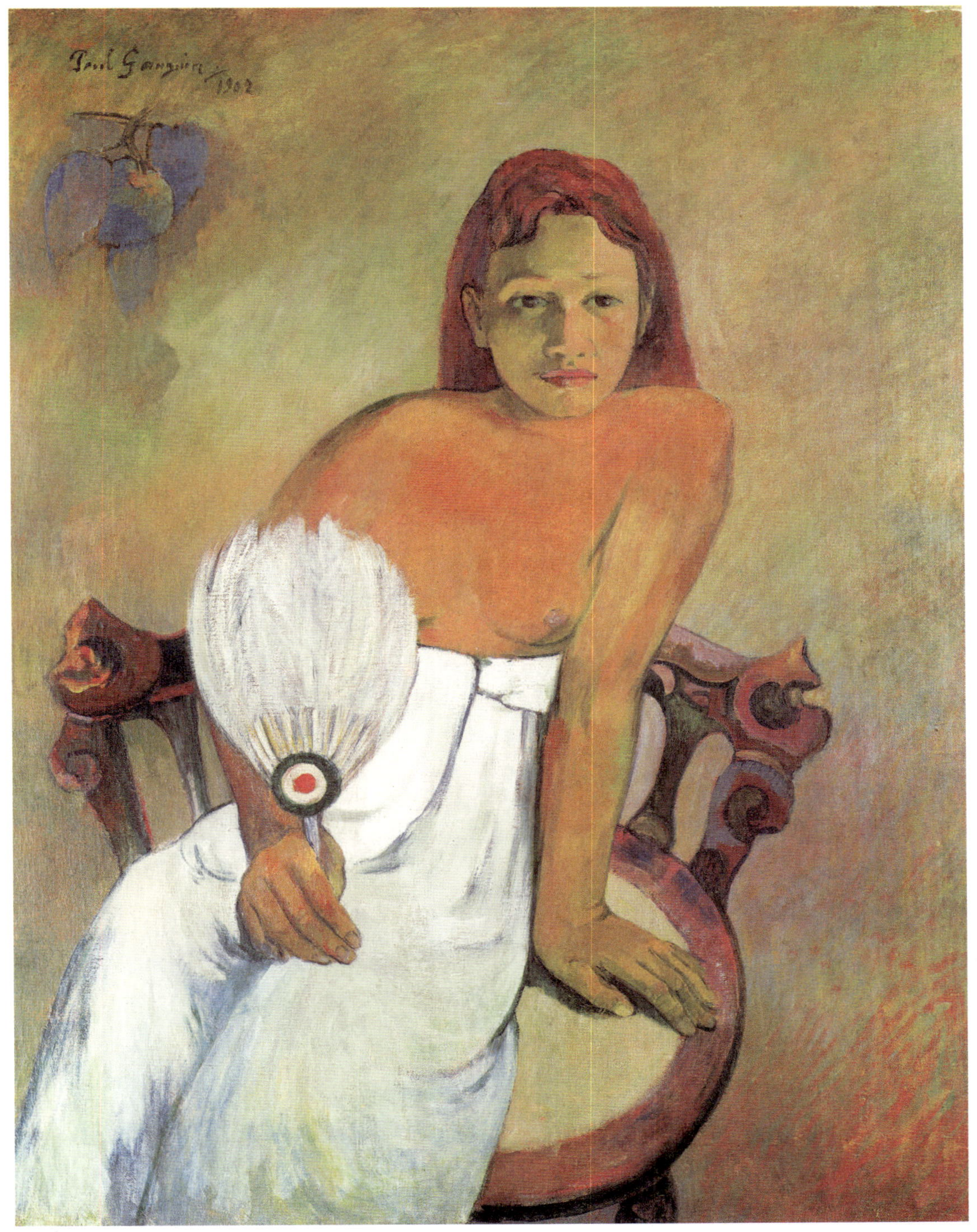

Girl with a Fan, 1902
Oil on canvas, 91 x 73 cm (35⅞ x 28¾ in)
• Museum Folkwang, Essen, Germany

Perhaps the most exquisite, natural portrait of a Tahitian girl that Gauguin created, it was painted from life, with a photograph taken as he worked. His model was Tohotaua, wife of the Hiva Oa witch doctor.

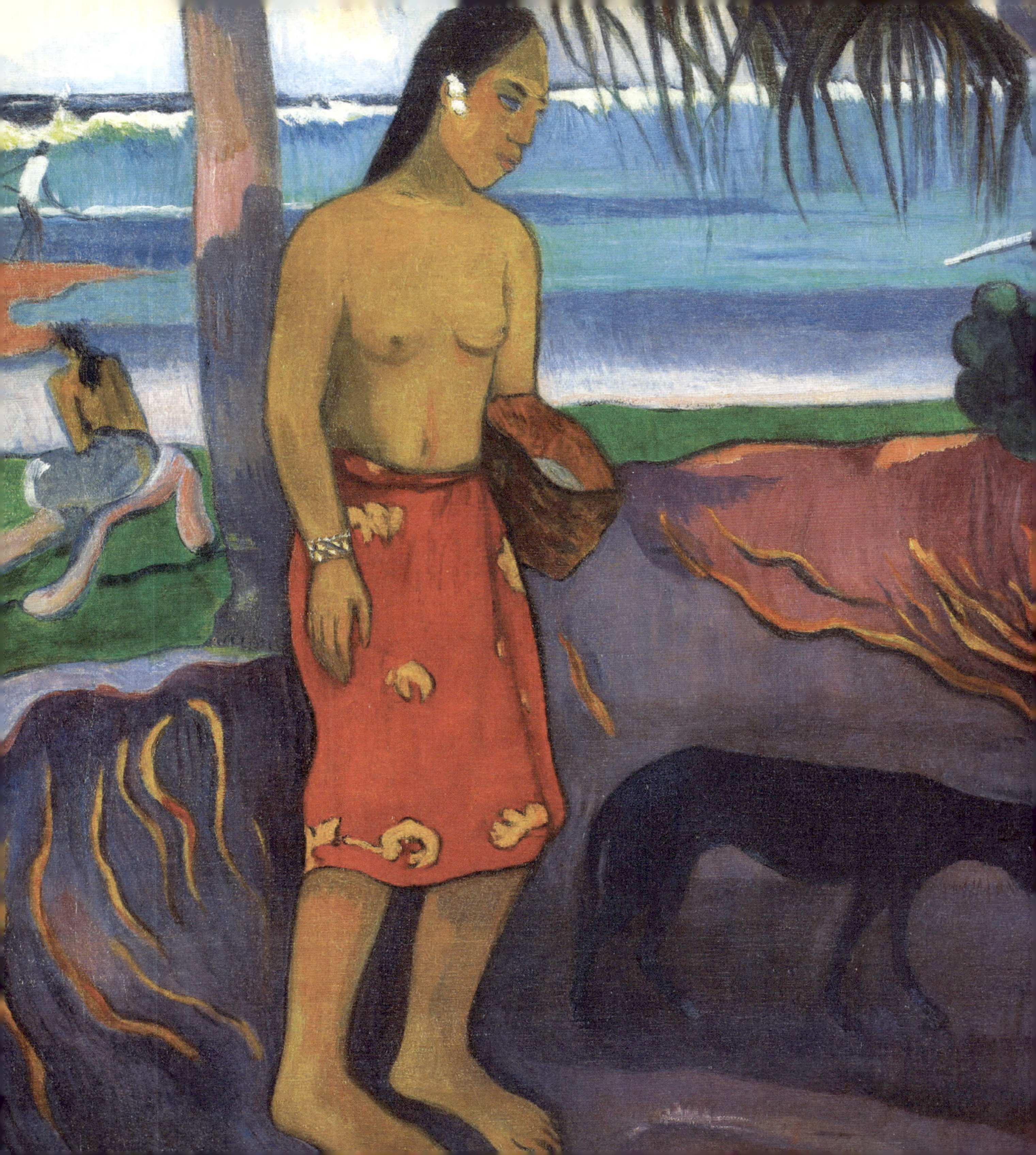

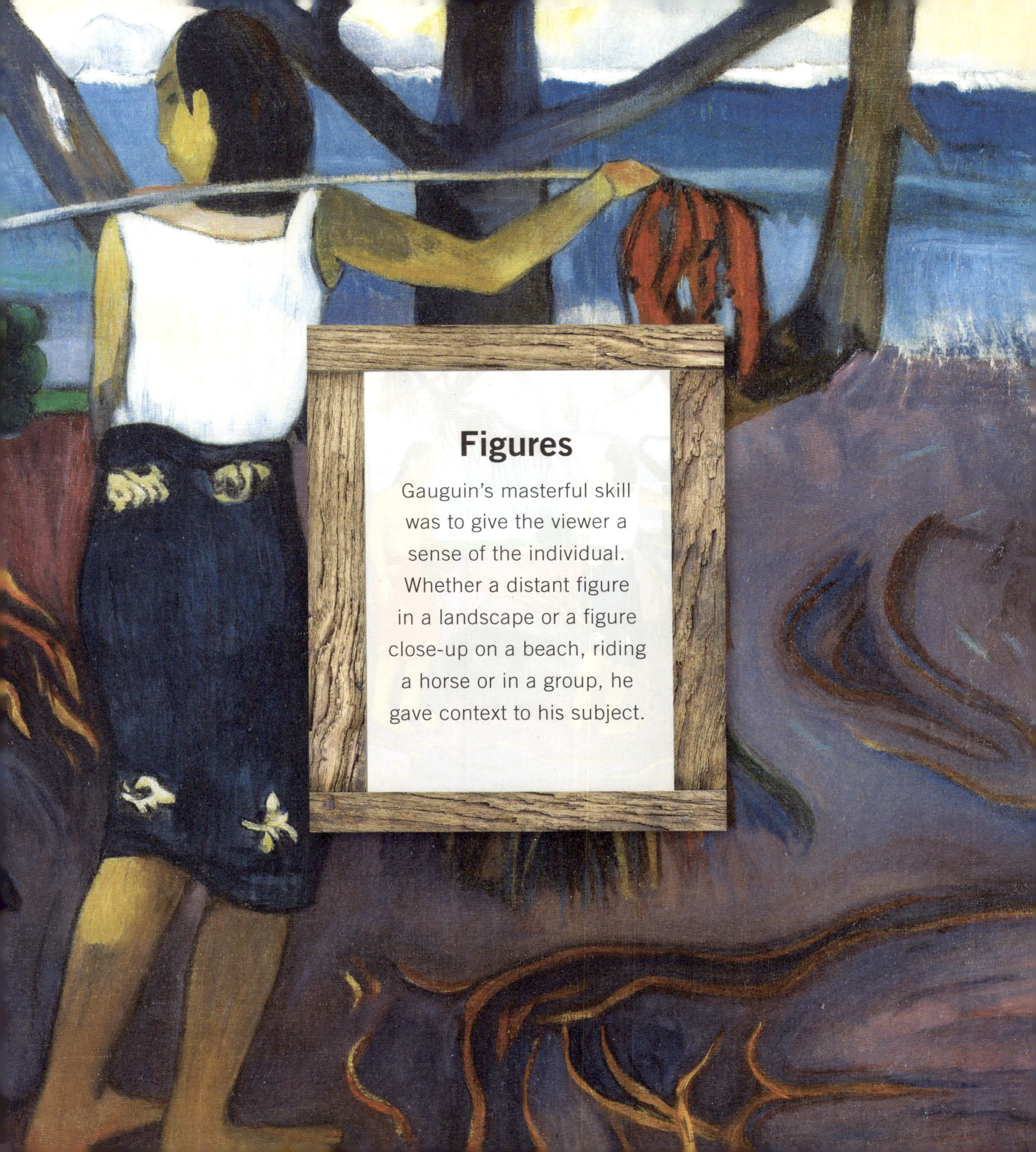

Figures

Gauguin's masterful skill was to give the viewer a sense of the individual. Whether a distant figure in a landscape or a figure close-up on a beach, riding a horse or in a group, he gave context to his subject.

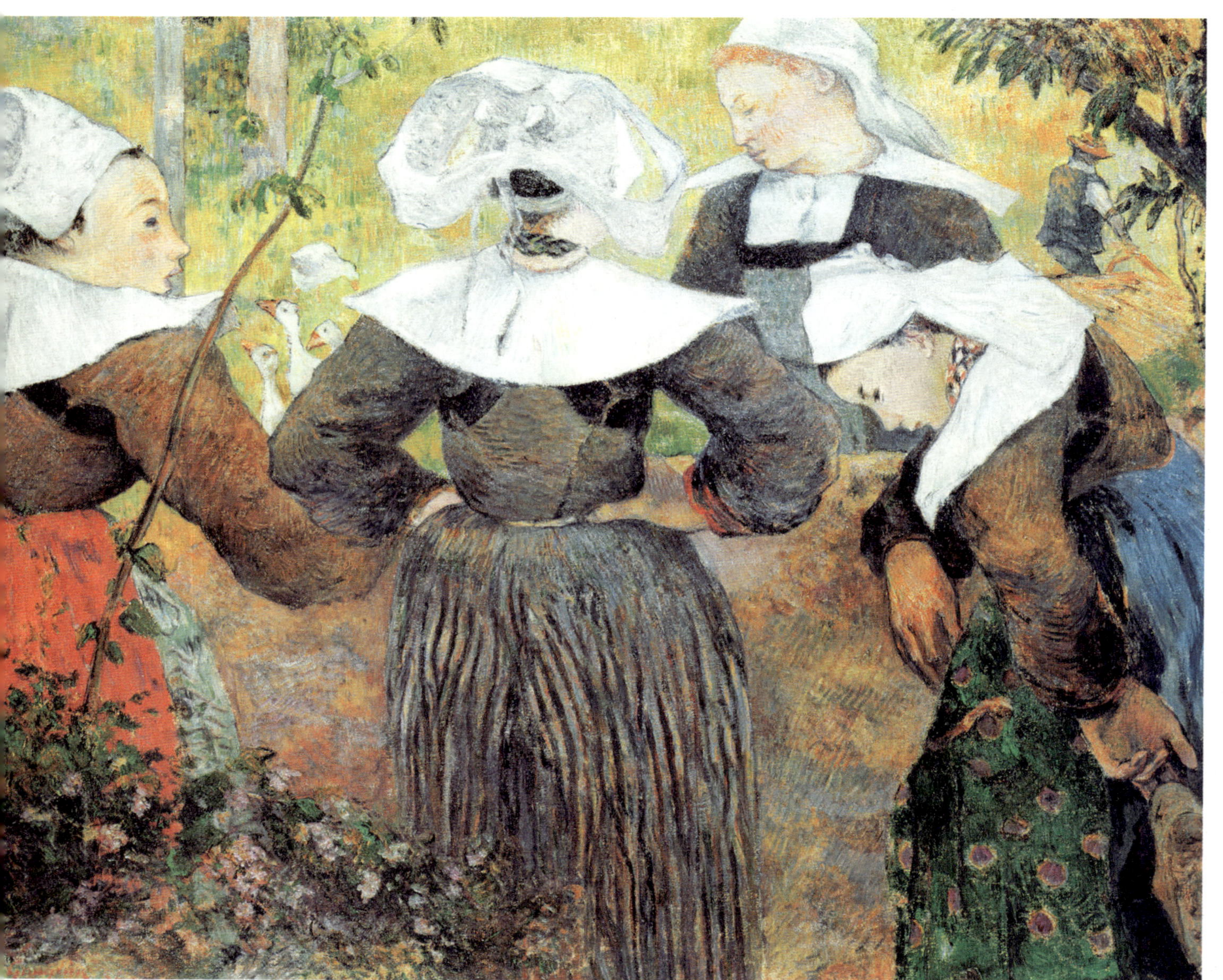

Four Breton Women, 1886
Oil on canvas, 92 x 73 cm (36¼ x 28¾ in) • Neue Pinakothek, Munich

Capturing the rhythm of Breton life within the rhythm of its rural landscape, four Breton women, in traditional costumes, meet and talk.

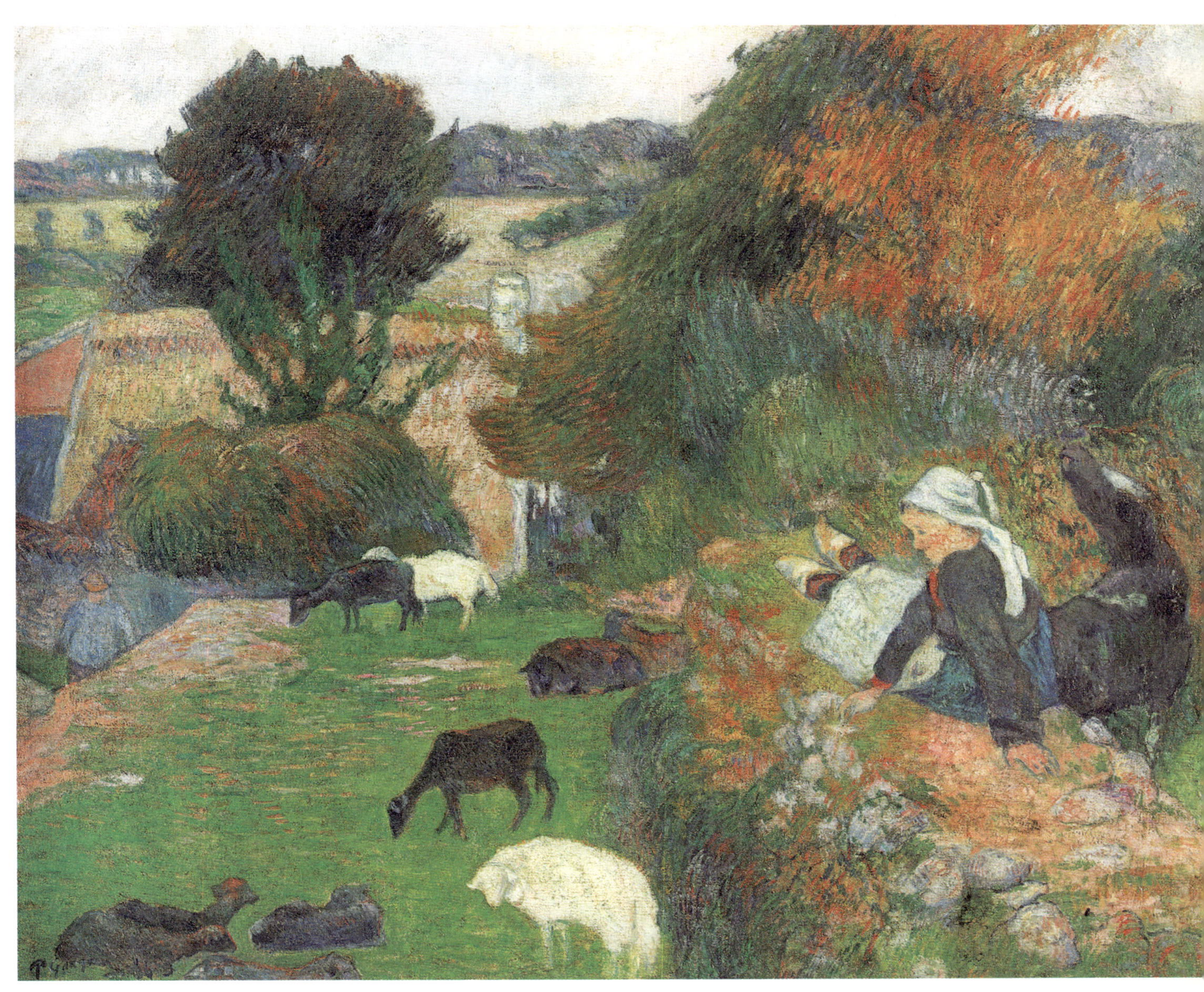

The Breton Shepherdess, 1886
Oil on canvas, 60.4 x 73.3 cm (23¾ x 28 in)
• Laing Art Gallery, Newcastle upon Tyne

In the style of Pissarro, one of his favourite painters, Gauguin captures the essence of traditional Breton life, its landscape and people.

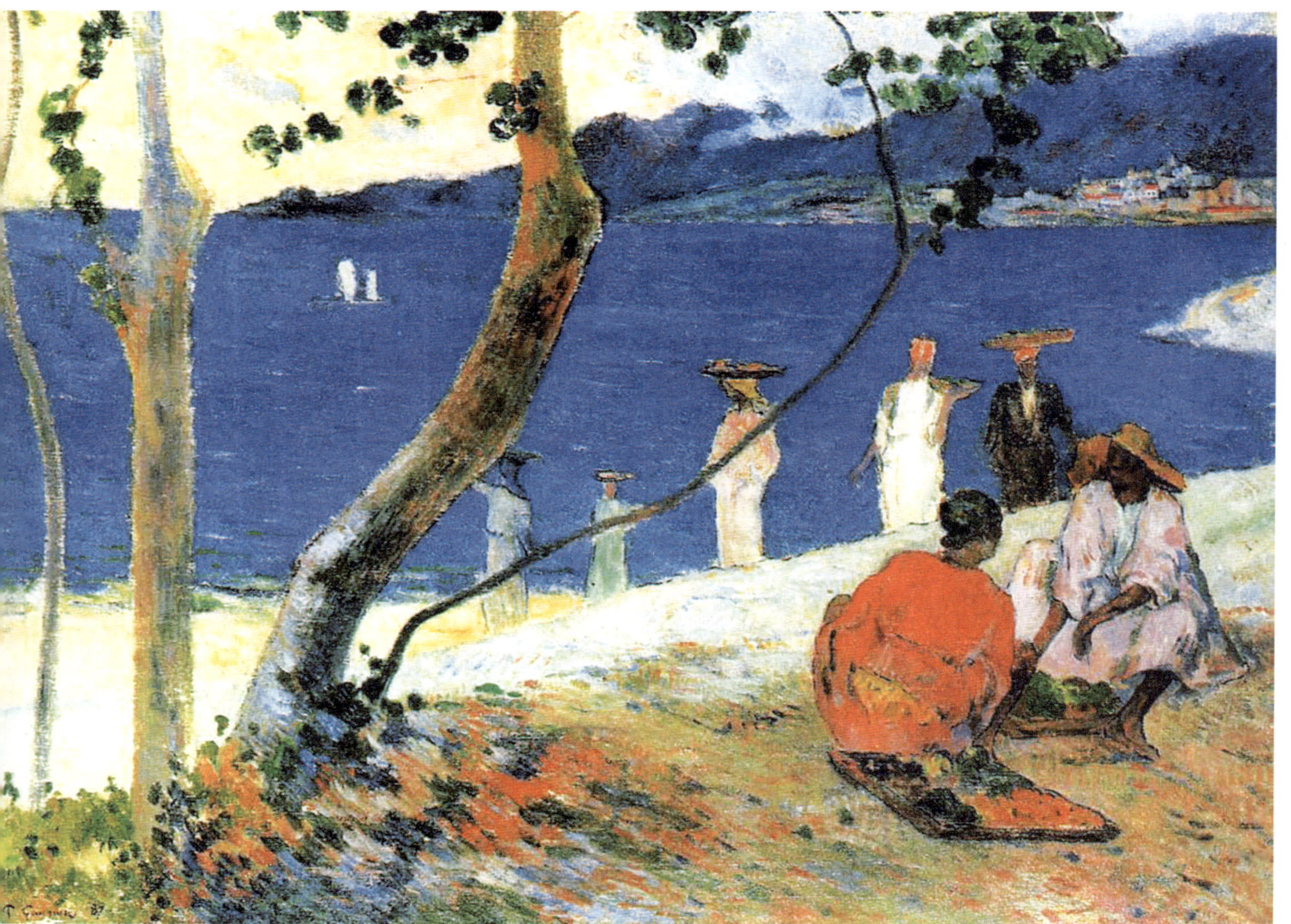

Seashore, Martinique Island, 1887
Oil on canvas, 46 x 61 cm (18⅛ x 24 in) • Private Collection

Using a palette of rich, pure colours, Gauguin's painting captures the island beauty of Martinique. Its content is informed by Japanese prints, from the trees cutting across the picture plane to the seated group of people.

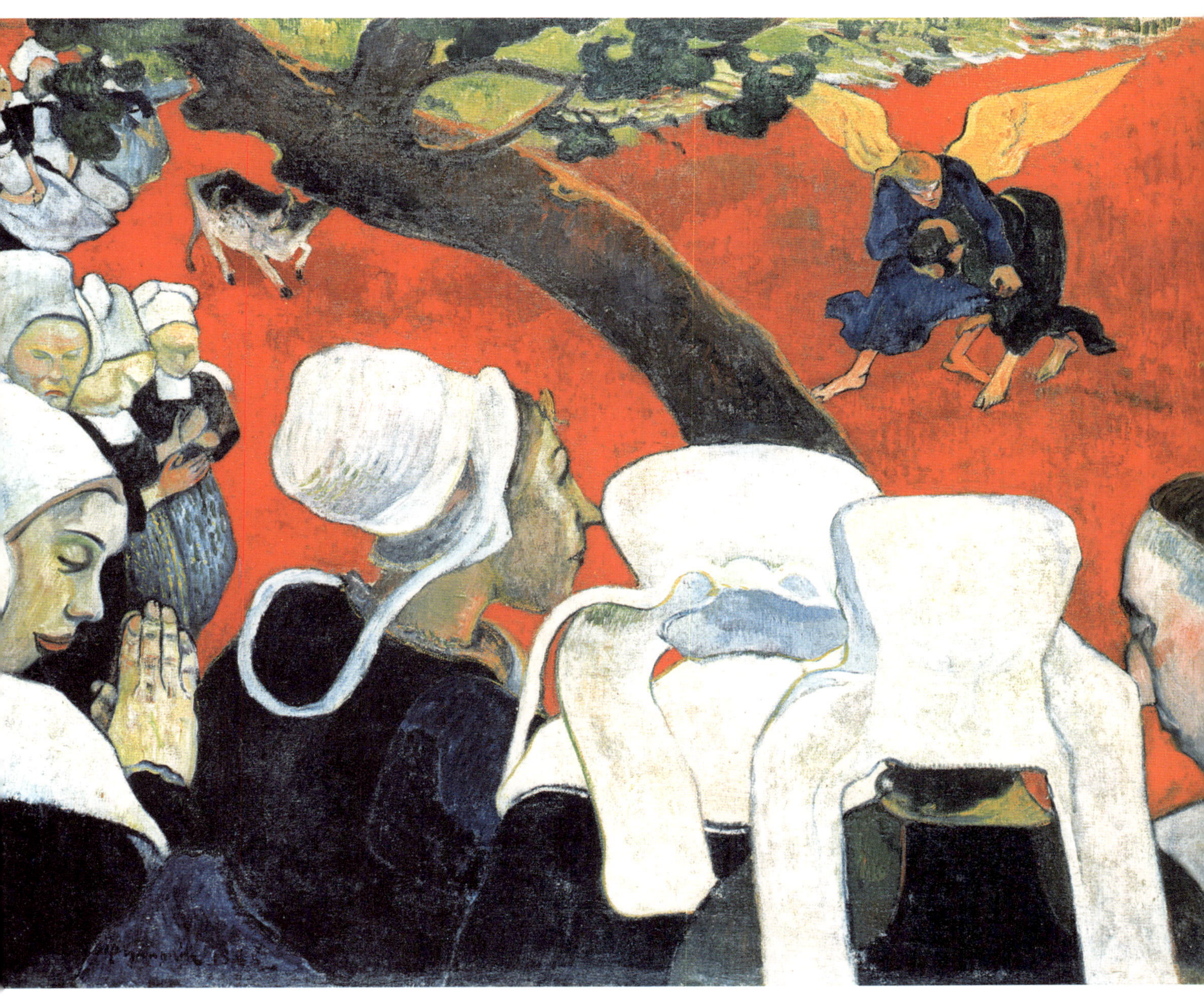

Vision after the Sermon (Jacob Wrestling with the Angel), 1888
Oil on canvas, 74.4 x 93.1 cm (29⅓ x 36⅔ in)
• National Galleries of Scotland, Edinburgh

This painting marked a groundbreaking moment in Gauguin's art. Writing to Van Gogh, he stated '… I think I have achieved in the figures a great simplicity, rustic and *superstitious*….'

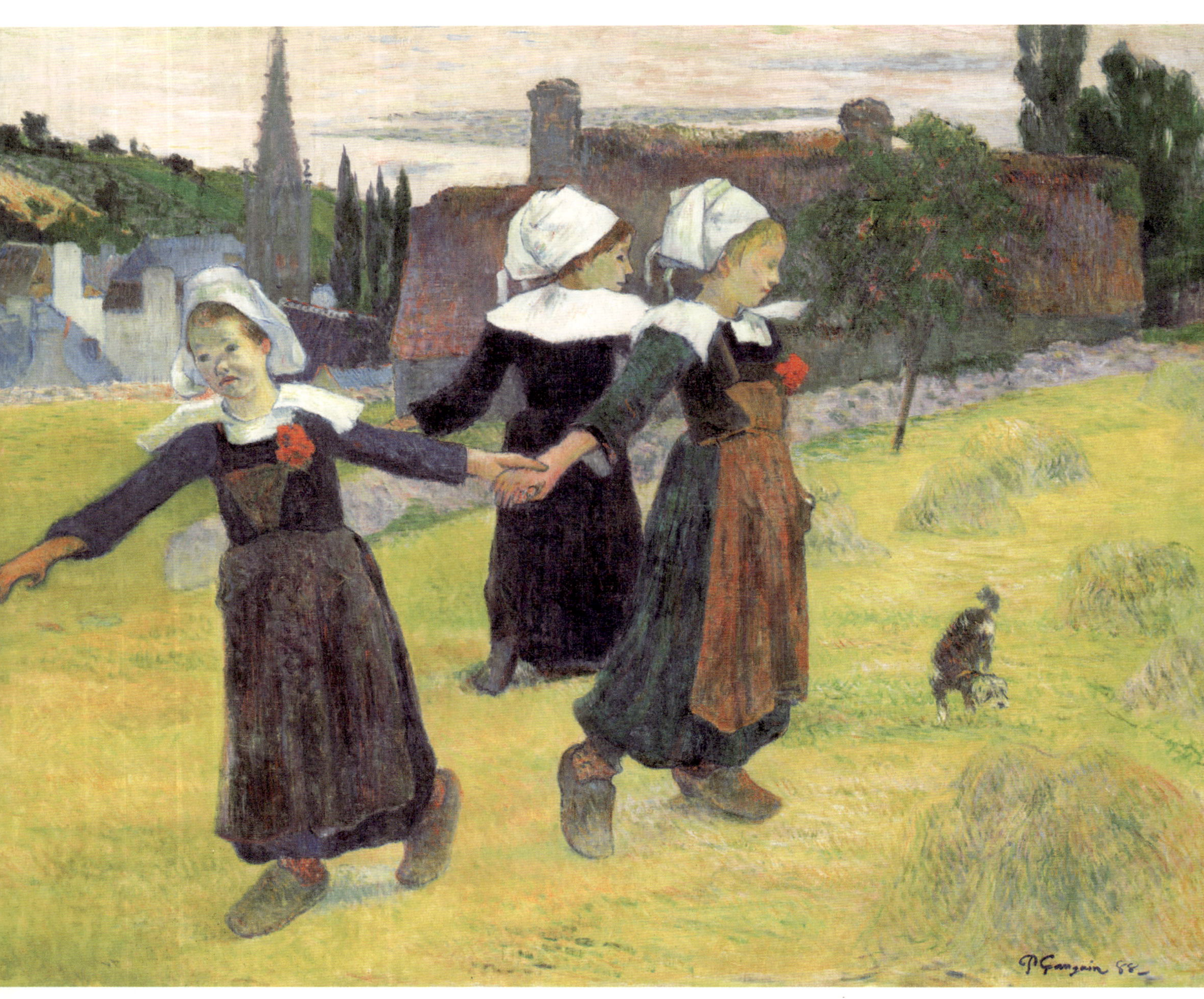

Breton Girls Dancing, Pont-Aven, 1888
Oil on canvas, 73 x 92.7 cm (28¾ x 36½ in)
• National Gallery of Art, Washington D.C.

Painted in mid-June 1888, when Gauguin wrote to Van Gogh, 'I am in the middle of a Breton gavotte danced by three girls amid the hay....' The young girls are wearing traditional Breton costume with *coiffe* headdress.

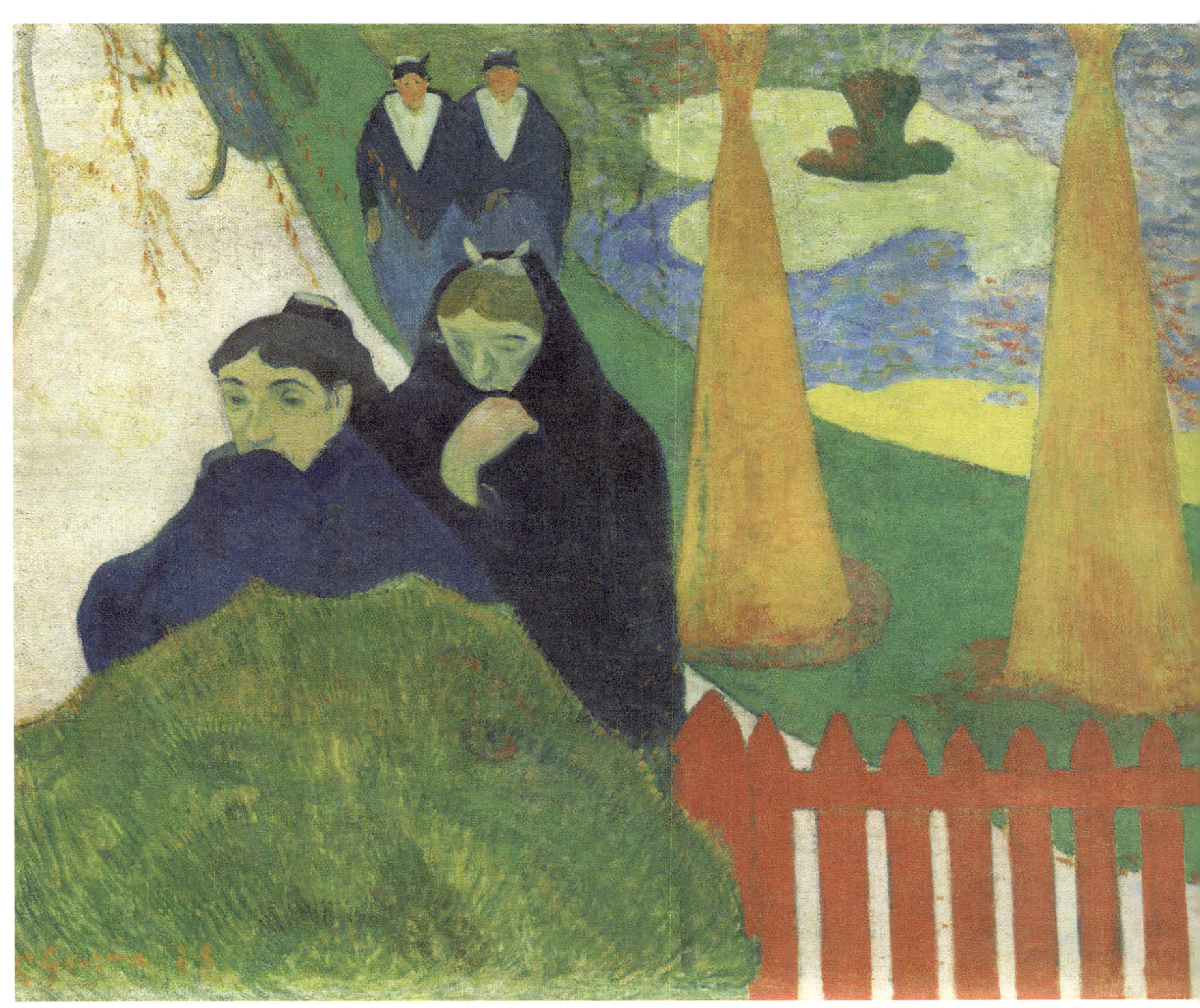

Arlésiennes (Mistral), 1888
Oil on jute, 73 x 92 cm (28¾ x 36⅓ in) • The Art Institute of Chicago

Flattened perspective and a rich use of pure colour connotes Gauguin's masterful engagement with *Japonisme*. The title comes from Gauguin's 1888–90 sketchbook, depicting local women in a wintry scene in a public park in Arles, its trees protected with cone-shaped straw.

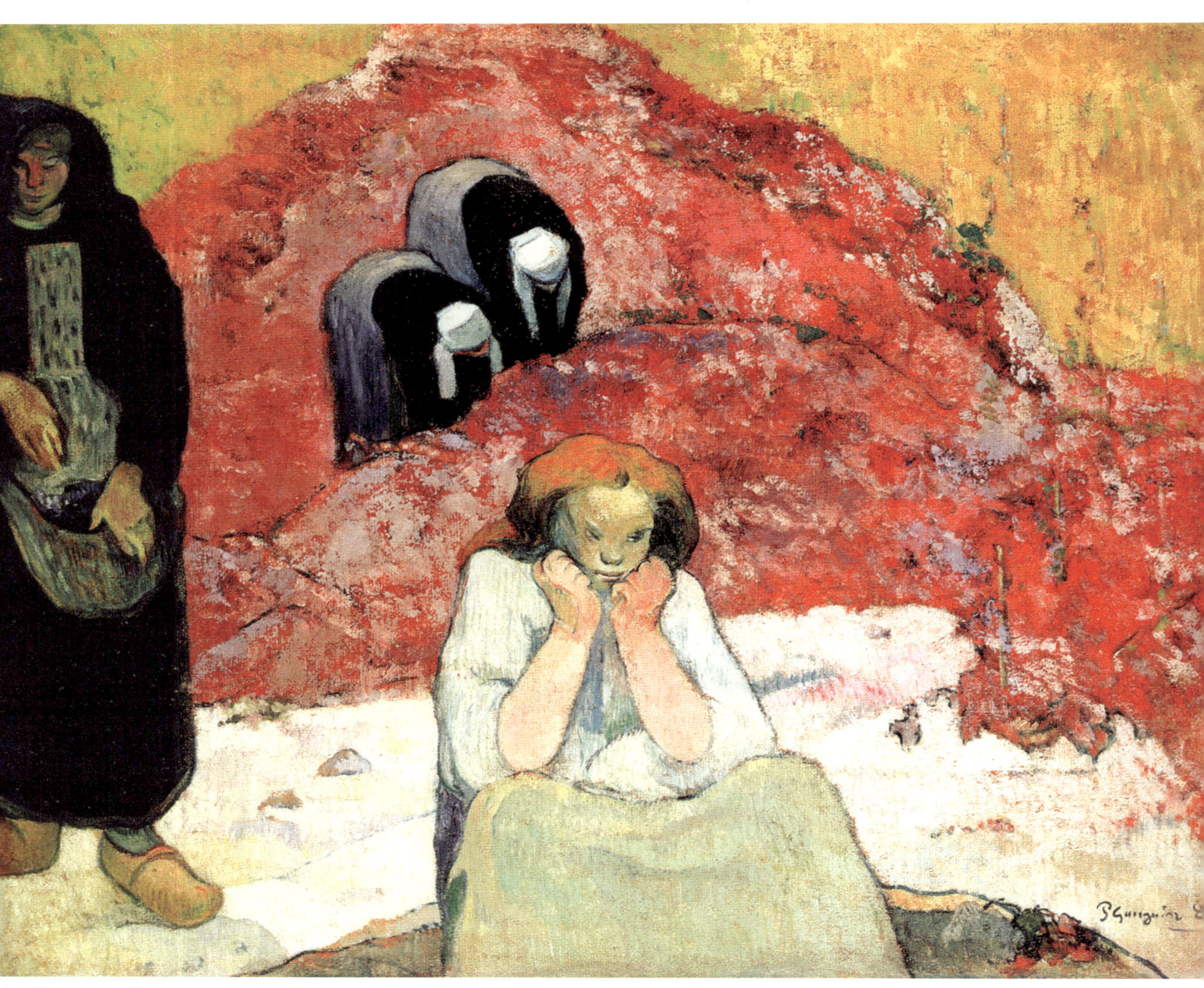

Grape Harvest at Arles (Les Misères humaines), 1888
Oil on sackcloth of jute, 73 x 92 cm (28¾ x 36⅓ in)
• Ordrupgaard, Copenhagen

In November 1888, Gauguin wrote to Theo van Gogh, 'I have done a painting from memory of a really bewitched poor wretch in the middle of a red vineyard, and your brother, who is very generous, thinks it's good....'

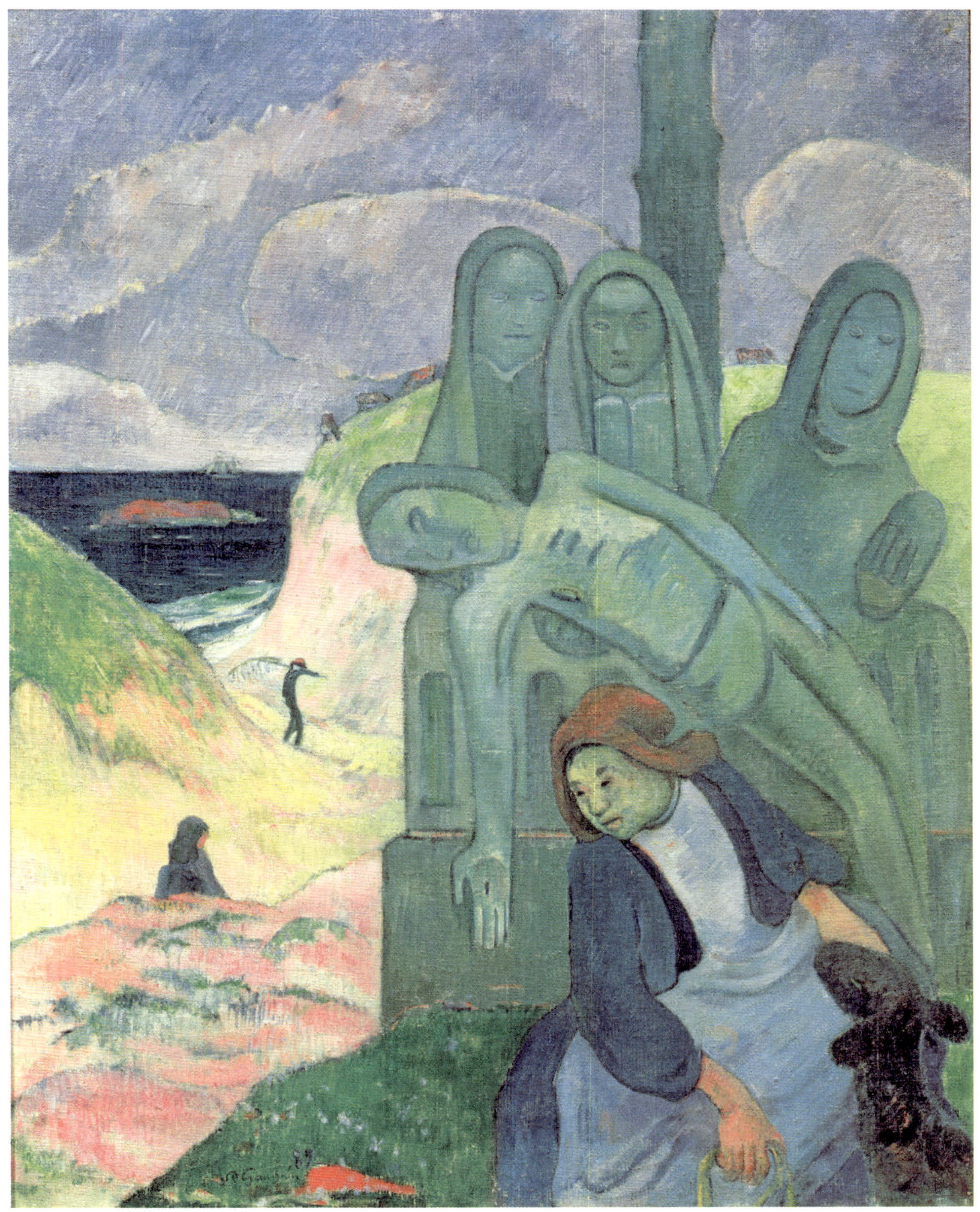

The Green Christ (Breton Calvary), 1889
Oil on canvas, 92 x 73 cm (36⅓ x 28¾ in)
• Musées Royaux des Beaux-Arts de Belgique, Brussels

In a Breton landscape, the body of Christ is removed from the Cross. Gauguin's depiction was informed by a stone statue he saw at Nizen, near Pont-Aven. The green-tinged aura expounds the feeling of sorrow and parting.

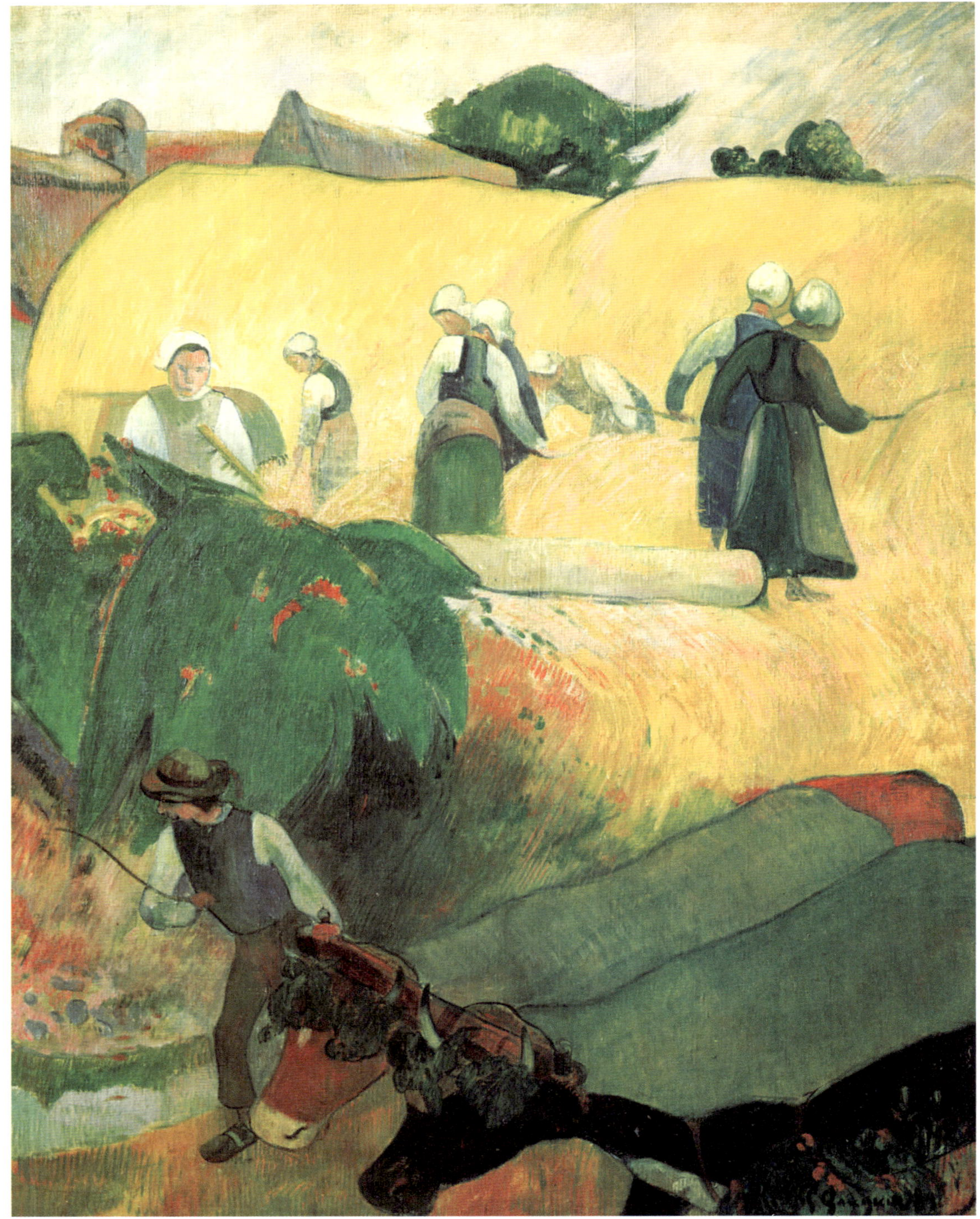

Haymaking, 1889
Oil on canvas, 92 x 73.3 cm (36⅓ x 28¾ in)
• The Courtauld Gallery, London

In this painting one witnesses the remarkable change in Gauguin's technique from picturesque Impressionism to Synthetism, using pure colour and a near-vertical picture plane informed by Japanese prints, where colour and line synthesizes to educe intense sensation.

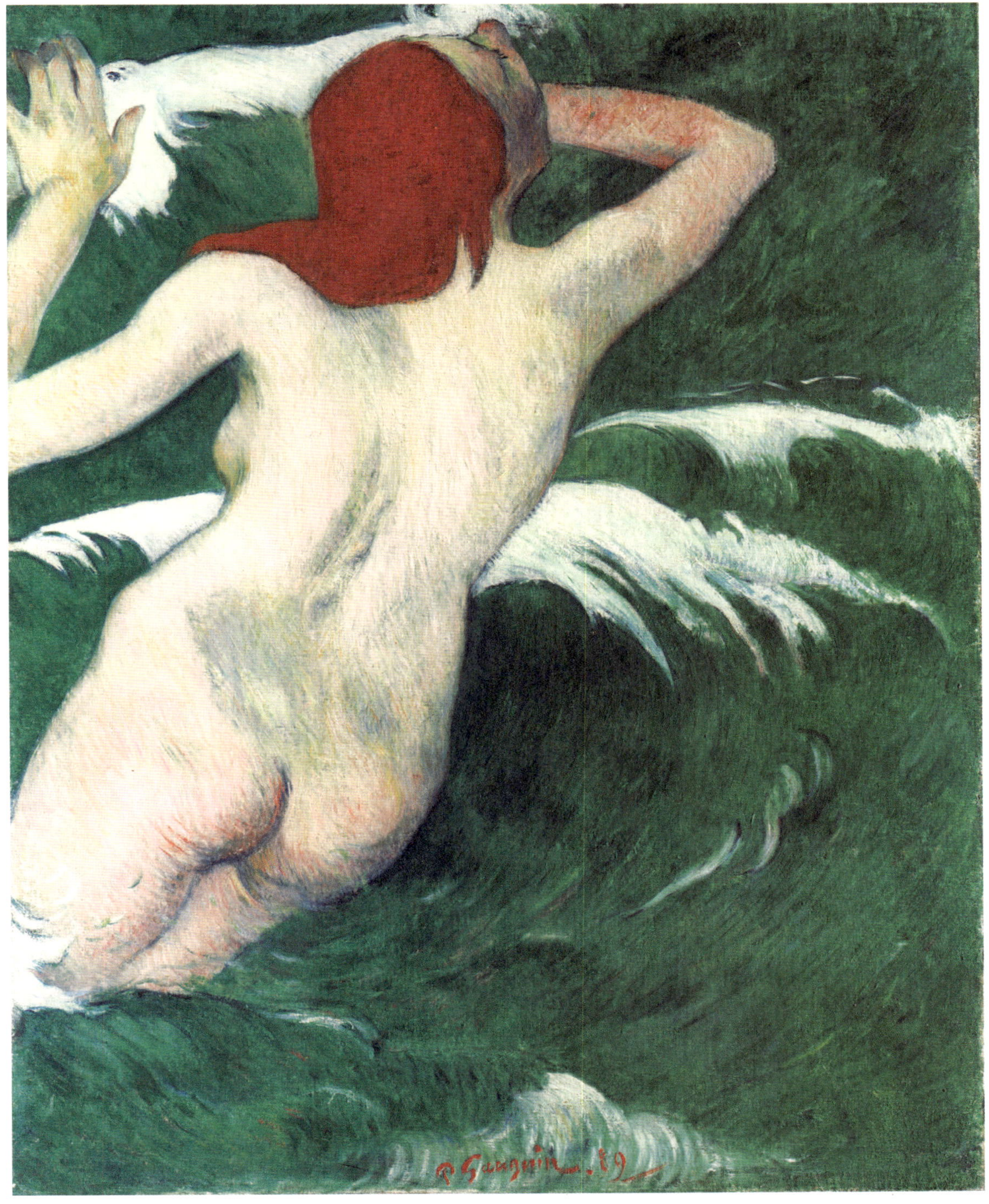

In the Waves (Dans les vagues), 1889
Oil on fabric, 92.5 x 72.4 cm (36⅜ x 28½ in)
• Cleveland Museum of Art, Ohio

A voluptuous redhead splashes naked in the waves of deep green water. Painted in Pont-Aven and exhibited at the Café Volpini, Paris the same year, Gauguin's use of strong complementary colours underlines its life-death symbolism.

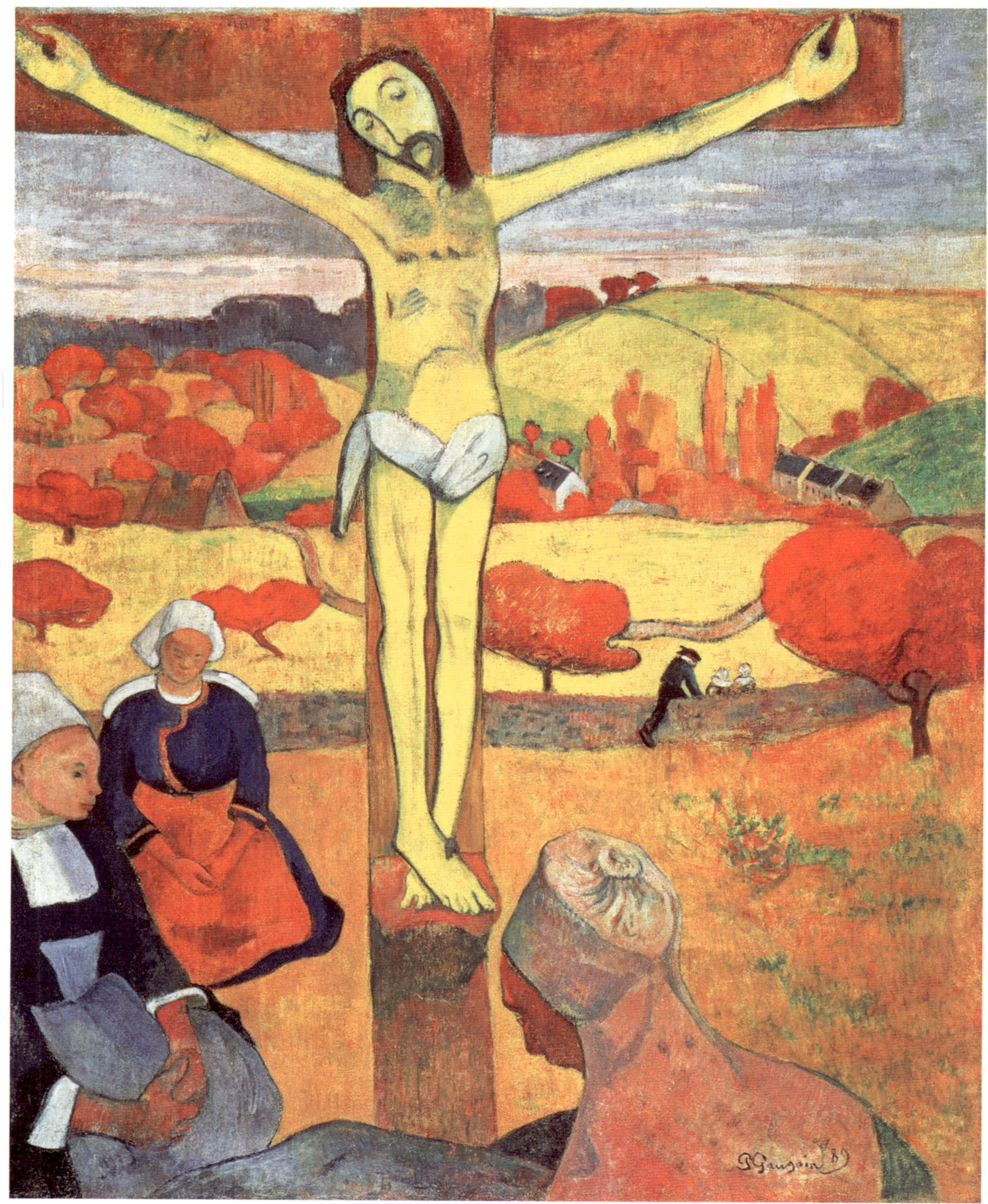

Yellow Christ, 1889
Oil on canvas, 92 x 73 cm (36 x 29 in)
• Albright-Knox Art Gallery, Buffalo

A self-portrait of Gauguin as a martyred man, castigated by friends for neglect of his family. Set in Brittany, Breton women in traditional costume gather at Christ's feet. Gauguin tried to give this painting to a church, without success.

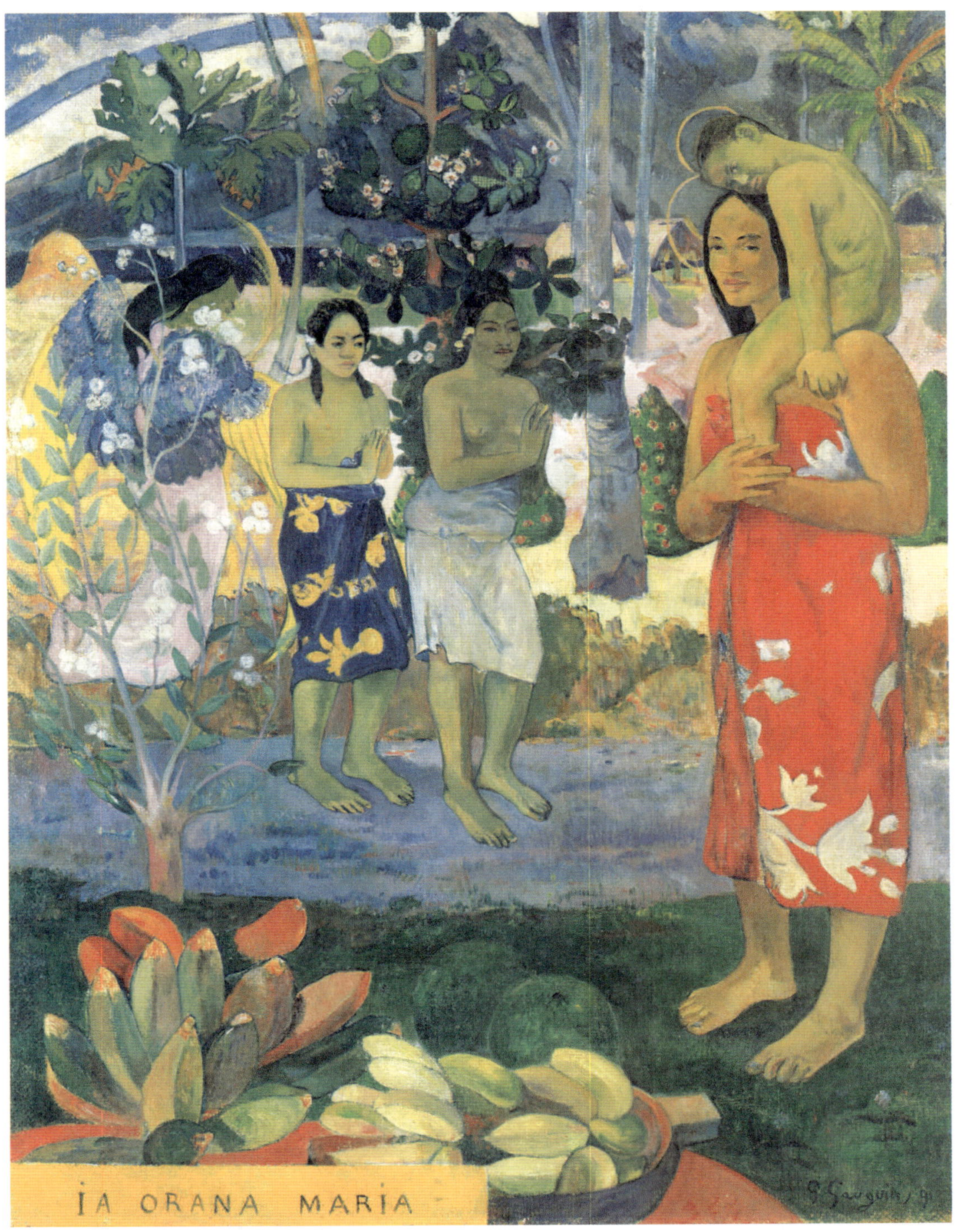

Hail Mary (Ia Orana Maria), 1891
Oil on canvas, 113.7 x 87.6 cm (44¾ x 34½ in)
• Metropolitan Museum of Art, New York

Painted in glowing orange, lilac, pink and indigo, Gauguin's first major work in Tahiti derives from Christian iconography of Mary, mother of Jesus. Tahiti became a Christian country in 1880. The painting was exhibited at Gauguin's Paris show in 1893.

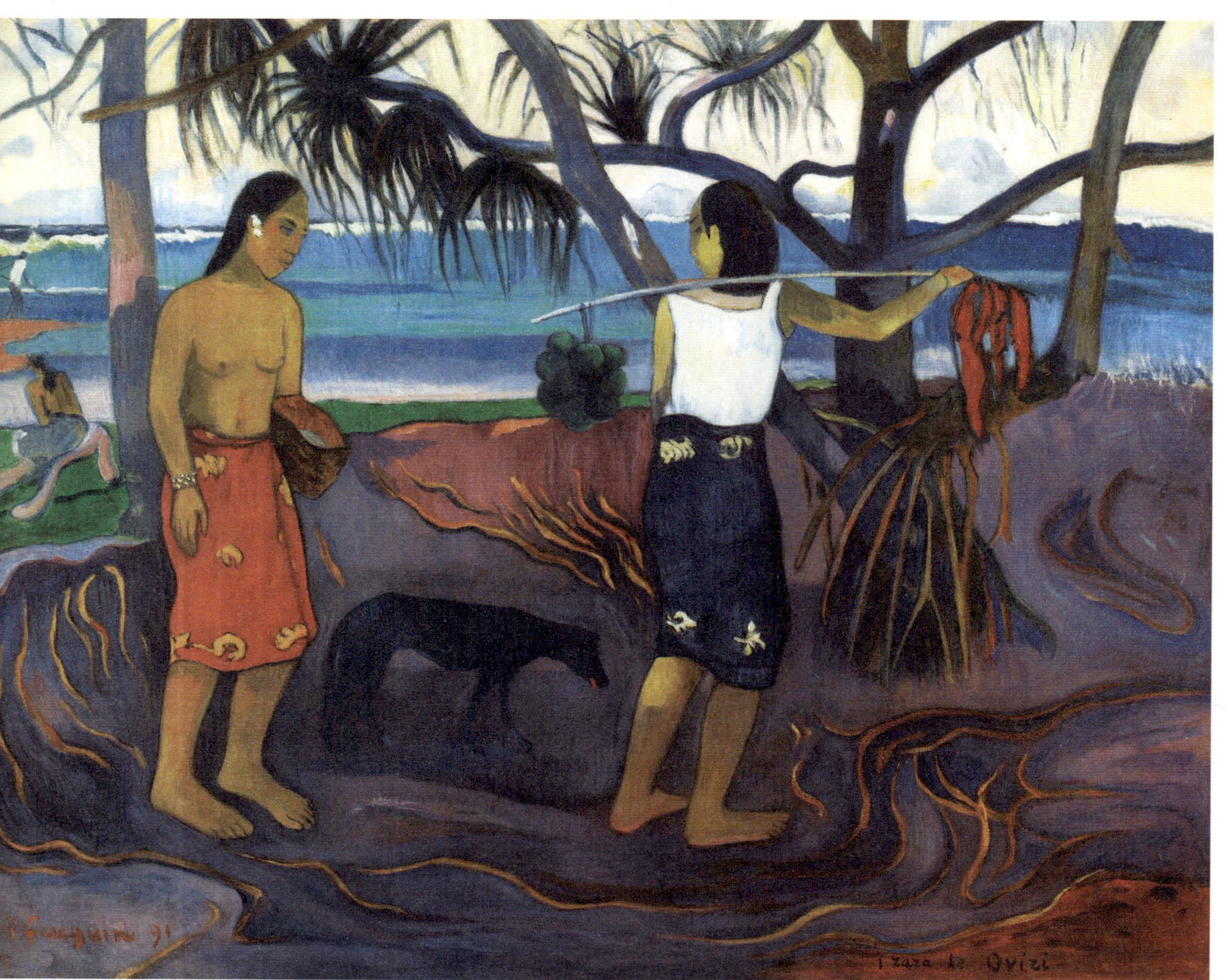

Under the Pandanus (I Raro te Oviri) 1891
Oil on canvas, 73 x 91.4 cm (28¾ x 36 in)
• Minneapolis Institute of Art, Minnesota

Horizontal bands of rich colour depict the sea, the trees and vegetation within this tranquil setting. Two young women walk under the Pandanus pines, with their slender, delicate palm leaves, found in marshy land and seacoasts in tropical regions.

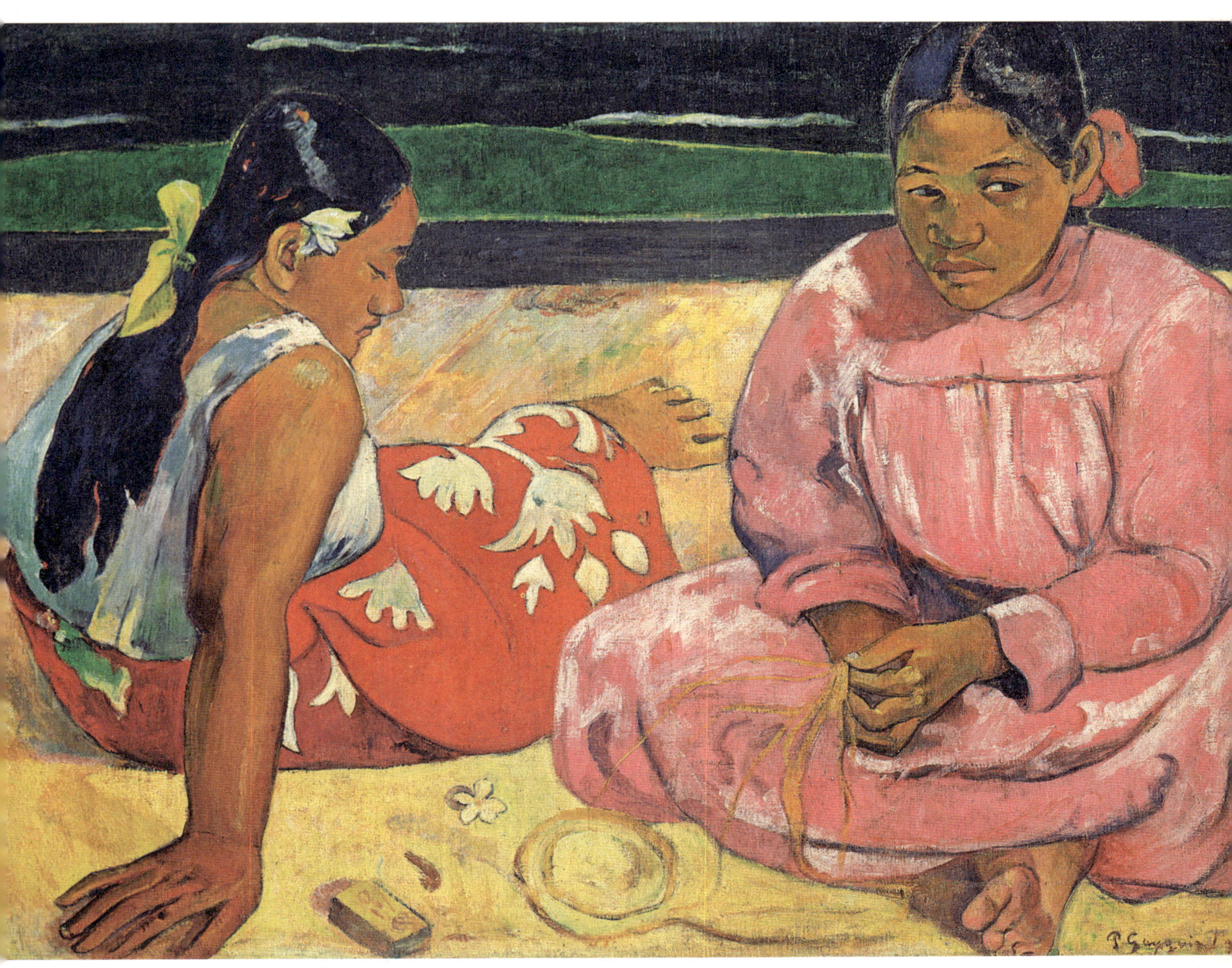

Women of Tahiti, On the Beach, 1891
Oil on canvas, 69 x 90 cm (27⅛ x 35⅜ in) • Musée d'Orsay, Paris

One of several paintings depicting Tahitian young women on a beach, Gauguin's focus on the women of the island was to heighten interest from European buyers. He liked this work and produced another version, *Parau Api* (1892).

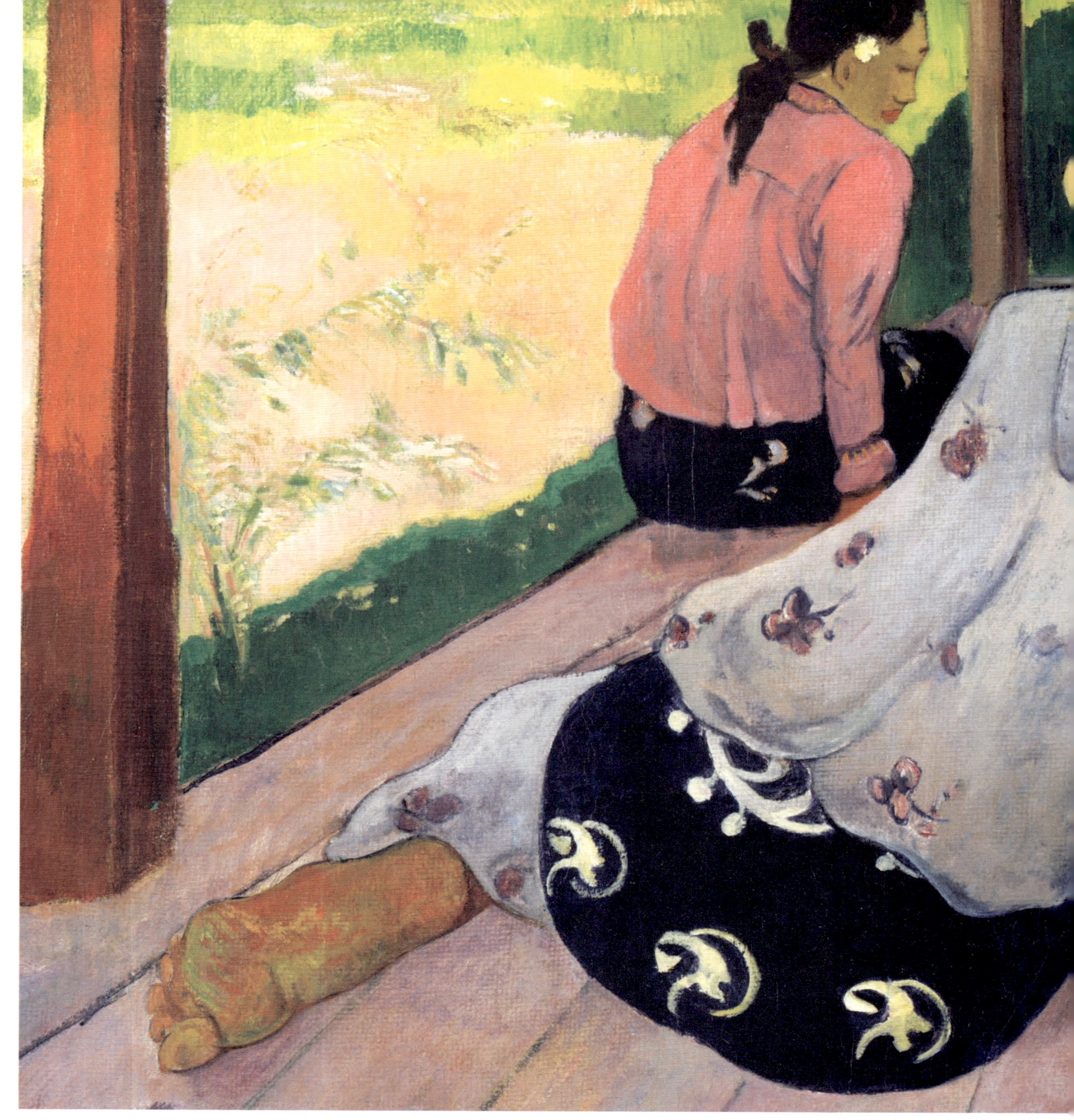

The Siesta, *c.* 1892–94
Oil on canvas, 88.9 x 116.2 cm (35 x 45¾ in)
• Metropolitan Museum of Art, New York

Gauguin captures local life in a domestic scene on a shaded veranda, where one girl irons clothes and friends relax out of the heat of the sun while chatting with a visitor.

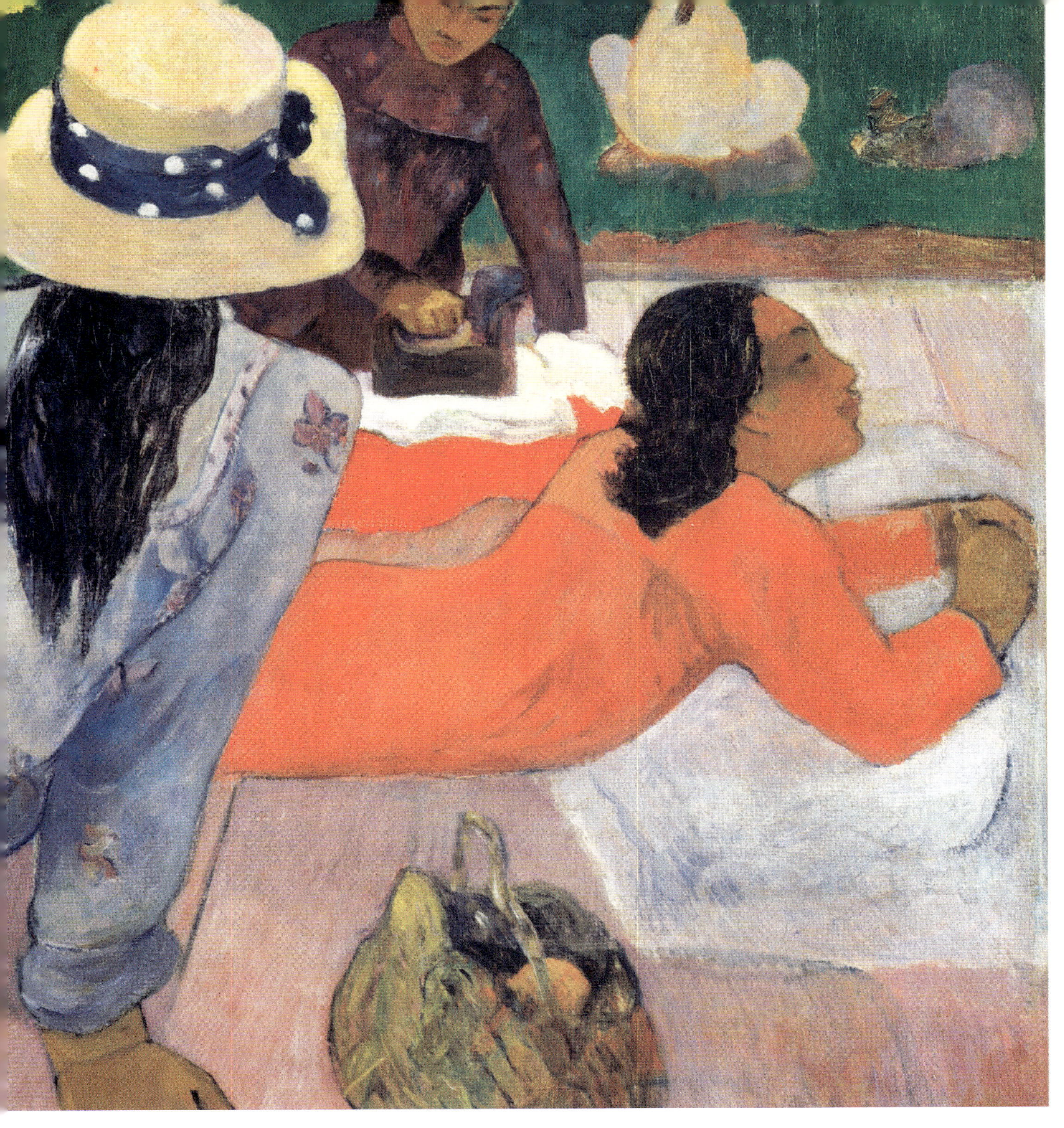

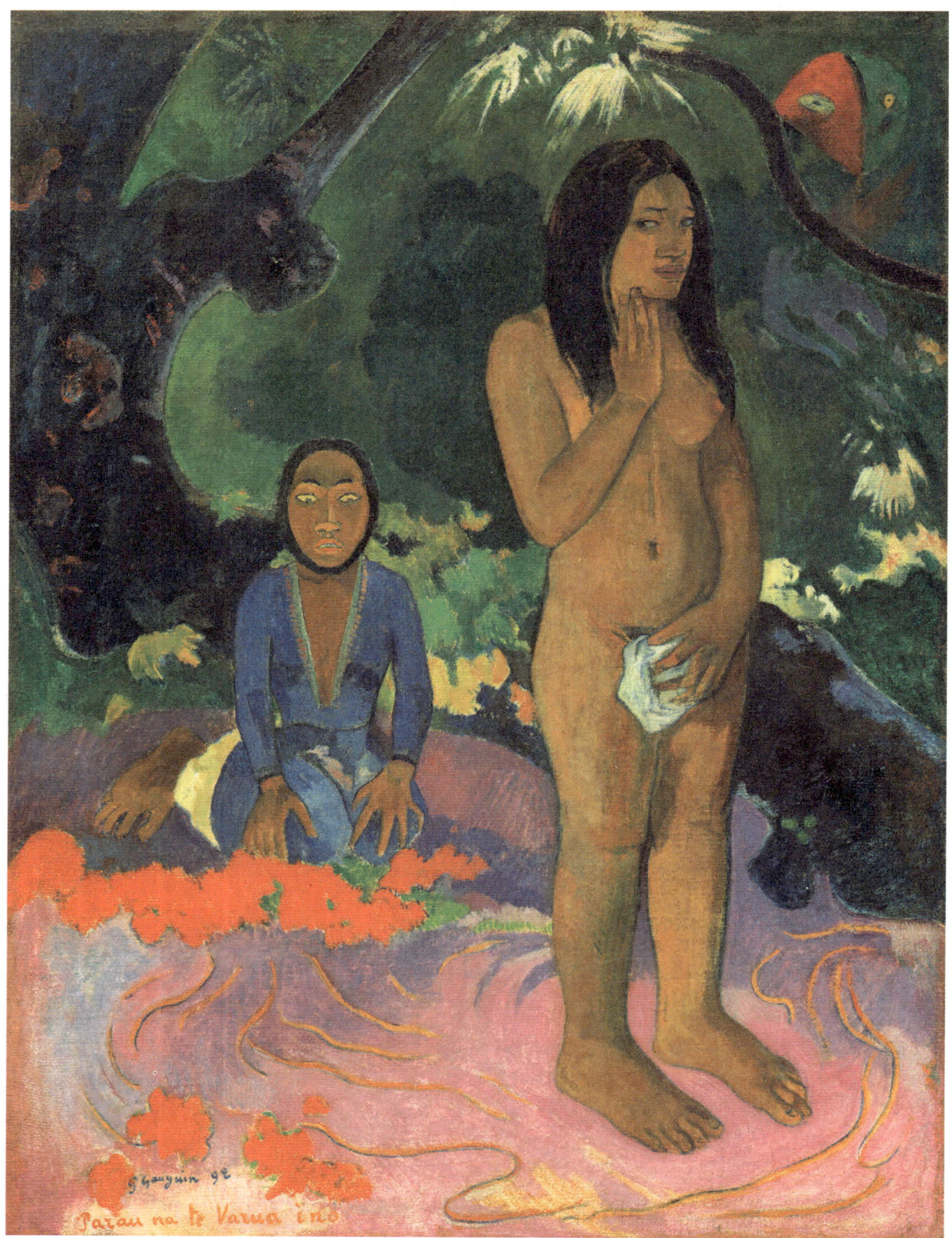

Words of the Devil (Parau Na Te Varua ino), 1892
Oil on canvas, 91.7 x 68.5 cm (36⅛ x 27 in)
• National Gallery of Art, Washington D.C.

Tropical colours accentuate Gauguin's symbolic interpretation of a complex Tahitian spiritual myth. *Varua ino* is a Tahitian masked evil spirit in human form. The young woman possibly represents the spiritual and human morality of Eve in the Garden of Eden.

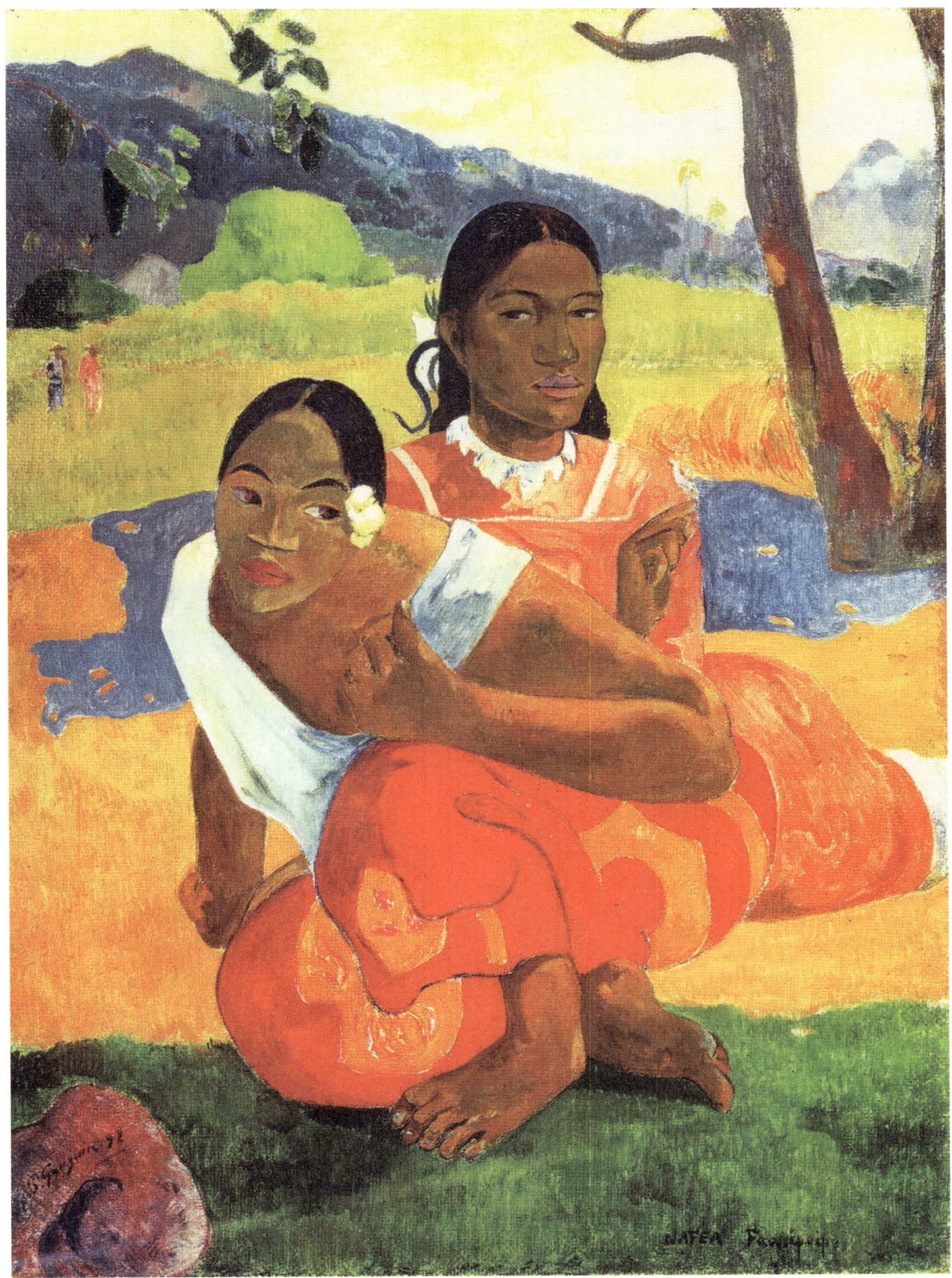

When Are You Getting Married? (Nafea Faa Ipoipo?), 1892
Oil on canvas, 105 x 77.5 cm (41⅓ x 30½ in)
• Fondation Rudolf Staechelin, Basel

A young woman wears a flower behind her ear, a Tahitian tradition when eligible for marriage. Gauguin had read a popular autobiography, *Marriage of Loti* (1880), which centred on an exotic marriage between a Tahitian girl and Frenchman Pierre Loti.

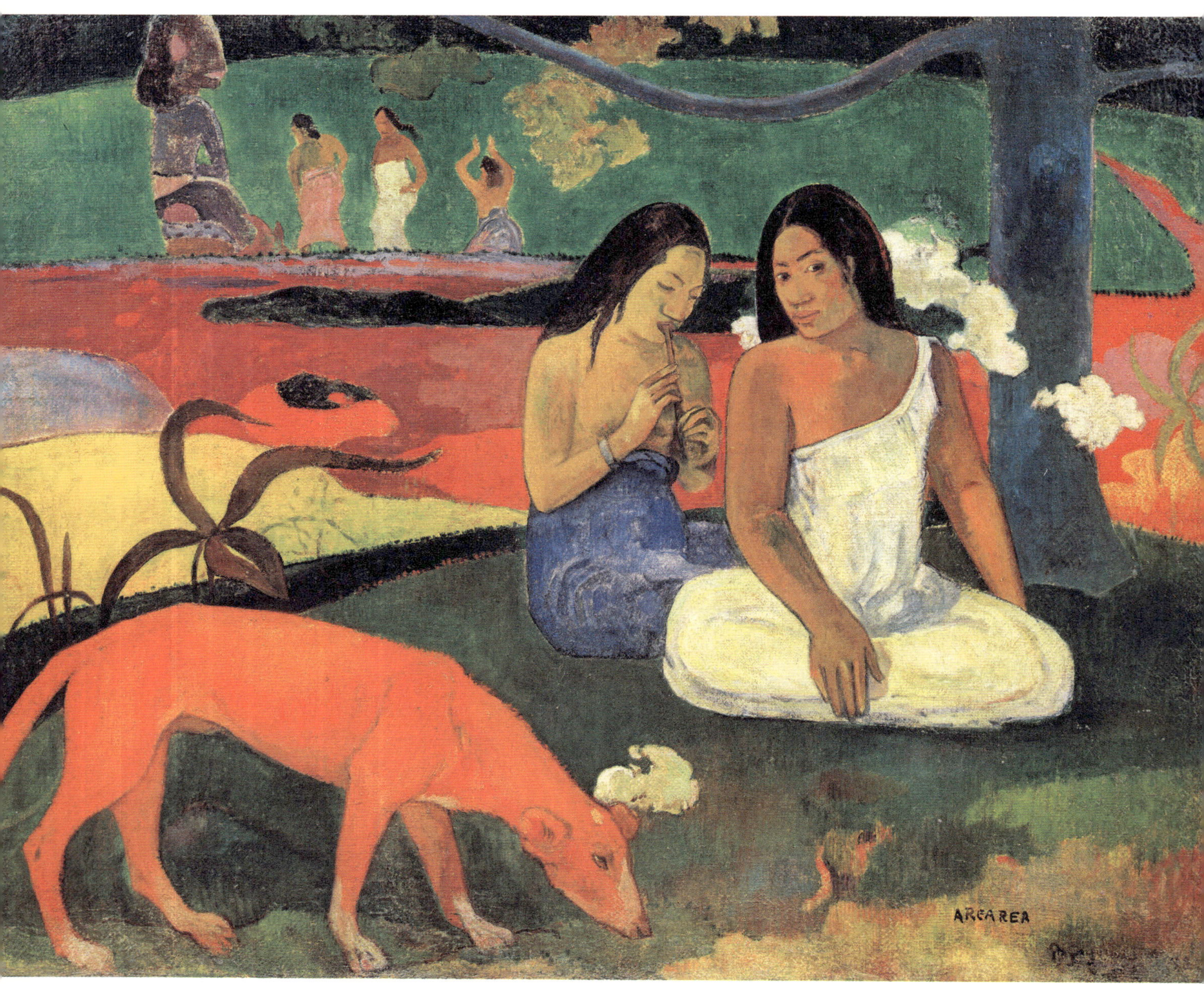

Joyousness (Arearea) or The Red Dog, 1892
Oil on canvas, 75 x 94 cm (29½ x 37 in) • Musée d'Orsay, Paris

By a lagoon, *arearea* (joyousness) abounds. Within a rich landscape of pure colour, women happily worship at a Maori statue. In the foreground, young women sit, one playing a Tahitian flute while a red dog (Gauguin?) ambles along.

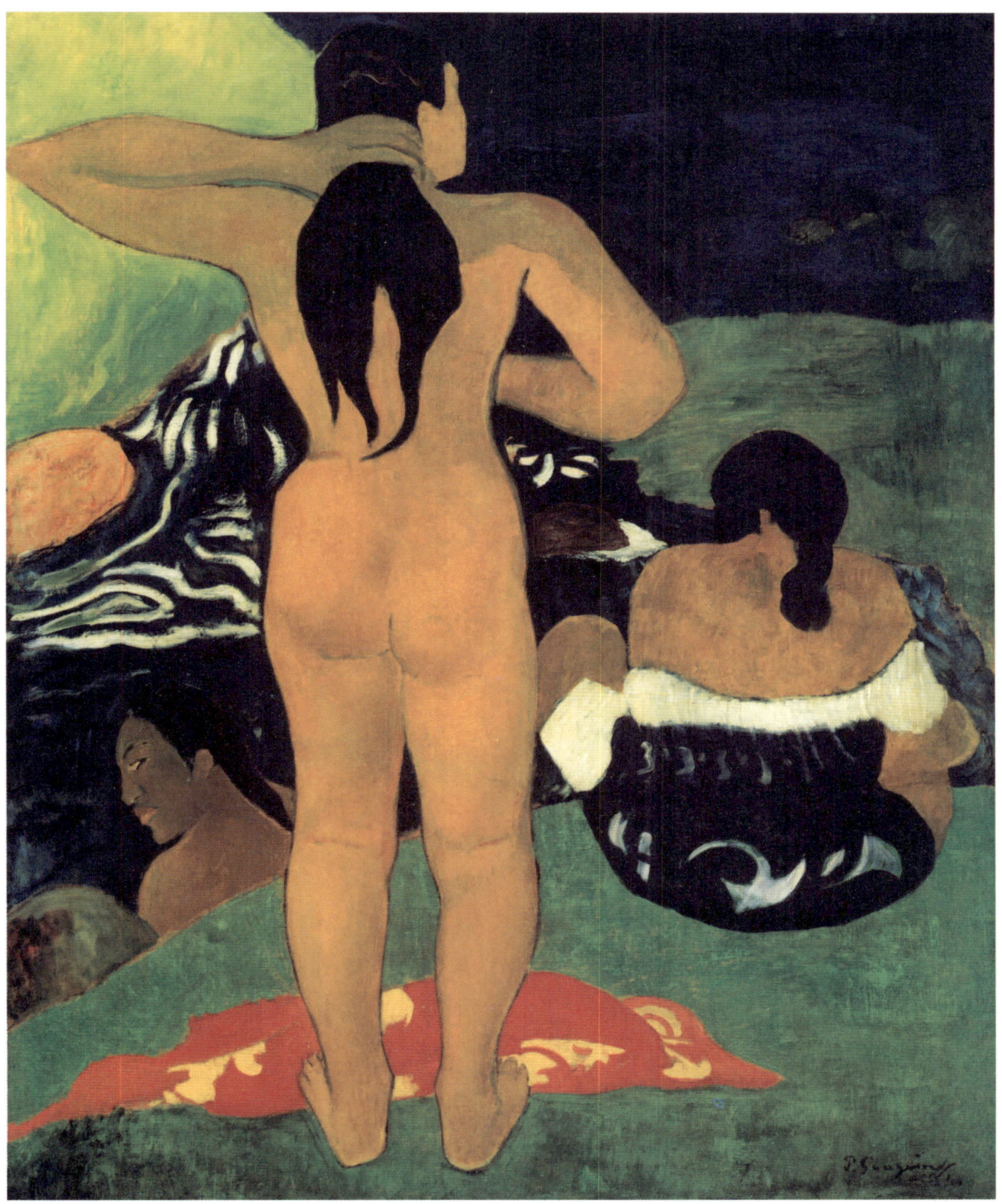

Tahitian Women Bathing, 1892
Oil on paper laid down on canvas, 111.1 x 89.2 cm (43¾ x 35⅛ in)
• Metropolitan Museum of Art, New York

One in a series of works of Tahitian women bathing; in Gauguin's creation of an exotic pastoral paradise, the large-scale format accentuates the dynamic use of colour and line.

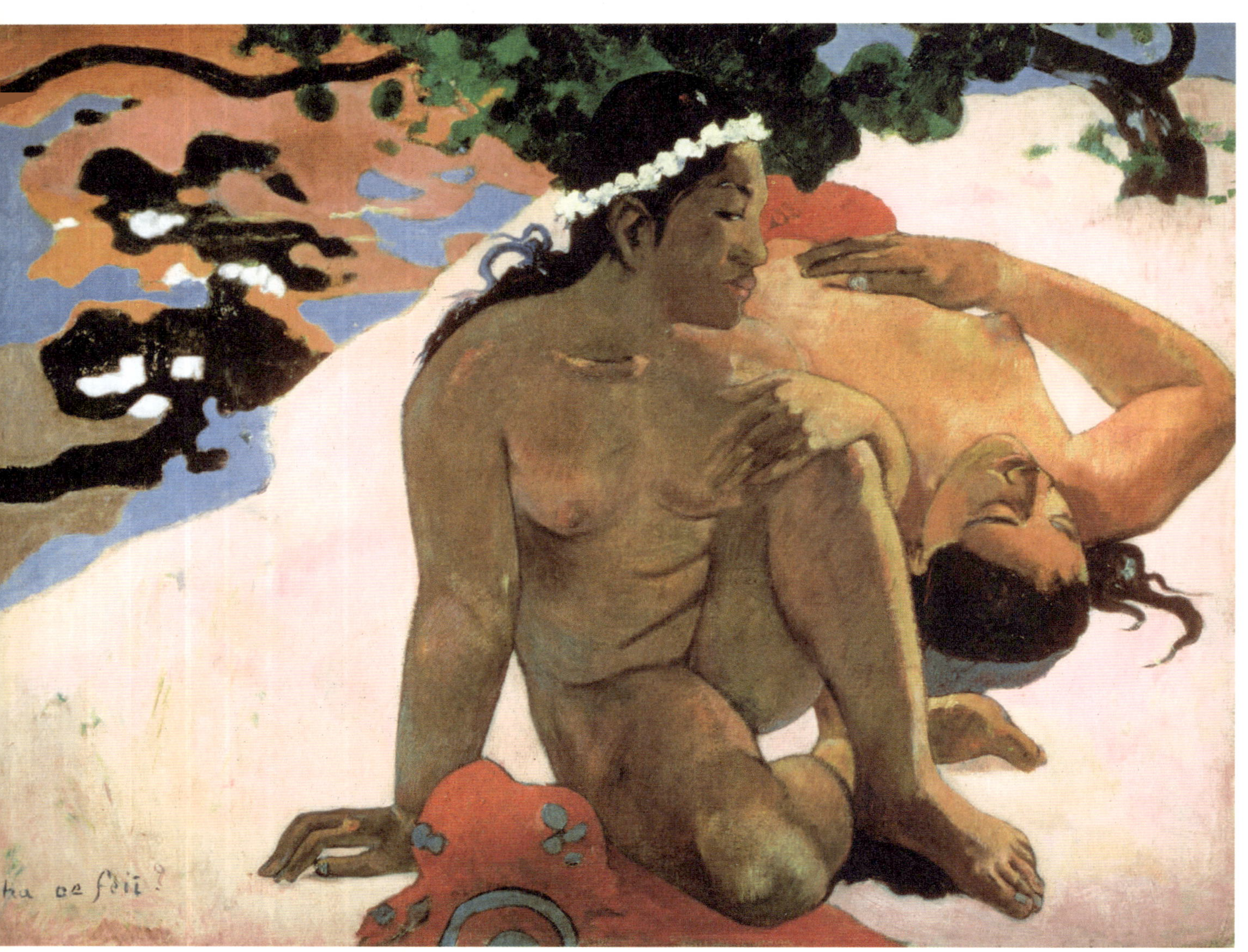

Are You Jealous? (Aha Oe Feii?), 1892
Oil on canvas, 66 x 89 cm (26 x 35 in) • Pushkin Museum, Moscow

Gauguin liked to use Tahitian titles for his paintings, not always as accurate as he intended, which annoyed European critics. However, he wanted the indigenous language to impart the sensation of Polynesian life, both in words and visual depiction.

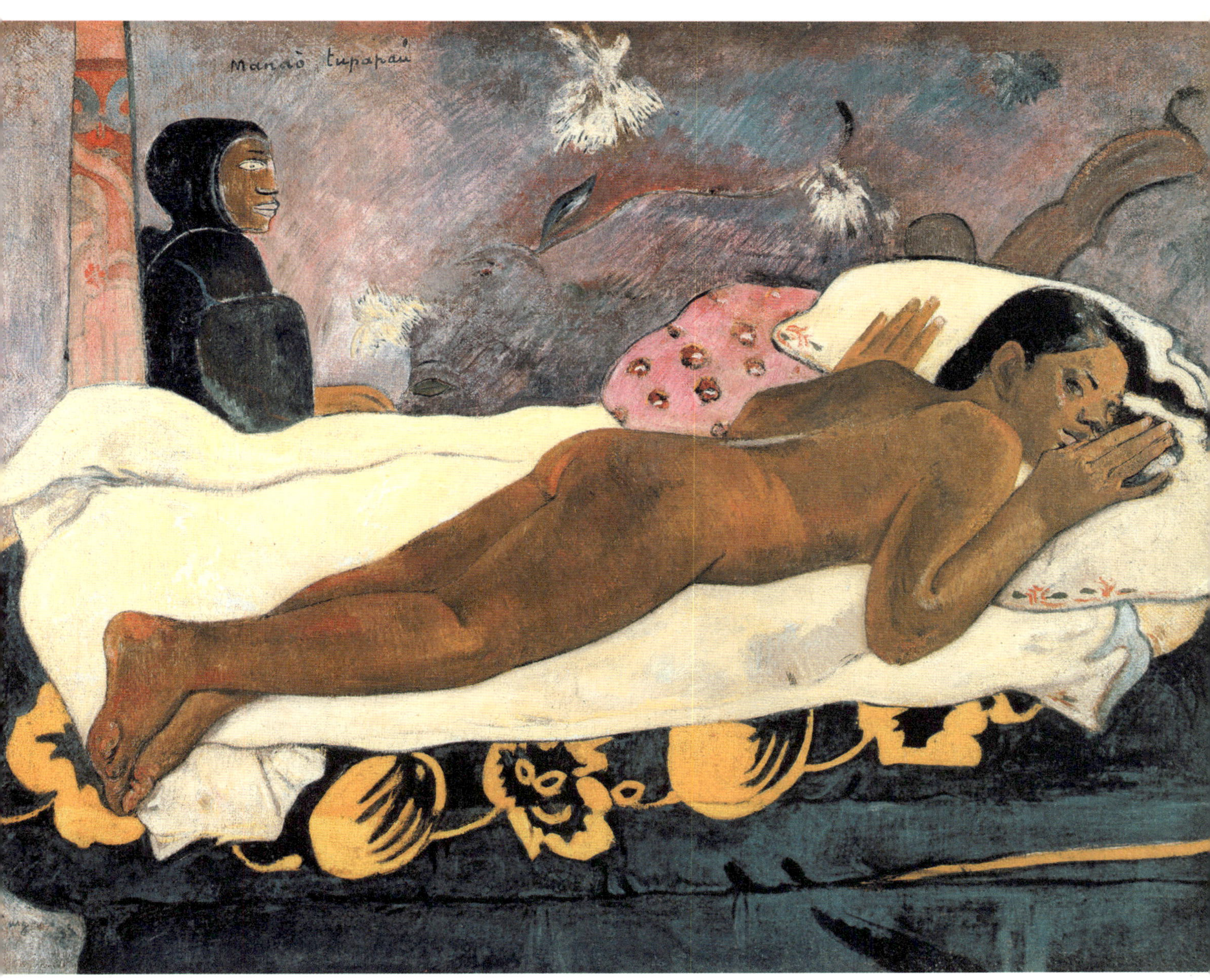

The Spirit of the Dead Watching (Manao Tupapau), 1892
Oil on canvas, 73 x 92 cm (28¾ x 36⅔ in)
• Albright-Knox Art Gallery, Buffalo

Tehamana, Gauguin's teenage 'wife', lies naked on a bed, watchful for the Spirit of the Dead. In this work, full of symbolism and fearfulness, Gauguin captured not only Tahitian mythology but also the insecurities Tehamana faced as the artist's muse.

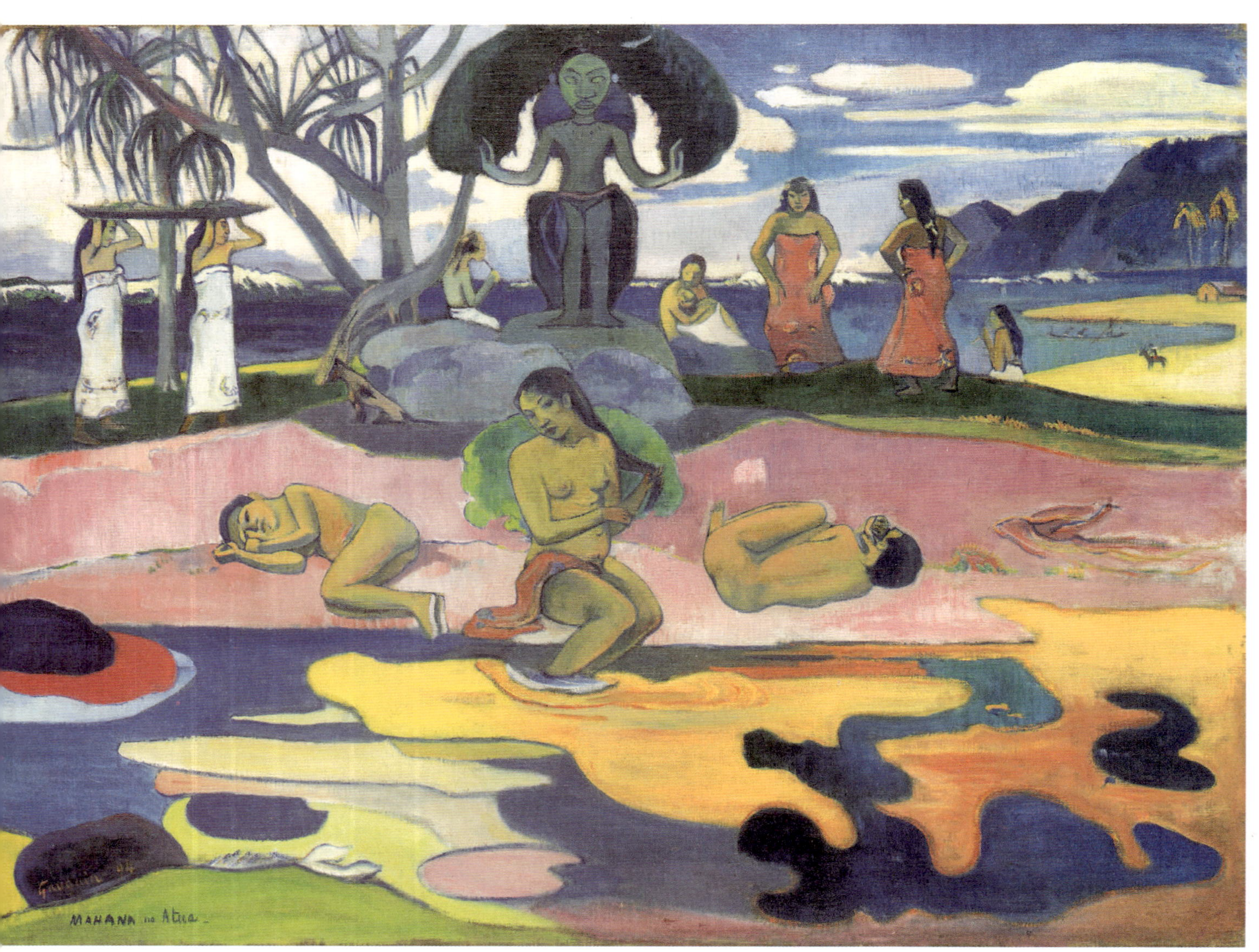

Day of the God (Mahana no Atua), 1894
Oil on canvas, 66 x 87 cm (26 x 34⅓ in) • The Art Institute of Chicago

In paintings of Tahiti, Gauguin wanted to express the primitive but created primitivism, a Western view of 'savage' nations. In this work, created in Paris from Gauguin's imagination, islanders gather near a vast sculpture of an ancient deity.

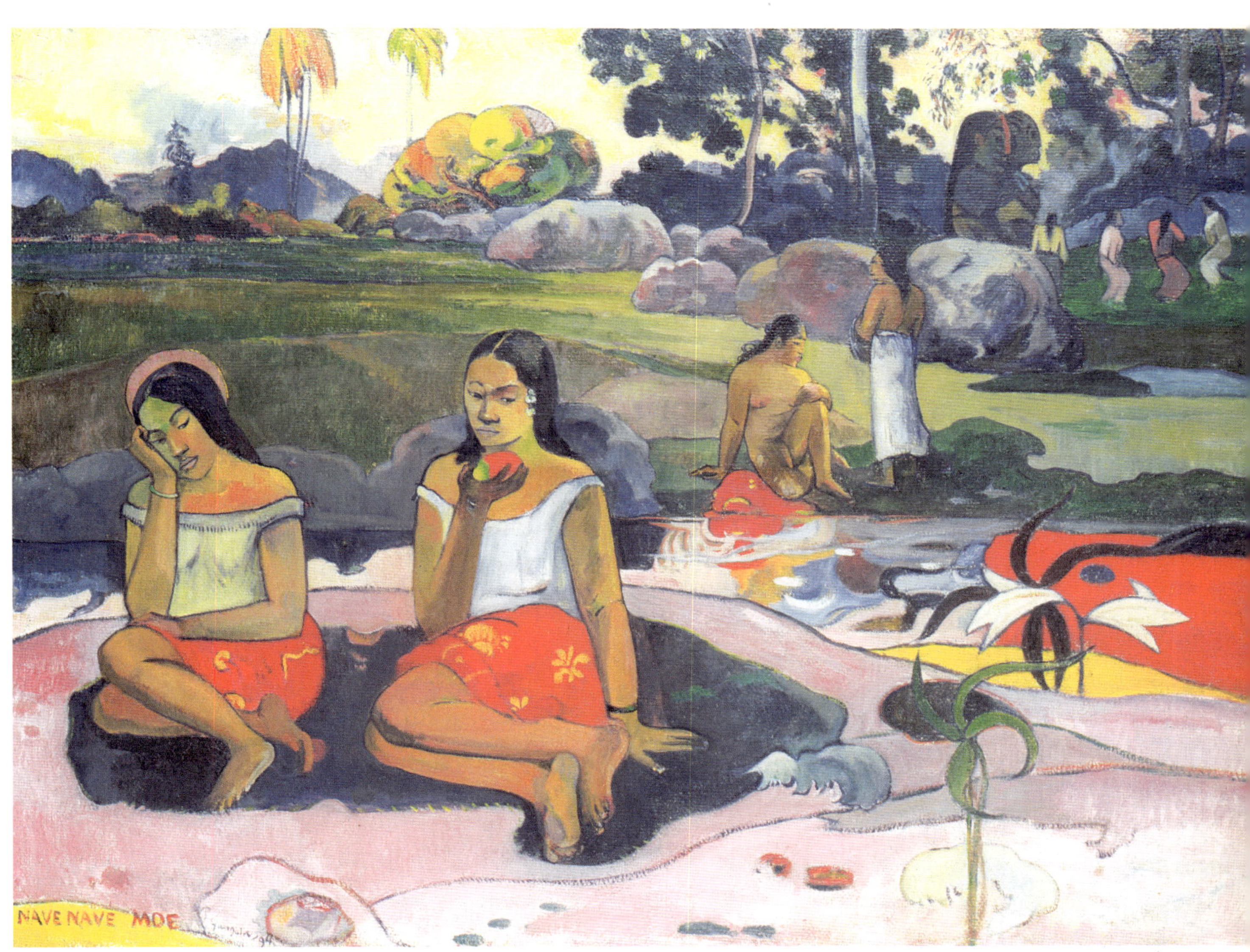

Sacred Spring (Nave Nave Moe), 1894
Oil on canvas, 73 x 98 cm (28¾ x 38⅗ in)
• The State Hermitage Museum, St Petersburg

Nava Nave Moe was created from memory and painted in Paris in 1894, between Gauguin's sojourns in Tahiti. It depicts Tahitians near a sacred spring worshipping a double deity, possibly the supreme creator god Ta'aroa and one of his wives.

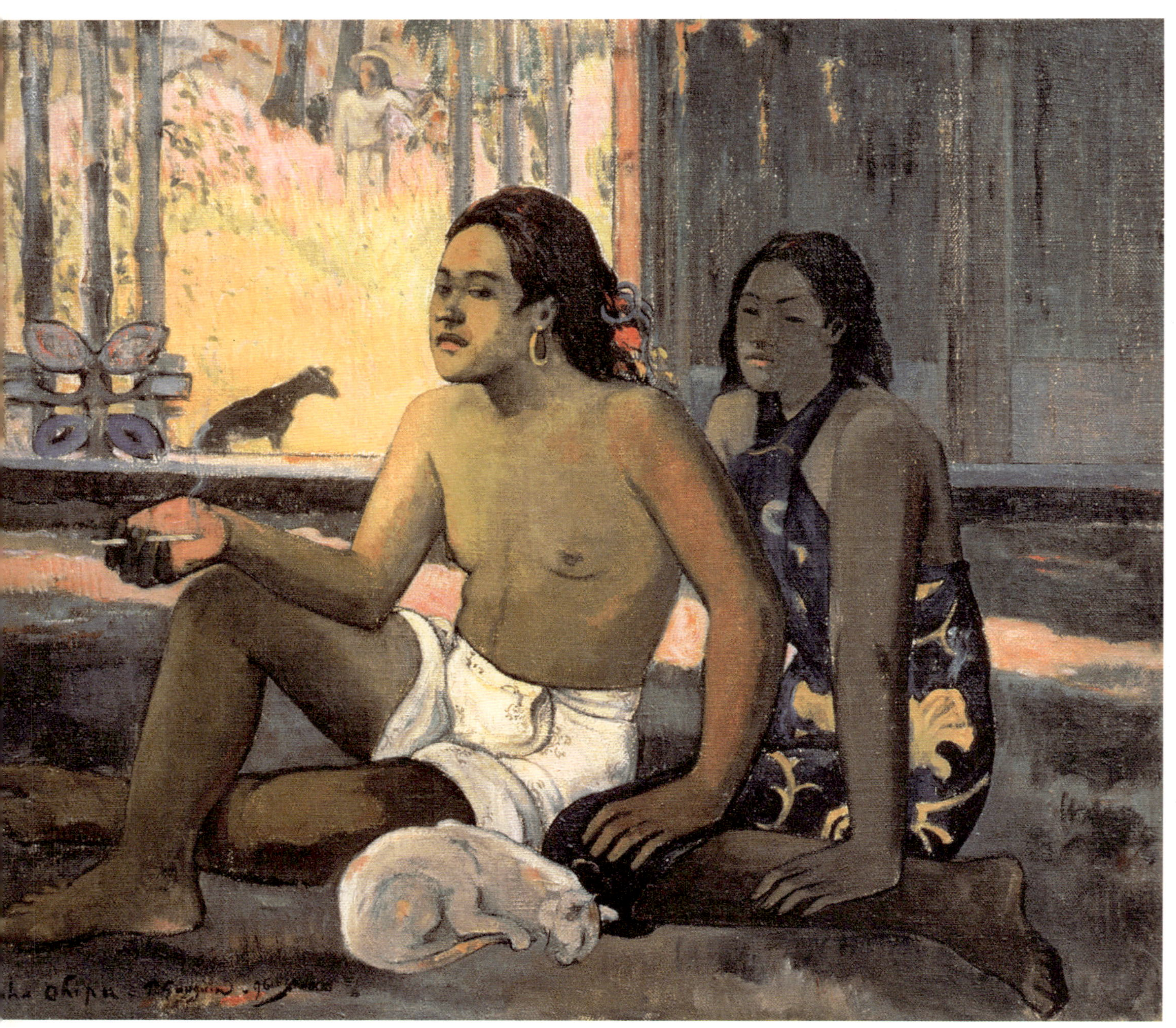

Not Working (Eiaha Ohipa) or Tahitians in a Room, 1896
Oil on canvas, 65 x 75 cm (25⅗ x 29½ in) • Pushkin Museum, Moscow

The composition may be informed by Gauguin's photographs of bas-reliefs in Borobudur. He depicts the relaxed lifestyle of a young couple preferring not to work in the heat of the day. Gauguin used complementary colours to contrast the cool of the internal room of the dwelling with the heat of the day outside.

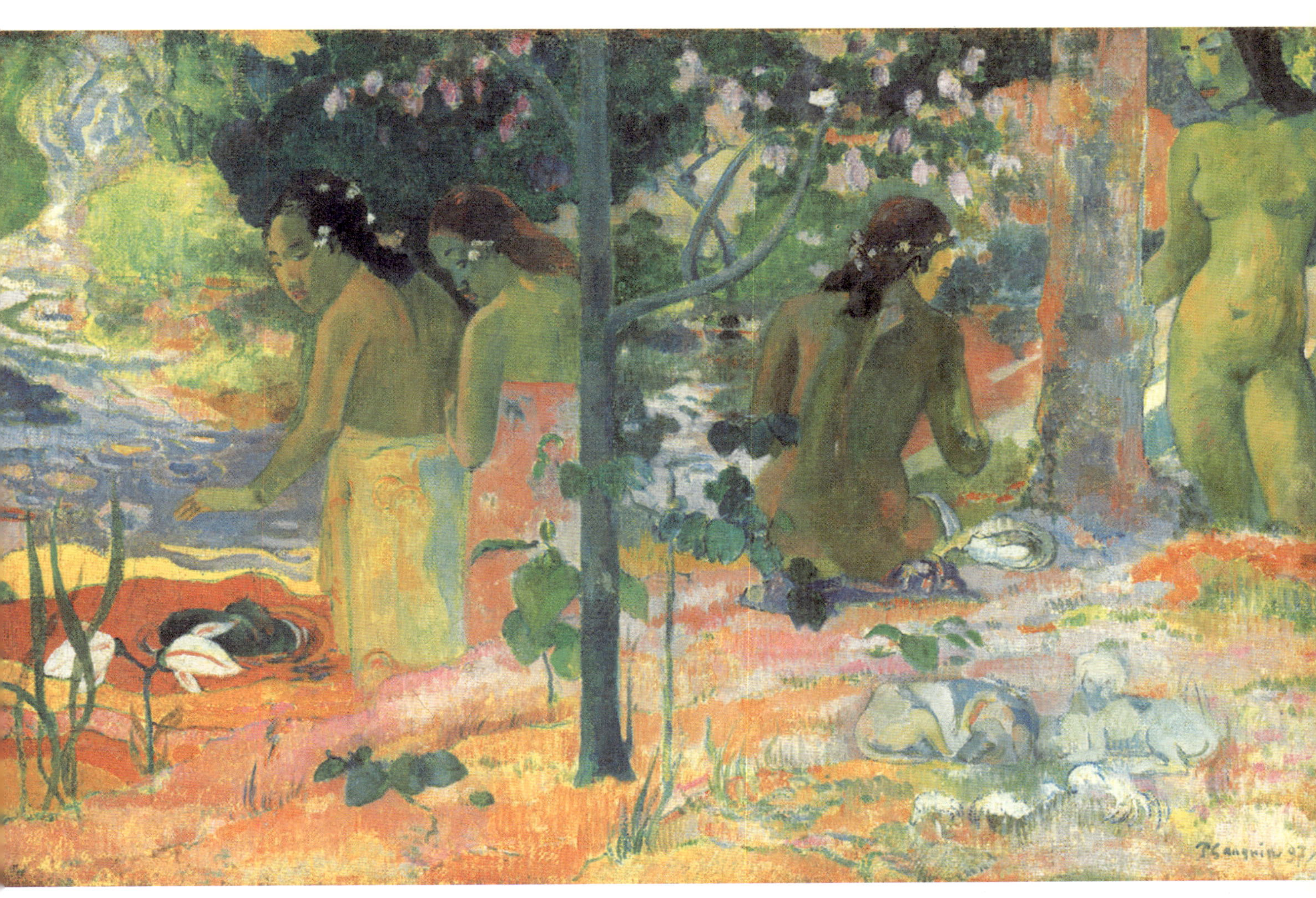

The Bathers, 1897
Oil on canvas, 60.4 x 93.4 cm (23¾ x 36¾ in)
• National Gallery of Art, Washington D.C.

In a close-up voyeuristic view of women bathing, Gauguin captures the intimacy of young women, naked and semi-disrobed, congregating to swim and bathe in the waters.

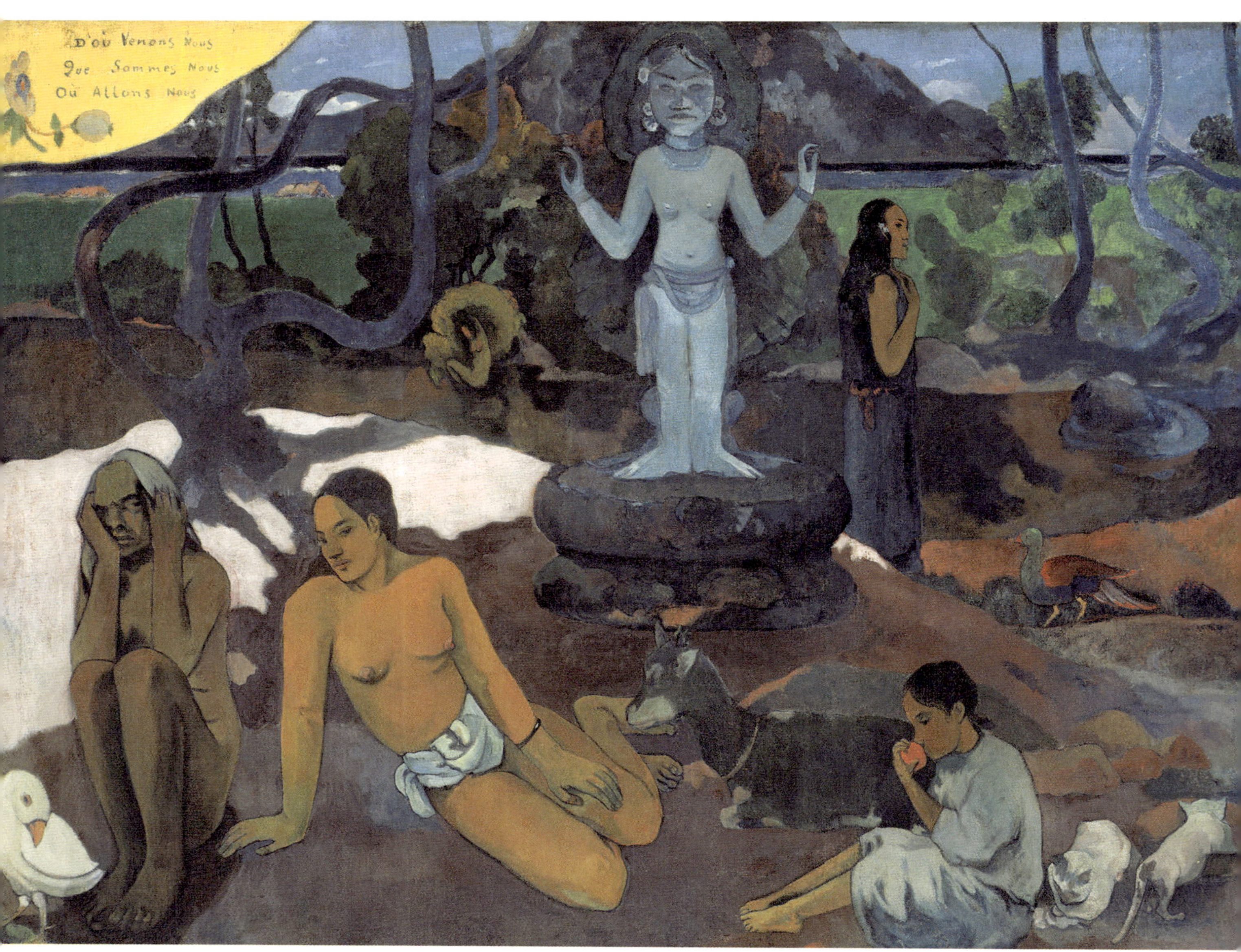

Where Do We Come From? What Are We? Where Are We Going? 1897
Oil on canvas, 139.1 x 374.6 cm (54¾ x 147½ in)
• Museum of Fine Arts, Boston

Set in an imagined spiritual world based on Tahitian mythology, Gauguin's powerful painting is full of symbolism, mystery and intrigue. In his largest artwork, he depicts the human life cycle from birth to death and asks three formidable, unanswerable questions.

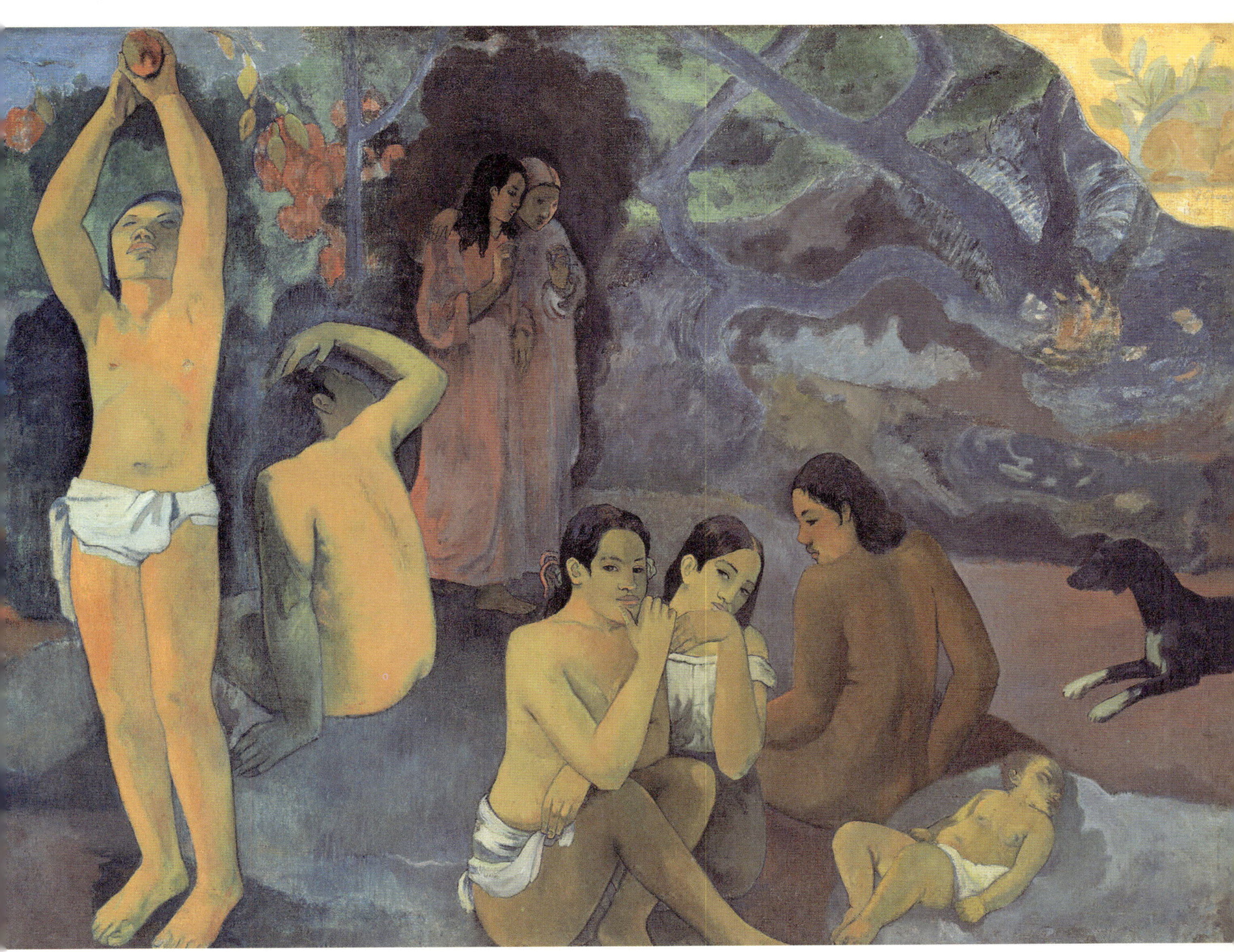

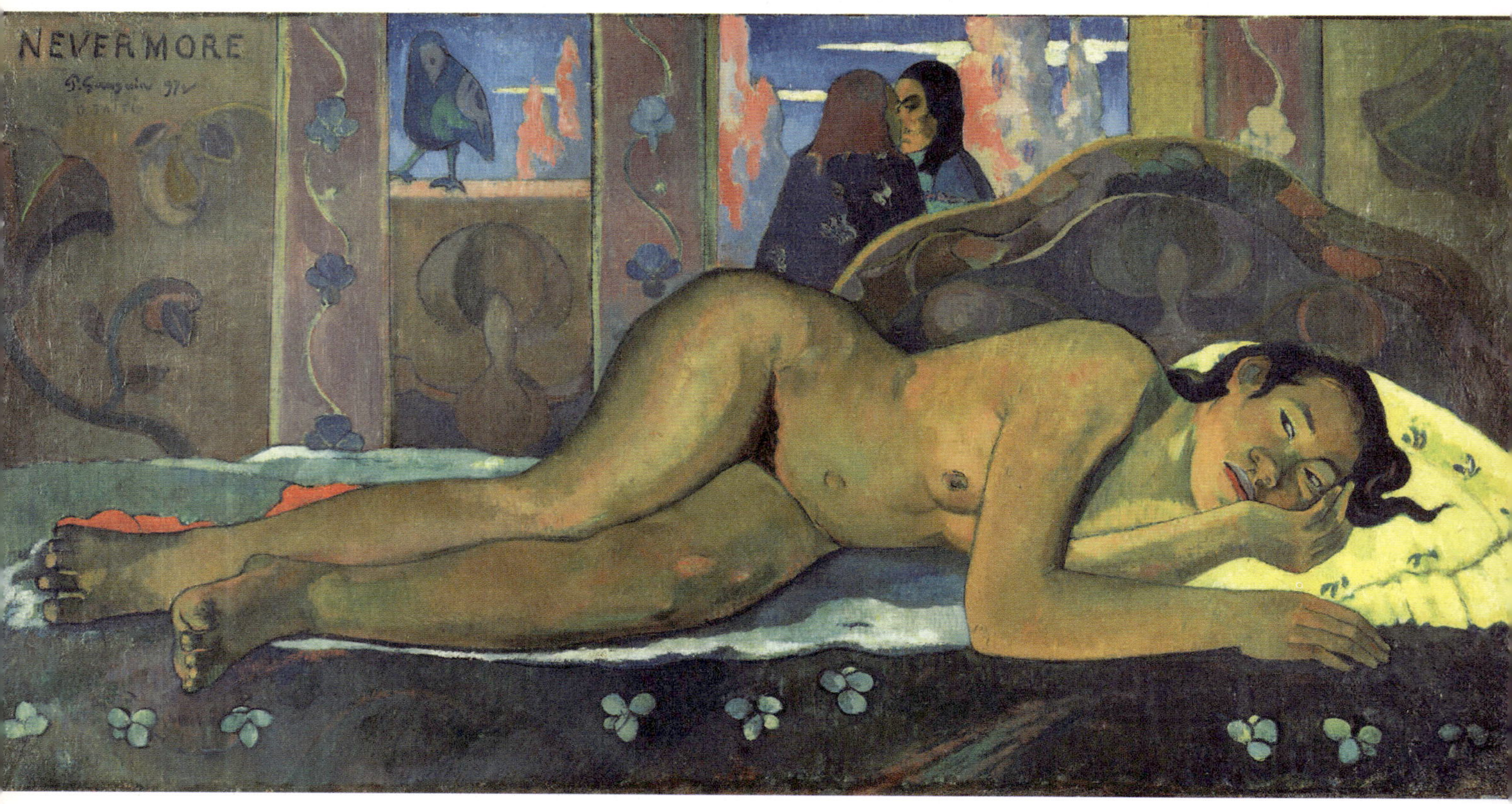

Nevermore, 1897
Oil on canvas, 60.5 x 116 cm (23¾ x 45⅔ in)
• The Courtauld Gallery, London

Gauguin portrays a Western view of the primitive native. In a letter to George-Daniel de Monfreid, of 14 February 1897, he wrote: 'I've tried to suggest, by means of a nude, a certain barbaric luxury of long ago … suffused with deliberately subdued and sad colours.'

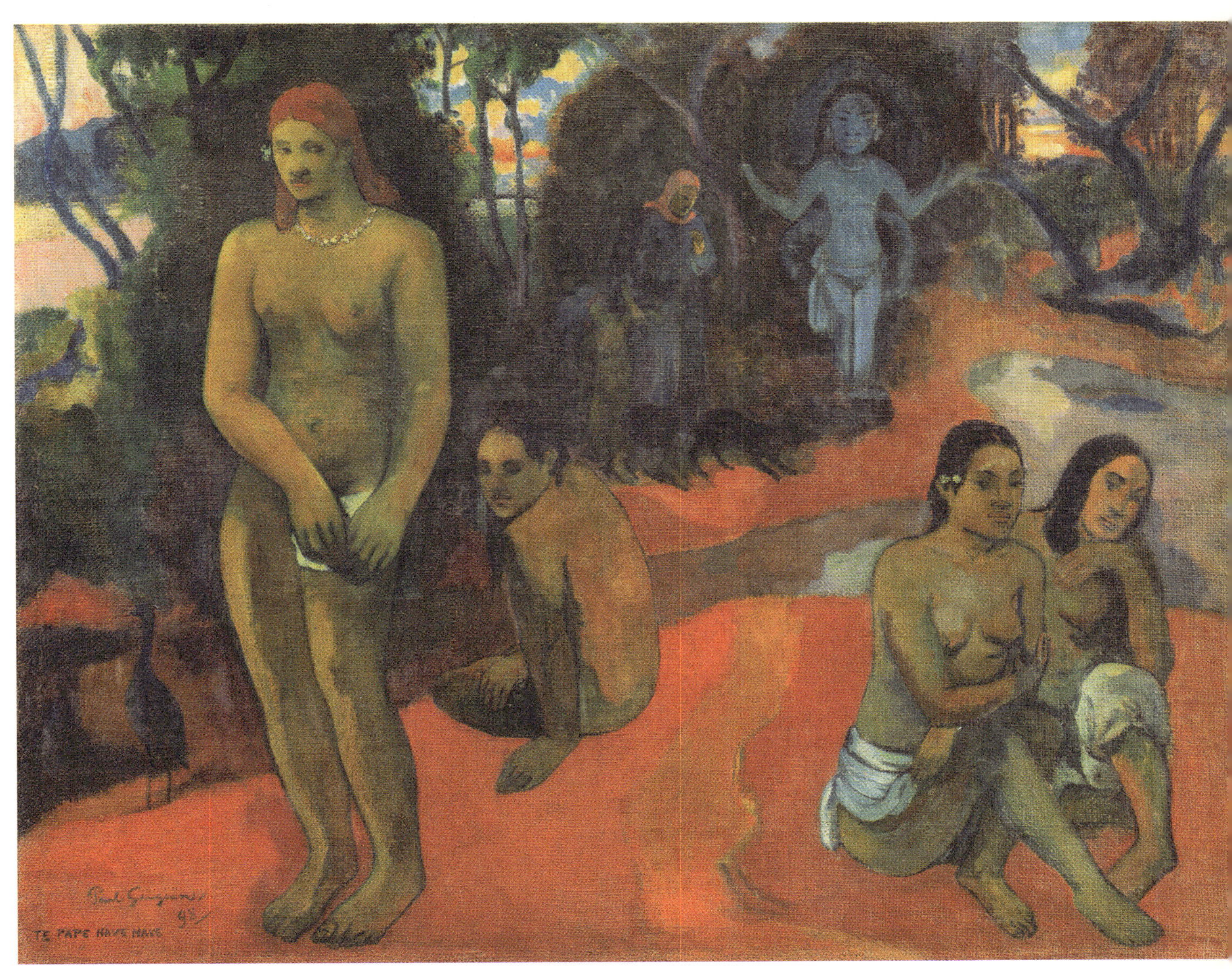

Delectable Waters (Te Pape Nave Nave), 1898
Oil on canvas, 74 x 95.3 cm (29⅛ x 37½ in)
• National Gallery of Art, Washington D.C.

First in a series of friezes that includes *Where Do We Come From? What Are We? Where Are We Going?* In a fire-red-orange glade near water, stands a blue statue representing the divine goddess Hina.

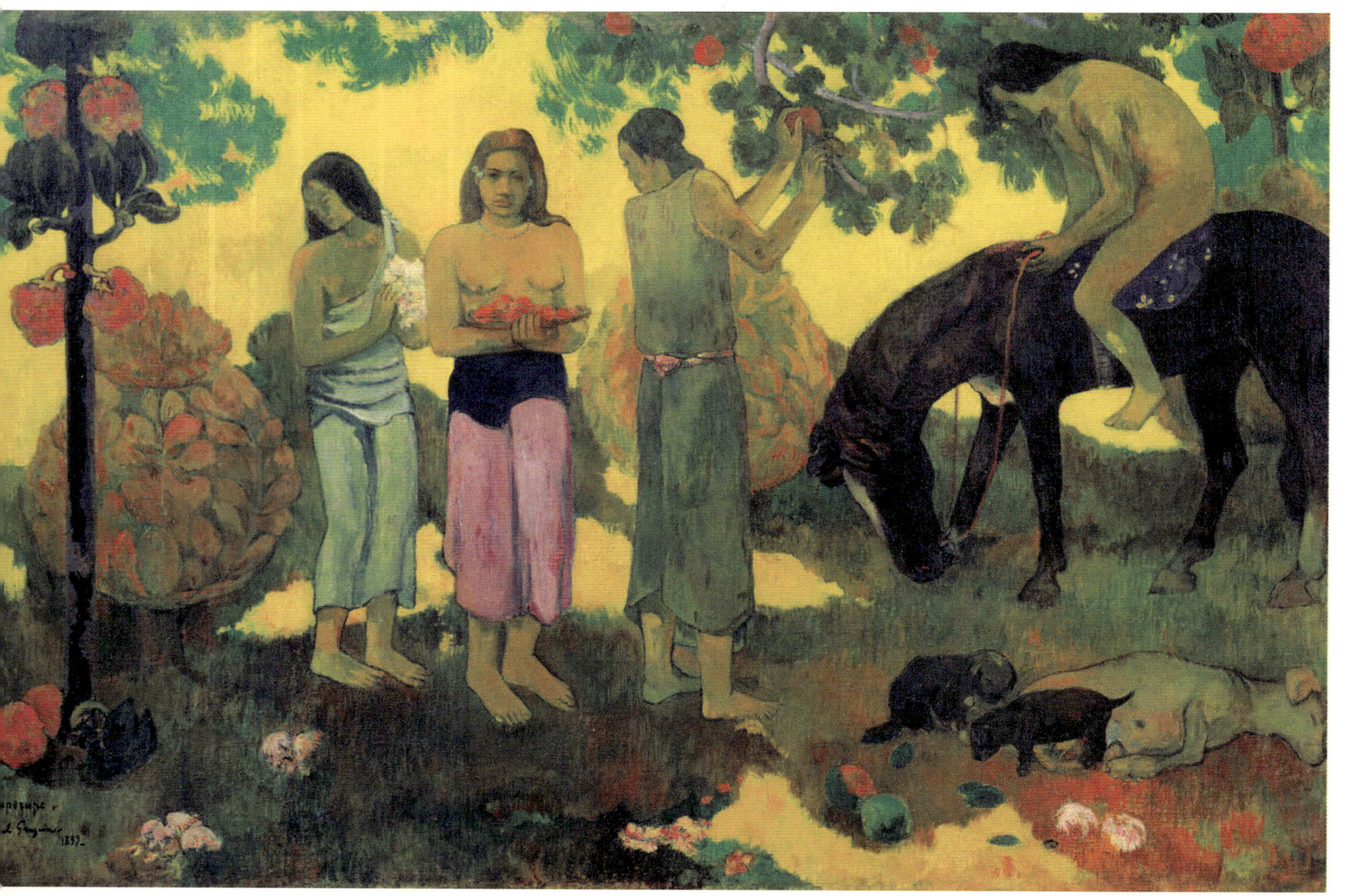

Fruit Gathering (Rupe Rupe), 1899
Oil on canvas, 128 x 191 cm (50⅔ x 75⅓ in)
• Pushkin Museum, Moscow

Two Tahitian women gathering fruit first appeared in Gauguin's vast frieze *Tahitian Pastoral* (*Faa Iheihe*) (1898) and again in *Two Tahitian Women* (1899). *Fruit Gathering* was created for the 1900 Exposition Universelle in Paris.

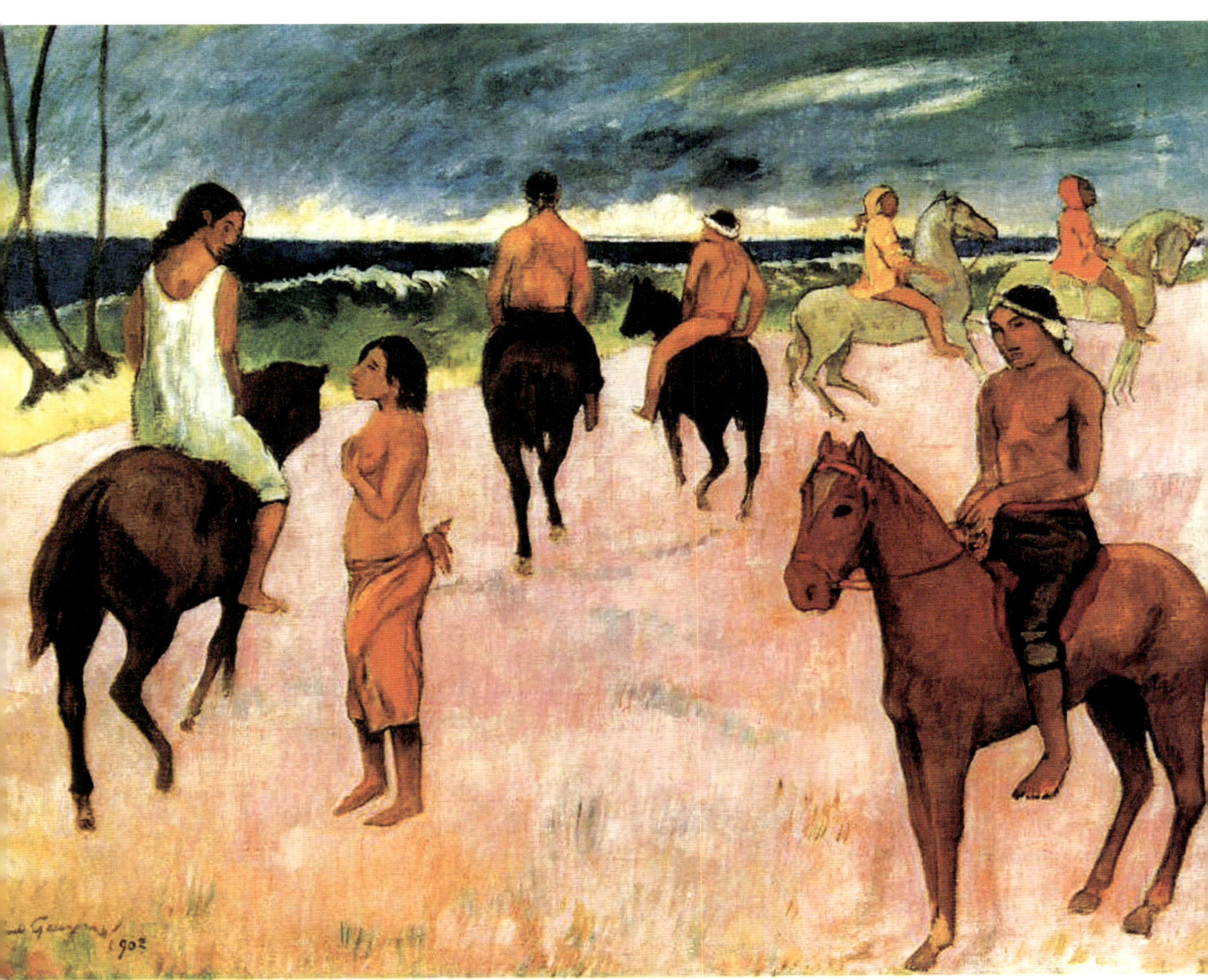

Riders on the Beach, 1902
Oil on canvas, 91 x 72 cm (35⅓ x 28⅓ in) • Musée d'Orsay, Paris

Reminiscent of a Degas racehorse painting, Gauguin depicts local riders exercising their horses on warm pink coral-dusted sands by the seashore in Atuona. Two white horses with hooded riders – possibly Polynesian spirits of the dead – lead the way.

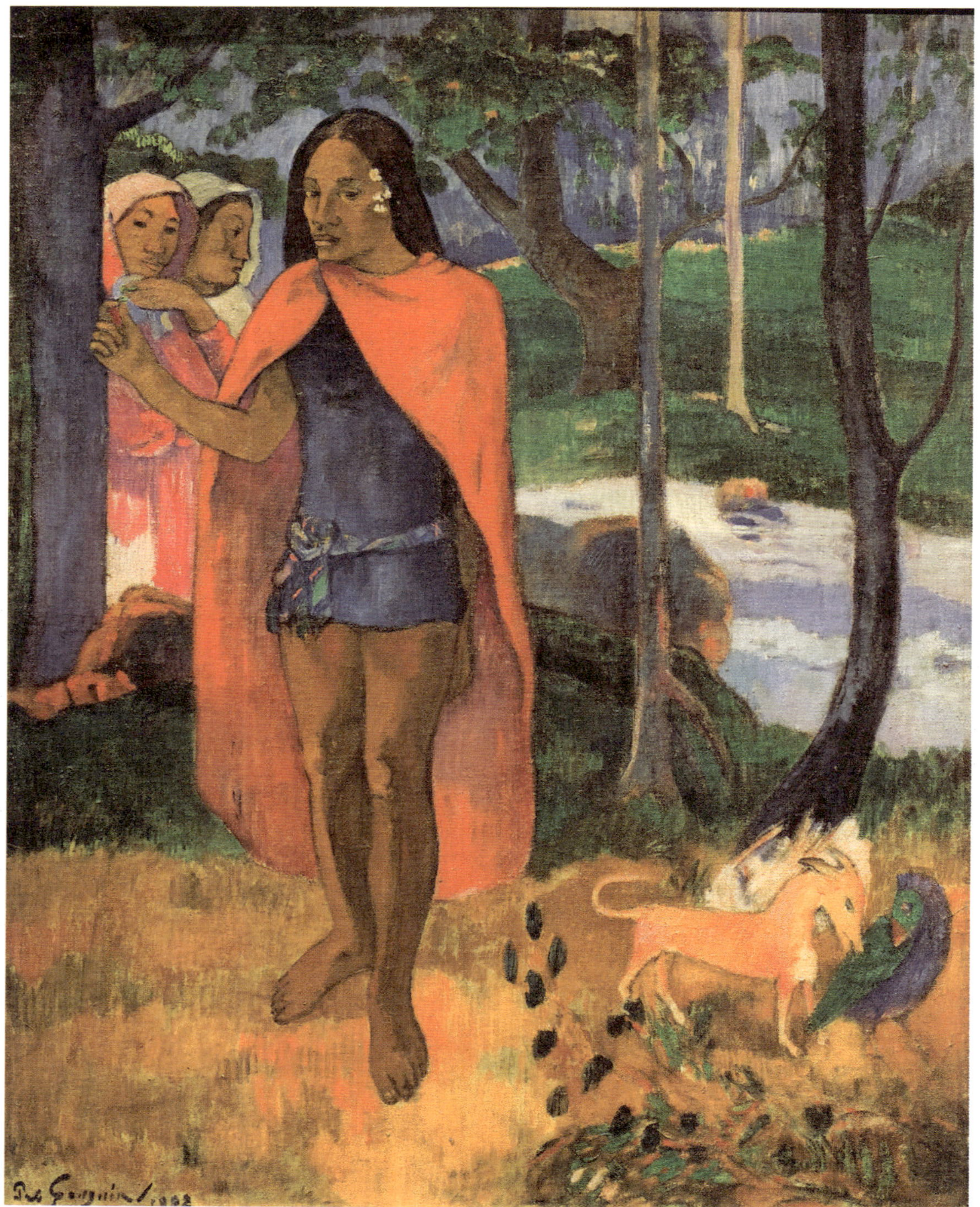

**The Sorcerer of Hiva Oa
(Marquesan Man in the Red Cape), 1902**
Oil on canvas, 92 x 73 cm (36⅕ x 28¾ in)
• Museum of Modern and Contemporary Art, Liège, Belgium

A remarkable painting, mixing mythology with the beauty of the Marquesan landscape and its indigenous people, Gauguin's intense colour palette of complementary rich hues sharply focuses attention on the red cloak of the mysterious sorcerer.

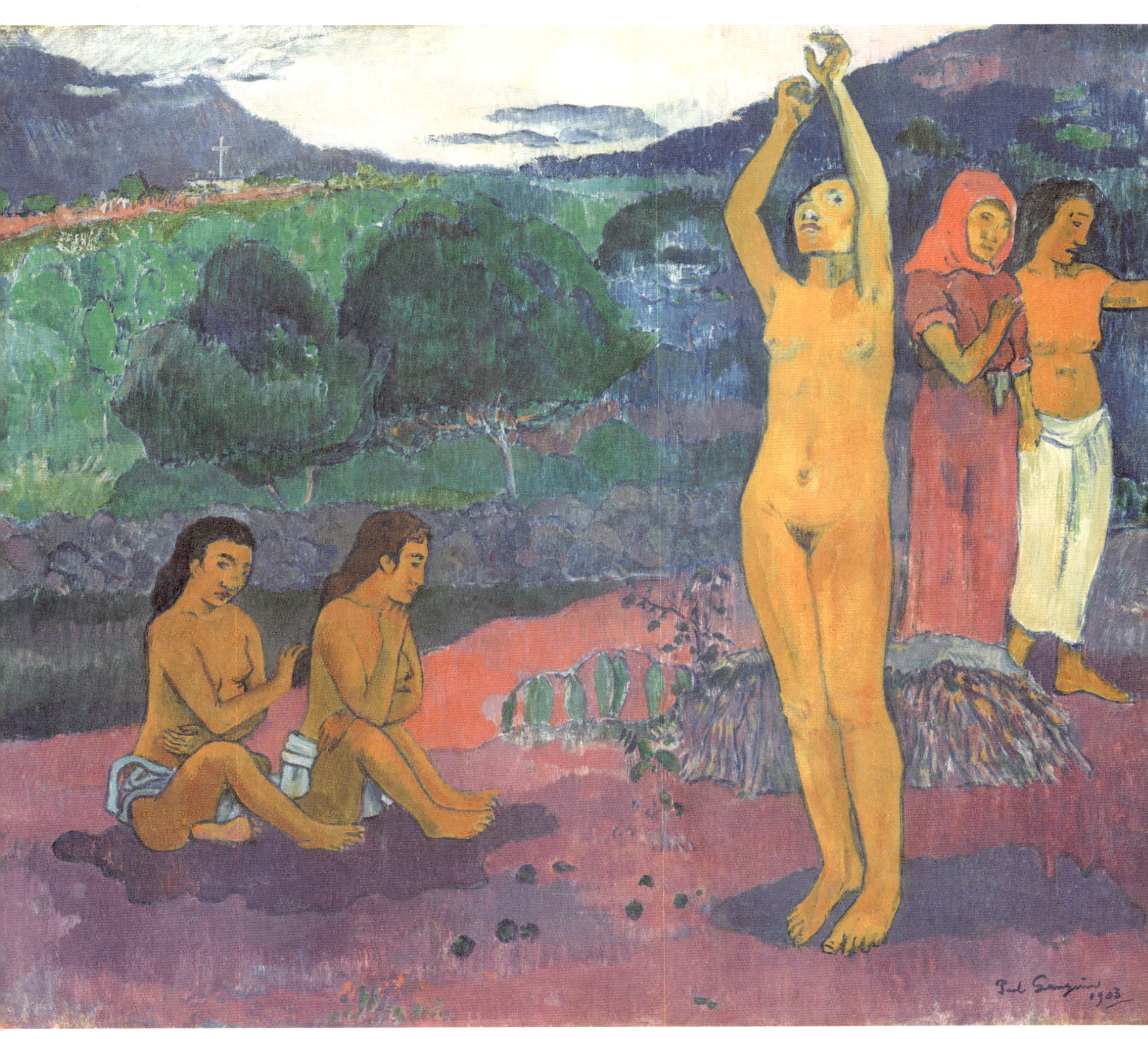

The Invocation, 1903
Oil on canvas, 65.5 x 76.6 cm (25¾ x 30⅛ in)
• National Gallery of Art, Washington D.C.

Gauguin died on 8 May 1903. This painting was one of his last works. The main figure standing was first seen in his monumental 1897 work *Where Do We Come From? What Are We? Where Are We Going?*

Indexes

Index of Works

Page numbers in *italics* indicate illustration captions.

General Index

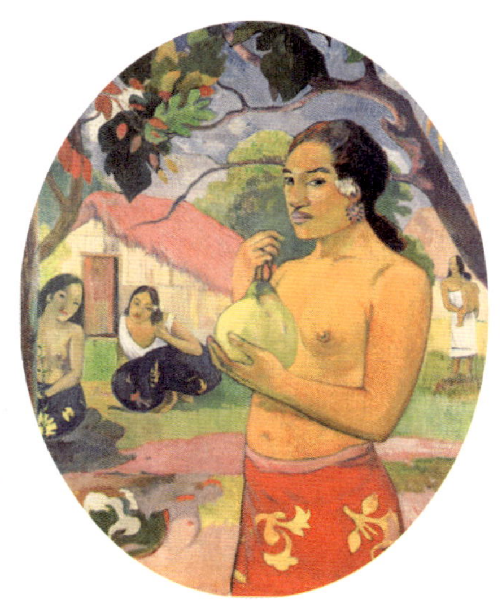

Masterpieces of Art
FLAME TREE PUBLISHING

A new series of carefully curated print and digital books covering the world's greatest art, artists and art movements.

If you enjoyed this book please sign up for updates, information and offers on further titles in this series at
blog.flametreepublishing.com/art-of-fine-gifts/